EDUCATING
AFRICAN AMERICAN MALES

*During my time at the Johns Hopkins University, I met many outstanding
people who played an important role in my quality of life there. Over the
span of my time at the Johns Hopkins University, CRESPAR lost the following
four people to various illnesses. I wish to dedicate this book to the memory of*

John H. Hollifield, my greatest cheerleader (CRESPAR JHU)

*Viola Mason, one of the friendliest and most positive
people at CSOS (CRESPAR JHU)*

*Sylvia Johnson, an incredible scholar and wonderful
mentor (CRESPAR HOWARD)*

*Kevin Cuffie, a wonderful friend and colleague and
an eternal optimist (CRESPAR JHU)*

Edmund W. Gordon | C. K. McGuire | Robert Cooper | Will J. Jordan
Pedro A. Noguera | Ronald F. Ferguson | James Earl Davis
Melissa Roderick | Dena Phillips Swanson | Michael Cunningham
Margaret Beale Spencer | Jomills Henry Braddock II

EDUCATING
AFRICAN AMERICAN MALES

VOICES FROM THE FIELD

Edited by Olatokunbo S. Fashola

CORWIN PRESS
A SAGE Publications Company
Thousand Oaks, California

For information:

Corwin Press
A Sage Publications Company
2455 Teller Road
Thousand Oaks, California 91320
www.corwinpress.com

Sage Publications Ltd.
1 Oliver's Yard
55 City Road
London EC1Y 1SP
United Kingdom

Sage Publications India Pvt. Ltd.
B-42, Panchsheel Enclave
Post Box 4109
New Delhi 110 017 India

Printed in the United States of America

Library of Congress Cataloging-in-Publication Data

Educating African American males: Voices from the field / edited by Olatokunbo S. Fashola.
    p. cm.
Includes bibliographical references and index.
ISBN 1-4129-1433-7 (cloth) — ISBN 1-4129-1434-5 (pbk.)
    1. African American men—Education. 2. African American students—Social conditions. 3. Urban schools—United States. I. Fashola, Olatokunbo S.
LC2731.E34 2005
371.829'96073—dc22

                                        2004024084

This book is printed on acid-free paper.

    06   07   08   09   10   9   8   7   6   5   4   3   2

Acquisitions Editor:	Elizabeth Brenkus
Editorial Assistant:	Candice L. Ling
Production Editor:	Diana E. Axelsen
Typesetter:	C&M Digitals (P) Ltd.
Cover Designer:	Anthony Paular
Graphic Designer:	Lisa Miller
Indexer:	David Luljak

Contents

Foreword

These presentations from the Conference on African American Male Achievement are more than welcome. So much of the attention given to this issue has been directed at documenting the failures and describing the endangered status of this species. In general, this literature is severely limited in its conceptualization of the issues and in its coverage of the range of adaptations, behaviors, characteristics, and conditions manifested in the lives of African American males. It is primarily a literature of Black male failures and dysfunctional behaviors and is most charitably described as a response to oppression and disadvantage. It is a literature of life in depressed inner cities where African Americans are overrepresented. Because this picture appropriately applies to a minority of the Black males in the United States, these foci suggest that the majority of members of the targeted group are being overlooked (Gordon, 1997). These foci also mean that issues such as age, class, gender, and geographic differences are neglected. That the full range of adaptive and maladaptive behaviors and conditions is largely undocumented and has not been subjected to analysis is of even greater significance. Given the remarkable achievements of this group, just a century removed from enslavement and continuing to experience racism, this truncated picture provides a distorted popular view and an inadequate knowledge base for both public policy and the continued production of knowledge. Gordon (1996) has referred to the "African American male Problematique" to reflect the view that this generalized distortion of the conditions and status of Black males in the United States is an artificial or at best manufactured problem. Some African American males are in trouble, but the African American male condition is not one of universal failure.

The research literature specifically concerning African American males is a product of the latter half of the 20th century. This emerging literature tends to focus on questions having to do with dysfunctional males and their contribution to what was considered to be the problems with Black families, the legacies of slavery, and their impact on Black males to exercise responsibility for themselves and their families. Toward the mid-20th century, attention turned to studies of urbanization, poverty, and single-parent families. Since the early 1980s, the focus of much of this work has been on political/economic and social/psychological issues. Much of the emphasis has shifted to unemployment, lack of opportunity for meaningful participation in the political economy of the nation, institutionalized racism, and the impacts of these structural phenomena on the attitudes and behavior of African American males.

The general causes of the crisis for African American males addressed in the literature are often incorrectly addressed as separate issues in the psychosocial, economic, and educational domains. In the psychosocial literature, emphasis is given to how African American males behave and react to societal conditions, particularly to discrimination, poverty, and marginalization. Some attention has been given to Black male coping strategies or the lack thereof. Several studies address African American males' relationships with their families, their underground economies, and alternative lifestyles. A growing number of studies provide cultural analyses as well as psychological assessments. Indeed, among the strongest recent developments in this literature is the emergence of ethnographic analyses of African American males' life experiences and the recognition of subcultural norms unique to segments of this population.

The conference presentations presented in this volume build on the extant literature on Black males. Our concerns focus on academic achievement issues, schooling, and the social contexts in which such achievement must be developed. The first chapter looks at the relationships between cultural identity and many efforts at school reform. Other chapters address several interventions that Gordon (2000) has referred to as "supplementary education." These chapters reference a variety of interventions, deliberate and incidental, that some of us think are not simply supplemental but that may better enable schools to do their work. Another chapter addresses the relationship between teacher expectations and student achievement. We hope that these deliberations contribute to our understanding of and our capacity to address some problems identified.

—Edmund W. Gordon

*Professor Emeritus of Psychology at Yale
University and Richard March Hoe Professor of
Psychology and Education Emeritus at Teachers College*

Preface

A friend and colleague asked me the following question: "If I brought a 70-year-old illiterate man to you, could you teach him to read?" My answer was "yes," for I had taught reading to beginning readers. He asked me the same question referring to a 40-year-old man, and my response was "yes," again. He asked me the same question a third time pertaining to a teenager, and I said, "Yes, of course." My colleague's final question was, "Then why can't our African American males read in our public schools?" I did not have a response, but I did a lot of thinking about that question, and I continue to do so. As we introduce this edited volume dedicated to African American males, we encourage the readers to ask themselves the same question. Why are African American males not succeeding academically in schools?

The crisis of African American male lack of educational achievement has become such an important topic that in the year 2000, the U.S. Department of Education had cause to sponsor a conference specifically dedicated to this topic. As a researcher, one cannot help but wonder, If this topic is such a crisis for adults, are young African American males themselves aware of the odds against their succeeding academically in our schools today? More specifically, what is going on in the minds of African American male students who are not succeeding in school? At what point in their young academic lives do they realize that because of sociological, psychological, educational, and environmental factors that count against them, they are really not supposed to be successful in the classroom?

Does this begin in September when the summer ends, the weather begins to change, and around Labor Day, the theme for school-aged children is "back to school?" For families of all school-aged children, there is much anticipation about the upcoming new school year. During the back-to-school period, television, newspaper, magazine, and radio commercials flood the public with pictures of smiling school-aged students clad in new uniforms, carrying new books, and eager and ready to learn. But then, as many of us know, television commercials often have a way of not reaching an entire audience.

If one attempted to paint a realistic picture of the back-to-school period, one would realize that not all school-aged children are always excited about returning to school. Some students are returning to school after having been retained in grade. Some are returning to school after having numerous suspensions during the previous school year, and they wonder what, if anything, will change during the upcoming school year to make school a more enjoyable experience. Others are returning to school ill-equipped to succeed behaviorally, academically, economically, culturally, or socially, and therefore it is only a matter of time before these students join the nation's population of dropouts.

This makes one wonder, What is taking place in the minds of students who are not succeeding in school? How many of them are actually dreading attending school in the fall? When do students begin to associate school with negative feelings, and can some of these negative experiences and feelings be erased or improved?

One might also ask, Do these feelings begin to accumulate in the spring time? During the spring season, we once again see signs of hope in the natural environment. The trees begin to grow leaves, the grass begins to turn green, April showers begin to produce May flowers, the days grow longer and the nights are shorter, and the days are also warmer. The advent of the spring also signifies the beginning of testing season in many schools, and this can also be a traumatic time for students facing academic achievement challenges. This is the case not only for standardized tests but also for school-based tests that eventually determine whether or not students will be promoted to the next grade. One cannot help but wonder what takes place in the minds of young African American male students who are struggling to find answers to questions that they might not even understand. This reflects not only questions in the classroom but also questions about life, role models, presence of positive males, the relationship between academic achievement and masculinity or race, constructive outlets for displaying frustration, joy, sorrow, misunderstanding, and pain. The authors of the various chapters in this volume attempt to address many of these issues individually and uniquely.

The chapters in this edited volume are rich and informative scholarly insights into many of the obstacles that adjust the expectations, standards, and goals of academic achievement for African

American males. They attempt to provide insight about cultural, behavioral, emotional, and cognitive struggles faced by the academic community at large. The work, however, does not end here. In fact, the work has just begun. One of the next steps for people in higher education is to begin to create infrastructures in the educational community that will continue the important work in this area and to stay in constant communication with practitioners, fellow researchers, legislators, and policy makers.

The chapters in this volume approach this serious issue from various perspectives, suggesting improvements in different aspects of the educational process. Edmund W. Gordon's foreword makes the case that the existing literature about African American males must be added to, including areas that pertain to education and schooling. Rather than show African American males as a lost cause, he asks that we begin to investigate different ways that we as a community of educators and researchers can come together and explore better ways to improve the educational achievement, attainment, and experiences of African American males.

Robert Cooper and Will Jordan address this issue by discussing sociological aspects of the classroom, such as the racial and gender interactions between students and teachers, the shortage of African American male teachers in public schools, and appreciation of the talents of African American males.

Fashola's chapter presents alternative ways of intervening in the lives of young African American males by providing them with opportunities for mentorship, positive enrichment experiences, academic enrichment and achievement, and positive peer interaction during the nonschool hours. She presents four programs that have successfully addressed the academic needs of African American male students during nonschool hours and also addresses community-based programs that have either had success with or show future promise working with African American males during the hours when they are not in school and not under the direct supervision of their parents or families.

Pedro Noguera's chapter addresses the issue by discussing the socioemotional, family/community support services, and the needs of the students.

Ronald Ferguson approaches this topic by specifically exploring teachers' interactions with students and paying close attention to their perceptions, expectations, and interactions with students. He addresses how these influence students' beliefs, behaviors, work habits, and ultimately, academic achievement.

James Davis addresses this issue by examining forces sometimes beyond the classroom. He specifically addresses the developmental and socioemotional aspects of gender definition—how these factors may contribute to the development of African American males and how they manifest themselves in educational settings.

Melissa Roderick presents an intricate study of four young African American males who aspired to succeed and tells their stories using case studies and interviews. She presents students with aspirations of success in the beginning of the school year who slowly but surely, as a result of loopholes in the school system, their communities, and sometimes society at large, are faced with the tough task of deferring their dreams of academic success.

Dena Swanson, Michael Cunningham, and Margaret Spencer also present societal and familial impacts on the education of African American males. They show how some males struggle to define themselves as young scholars, sometimes having to juggle academic achievement with masculinity and sometimes having to select one of the two in order to be successful. They also discuss the challenges that males are faced with when they choose to be scholars in terms of having strong survival mechanisms in and out of the classroom.

Jomills Braddock's chapter addresses the benefits and challenges of African American males participating in athletic events in school, and the extent to which this seems to enhance some students' academic performance, but not others.

Altogether, the various chapters in this edited volume are the proceedings from the conference on African American males presented at Howard University. The conference was cosponsored by Howard University and the U.S. Department of Education's Office of Educational Research and Improvement. The conference took place under the guidance of Dr. Kent McGuire and Ms. Sandra Steed, who also served as the main conference coordinator. As readers will note, the answers to many questions posed about the educational achievement of African American males are diverse. All the chapters in this volume are unique in their approaches, yet they all send a similar message: quality instruction, high expectations, and advocacy for the students. This is the first, and hopefully not the last, edited volume dedicated to the education of African American males.

Introduction

During the term that I served as Assistant Secretary of Education at the U.S. Department of Education (1998–2001), some of the staff members voiced concerns about a few issues that had previously gone unsupported. One of these topics struck such a chord of urgency that I agreed to sponsor a national conference addressing research concerns, findings, and ideas. This was the topic of the education of African American males.

I was, and still remain, concerned and disturbed about what the data reveal about the achievement disparities between majority and minority students. This information is even more troubling when the data are disaggregated between race and gender, and we find that this gap is largest among African American males. What is even more disturbing is that with the exception of a few scholars, there has really been relatively little attention given to solving this problem in the active educational realm. When I agreed to sponsor the conference, my sense was that while we have more than documented the problem, we seem to be "dragging our feet" in the direction of addressing the specific components of the problem and in creating and using powerful and effective interventions. In other words, there are numerous diagnoses but very few prescriptions, cures, or treatment plans.

Although it is well-known that socioeconomic status has been used several times as a factor that predicts academic achievement, the reality is that even when controlling for socioeconomic status, African American males still lag behind their Caucasian counterparts academically. Thus, even in communities where we would expect this racial- and gender-driven achievement gap to be virtually eliminated, we still find race-related discrepancies pertaining to the achievement of African American males. This suggests that the challenge lies just as much with the educators as it does with the students, and sometimes it lies even more with the educators.

What is particularly troubling is that many harbor beliefs that these students are actually capable of succeeding academically. There is no question about it. They are. It is incumbent on the academic community to cultivate and nurture the students' motivation to succeed academically. We do realize, however, that educators cannot "diagnose" and "prescribe treatments" alone but that they need help. This edited volume attempts to provide such greatly needed help to researchers and practitioners alike by addressing these issues from a multitude of perspectives and providing some possible solutions without being prescriptive. It is with great anticipation that I welcome this volume, because I believe that it should and will generate greater visibility for the scholars who have worked diligently over the years to continue to address this important topic. It addresses the main two factors affecting African American male achievement— motivation and performance—by delving into how these factors eventually address policy, theory, research, and practice.

I am hopeful that this volume will generate and stimulate greater interest in these issues; we could *certainly* use more investment in rigorous analysis of factors contributing to the achievement and detriment of the education of African American males. I am also hopeful that this volume will begin to help to bridge the gap between researchers and practitioners, policy makers, and all theoreticians in the areas of education. This volume should definitely be read by all stakeholders in education and, specifically, of the African American male community. In conclusion, it is my sincere desire that many of the questions and solutions that have surfaced in this volume will be pursued with vigor now and in the years to come.

—C. K. McGuire

Dean, College of Education
Temple University

Acknowledgments

I would like to take this opportunity to thank all of the contributing authors; this has been a long process. I thank my coeditors, Robert Jagers and Robert Cooper, and all the individuals at Sage Publications and Corwin Press. I thank Linda Mmayi and Stephanie Trkay for their patience and dedicated work on the articles as they appeared in their former formats. I also express thanks to Sandra Steed, currently at the U.S. Department of Education's Institute for Educational Studies, and Kent McGuire, now the Dean of the College of Education at Temple University, for their vision for the Conference on African American Male Achievement. I would be remiss if I did not thank the numerous individuals who assisted with the entire process from the retrieval of articles to proofreading to contacting individuals and asking them to sign forms for publications. They include my priceless graduate assistant Bedelia Richards, Lisa Ward from the U.S. Department of Education, and my wonderful research assistants at the Johns Hopkins University: Will Digs, Claire Whitner, Marcus Artis, Sean Coleman, and Adia Harvey. These undergraduate, graduate students, and now Ph.D.s invested a lot of time and effort to make this edition possible. I also wish to thank Christopher Anderson and Gautam Harjai, who spent countless hours proofreading the articles and corresponding with the authors. I thank Susan Tally, Ok Park Choon, Stephanie Trkay, Linda Mmayi, and Kofi Lomotey for their generous contributions of time and effort. I thank Douglas Rife, Lizzie Brenkus, and Kylee Liegl of Corwin Press for always making me feel appreciated and respected as an author. Finally, my deepest heartfelt thanks to Priscilla Drum and Richard Mayer of U.C. Santa Barbara, my adviser and mentor; Robert Cooper and Robert Jagers, my coeditors; and Robb Clouse of Corwin Press and the late John Hollifield, my mentors and cheerleaders. Some of us encounter individuals in life who serve as confidantes, friends, mentors, and supporters. Sometimes these roles are interchangeable and sometimes they are not. I am fortunate and honored to have many such people in my life. Priscilla, Richard, Robb, and John have served, and continue to serve, in all four roles. Their conversations, pep talks, comments, and advice have kept me inspired to continue to explore life outside my "comfort zone" and to apply myself to my fullest capacity. I thank you.

About the Editor

 **Olatokunbo (Toks) S. Fashola** is Senior Research Scientist and Research Director of the Comprehensive School Reform Center at the American Institutes for Research (AIR). She is primarily responsible for the evaluation and production of AIR-Reports. She has also served as an Adjunct Research Scientist at Johns Hopkins University. While at Johns Hopkins, she conducted research and published books and articles on the effectiveness of comprehensive school reform programs, including programs specifically geared toward middle and high school students. Dr. Fashola has written numerous articles on comprehensive school reform and is coauthor of the bestselling book *Show Me the Evidence! Proven and Promising Programs for America's Schools* (Corwin Press, 1998). She has also conducted research on effective reading programs for students in need of additional academic services in Grades K through 12 and also specifically geared toward middle and high school students. She is also author of *Building Effective Afterschool Programs* (Corwin Press).

Dr. Fashola is also involved in the National Longitudinal Study of the No Child Left Behind Act (NLS-NCLB). She serves as a senior content adviser for the What Works Clearinghouse in the area of high school dropouts. She is author of an entry in the *Corsini Concise Encyclopedia of Psychology and Neuroscience* on the topic of dropouts. She has served as principal investigator, evaluator, and adviser for several after-school programs and program evaluations across the country, and to reputable organizations such as the U.S. Department of Education's IES and the National Academy of Science's Committee on Research in Education. Her report titled *Effective Dropout Prevention*

and College Attendance Programs for Latino Students at Risk has garnered national attention. She has authored numerous articles on schoolwide reform, dropout prevention, and literacy. Her most recent work includes studies of randomized field trials of after-school reading interventions for students in need, and she has served as a resource to the Department of Education, and the National Academy of Science's Committee on Research in Education (CORE). Dr. Fashola is a recipient of the American Federation of Teachers Outstanding Contributions to Research award and is a member of Phi Delta Kappa International.

About the Contributors

Jomills Henry Braddock II received his PhD from Florida State University (1973). He has previously held faculty/research appointments at the Department of Sociology, University of Maryland Park and at The Johns Hopkins University, Center for Social Organization of Schools/ Department of Sociology. His broad research interests in issues of inequality and social justice have been supported by public and private grants and contracts addressing equality of opportunities in education, employment, and sports. His work on these topics typically involves secondary analyses of large-scale national longitudinal data and addresses public policy issues.

Dr. Braddock previously served two terms on the National Educational Research Policy and Priorities Board, which was established by Congress to develop a long-term research agenda and to set priorities to guide the work of the Education Department's Office of Educational Research and Improvement (OERI). He is also the Director of the Center for Research on Sport in Society. This center, working with individuals in South Florida and elsewhere, focuses on community-based projects that emphasize athletic activity and provide formative and summative evaluation expertise.

Robert Cooper is Assistant Professor in the Graduate School of Education at the University of California, Los Angeles. Driven by a passion to encourage poor and minority youth to view themselves as lifelong learners, his research interests center on increasing the college matriculation rates of these students through rigorous research pursuits and exploring avenues that ensure their graduation from higher education institutions.

Michael Cunningham is Associate Professor at Tulane University, where he holds a joint appointment in the Department of Psychology and the Program in African and African Diaspora Studies. Using an assets perspective in understanding resilience and vulnerability in adolescent populations, his primary research interests include examining adolescent development in diverse contexts.

James Earl Davis is Associate Professor in the Department of Educational Leadership and Policy Studies at Temple University. His research focuses on gender studies in education, sociology of higher education, educational policy, program evaluation, and the educational and social experiences of Black boys and men.

Ronald F. Ferguson is an economist and senior research associate at the Wiener Center for Social Policy. He has taught at Harvard University's John F. Kennedy School of Government since 1983. He participates in a variety of consulting and policy advisory activities on issues of education, employment, youth development, and urban development.

Will J. Jordan is a senior sociologist at the CNA Corporation, a private research and development center in Alexandria, Virginia, whose analyses and technical support provide information for government and nonprofit organizations in several areas, including education. He specializes in educational research focusing on urban education, program evaluation, alternative educational models for high school students, and educational policy.

Pedro A. Noguera is Professor in the Steinhardt School of Education at New York University. His research focuses on the ways in which schools respond to social and economic forces within the urban environment. He has also done extensive field research and published several articles on the role of education in political and social change in the Caribbean.

Melissa Roderick is Associate Professor in the School of Social Service Administration and Director of the Consortium on Chicago School Research at the University of Chicago. Her fields of special interest include education policy, urban high schools, adolescence, youth policy, human resources policy, and empirical analysis.

Margaret Beale Spencer is Professor of Education and Psychology at the University of Pennsylvania. Her adolescent-focused research explores resiliency, identity, and competence formation processes in youth. She serves as director of the Center for Health, Achievement Neighborhood, Growth and Ethnic Studies (CHANGES), as well as the Interdisciplinary Studies in Human Development (ISHD) Program and W.E.B. DuBois Collective Research Institute.

Dena Phillips Swanson is Assistant Professor in Human Development at Emory University. Her research addresses identity processes, adaptive strategies, and contextual supports of racial and ethnic minority youth.

CHAPTER ONE

Cultural Issues in Comprehensive School Reform

Robert Cooper

University of California, Los Angeles

Will J. Jordan

Temple University

As Cooper (1996) argued, American society remains stratified by both race/ethnicity and class. Being African American continues to have particularly negative connotations and consequences (Peters, 1981). Although African American students have made academic achievements and educational gains in recent years, public education in this country widely remains separate and unequal, even 50 years after *Brown v. Board of Education* (1954). Public education is separate to the extent that African American students, particularly males, are more frequently identified for special education than their peers or placed in vocational nonacademic classes in which they are neither intellectually stimulated nor challenged (Oakes, 1985). The educational experiences of these students often include low expectations, a feeling of inferiority, and a sense of defeat in their academic pursuits. Public education in this country remains unequal to the extent that the majority of African American students receive instruction from teachers who often lack experience, motivation, resources, and/or enthusiasm to effectively engage students in the learning process despite deteriorating school facilities that are both racially and economically isolated (Kozol, 1991).

On average, African American students disproportionately attend large, urban comprehensive or "zoned" schools with a high concentration of low-socioeconomic-status students. Academic achievement and graduation rates in many of these schools are very low in comparison to national averages (Balfanz & Legters, 1998). Many of these schools are located in communities that have relatively few resources and little social capital and political influence. Not only the schools but also many of the communities in which these schools are embedded have endured generations of poverty and racial isolation. These communities are marred by multiple social ills such as violence and crime, unemployment, drug abuse, poor public health, and teenage childbirth, along with an educational system that reproduces intergenerational poverty rather than transforming it. Unfortunately, schools serving African American students have historically legitimated inequality to a greater extent than they have fostered true social mobility (Bowles & Gintis, 1976; Jencks et al., 1972).

Research consistently concludes that disparate learning opportunities result in differing achievement outcomes for students. The lingering achievement gap between middle-class and financially disadvantaged students, as well as between White and Black students, has prompted many scholars to investigate the relationship between student achievement and such issues as schooling context, curriculum, and instruction (Cooper, 1999, 2000), educational policies and practices (Darling-Hammond, 2000; Elmore, 1996), parental involvement (Epstein, 1995; Sanders, 1996, 1998), and even intergroup relations (Cooper & Slavin, 2001; Schofield, 1991). Extant literature suggests the greatest and most persistent lag is between Black males and all other categories of students (Gibbs, 1988; Irvine, 1990; Polite & Davis, 1999). Educational statistics consistently reveal that Black males cluster at the top of the distribution of virtually every indicator of school failure, including dropout, absenteeism, suspension and expulsion, and low achievement (Garibaldi, 1992).

Many researchers and policy makers have denounced the use of deficit models to explain the negative schooling experiences of African American males and are engaged in research exploring and isolating the multiplicity of factors that contribute to the academic success of Black students (Cooper & Datnow, 2000; Sanders, 2000). They choose to shift the framing of their inquiry from a focus on the academic failure of African American students to an examination of alternative structures, organizations, and practices that lead to greater academic achievement. This line of inquiry flows from the educational resilience construct that focuses on success rather than failure (Wang & Gordon, 1994; Winfield, 1991). It views educational resilience not as a discrete, personal attribute but rather as the culmination of processes, mechanisms, and conditions that can be replicated across various school and family contexts. Utilizing such an approach helps to identify potential individual, school, and community factors that lead to and foster academic success among African American students (Winfield, 1991). In that tradition, this article explores ways in which the unprecedented amount of federal support for the comprehensive restructuring of schools with a large population of "at-risk" students can incorporate strategies to confront the unique educational challenges facing African American males. Researchers maintain that African American males must be guided to develop a positive sense of self and ethnic identity to be successful in school and in life (Boykin, 1986; Johnson & Johnson, 1981). If Black boys are to be sufficiently prepared to meet the challenges of the new millennium, it is important that they come to see themselves as intellectually and effectively competent in both academic and social circles and that they are able to enroll in as well as graduate from institutions of higher education.

BEING BLACK AND MALE IN AMERICA'S PUBLIC SCHOOLS

Cultural norms and values embedded in U.S. social, political, and economic institutions have resulted in the African American male becoming an "endangered" species (Gibbs, 1988; Hare, 1987; Jordan & Cooper, 2003). Not since the "lynching debates" of the early 20th century have Black boys and young men received so much attention and concern (Harris & Duhon, 1999). According to educational consultant Jawanza Kunjufu (1986), the endangered status is a result of African American boys' being systematically programmed for failure. Despite positive role models, such as Michael Jordan, Mohammed Ali, and Colin Powell, the majority of African American males, particularly those in urban centers, are categorized and stereotyped by the five Ds: dumb, deprived, dangerous, deviant, and disturbed (Gibbs, 1988). Although these words are seldom written or verbalized, they are often reflected in social policy and practice. Whether it is failure in the labor market or failure in educational pursuits, African American males are socialized to view themselves as less than, rather than equal to, their counterparts. Kunjufu (1986) cited the public school system as the most flagrant institution that contributes to the destruction of the African American boy. He claimed that educational institutions have established a myriad of policies and practices that unintentionally deny African American males equal access to high quality educational experiences, citing legislations, tracking, special education, and standard testing as examples. Moreover, Kunjufu maintained that the destruction of the African American male can be observed as early as the fourth grade when many begin to exhibit signs of intellectual retrogression, from which few recover, and proceed to find themselves ill prepared to survive in an innately racist educational system. Kunjufu contended that "the dominant cultural groups in American society, by control of key institutions, educational institutions being one of them, have systematically denied African American boys the fruits of their heritage, culture and rites of passage" (p. 15).

Numerous studies, such as the one released by the Committee to Study the Status of the African American Male in the New Orleans Public Schools (cited in Holland, 1991), confirm that African American males are disproportionately adversely affected by the public educational system. According to Holland (1991), the report reflects that although African American males represented only 43% of the public school population in the New Orleans public school system during the 1986 to 1987 academic year, they accounted for 57.7% of the nonpromotions, 65% of the suspensions, 80% of the expulsions, and 45% of the dropouts. Nonpromotions in the primary grades indicated that of the 1,470 first graders retained, 817 were African American males; of the 768 second graders retained, 440 were African American males; and of the 716 third graders retained, 438 were African American males (Holland, 1991). Experiencing similar statistics, many schools and districts are joining forces with researchers and policy makers to identify added resources and promising reform strategies and practices aimed at breaking the predictable cycle of failure for African American males in school. Because many scholars argue that little can be done within the context of the existing educational system, several innovative all-male academies have been established. These academies provide an African-centered curriculum that addresses the unique needs of urban juvenile and adolescent African American males and attempts to buffer them from potential pitfalls. Although this strategy has proven controversial, several Afrocentric all-male academies have been created during the past decade, beginning in the Milwaukee school district and spreading to other districts throughout the nation. However, the short- and long-term success of African American male academies has not been well established given the difficulty of controlling for self-selection and of finding adequate comparisons in regular public schools.

Moreover, numerically, the vast majority of African American males continue to attend regular public schools far more frequently than alternative, magnet, charter, religious, and private schools combined. Thus, to improve the conditions of education for African American males in this country, systemic changes must take place affecting regular community schools. Given the enormous costs, both financial and social, associated with school failure, particularly at the high school level, greater attention is being paid to high schools serving adolescents who are deemed the most at risk of school failure. School failure at the high school level translates into a variety of unproductive outcomes: dropping out of school, teenage pregnancy, crime, and drug use, all of which have serious implications for quality of life as an adult.

IMPROVING THE SCHOOLING EXPERIENCES OF AFRICAN AMERICAN MALES THROUGH COMPREHENSIVE SCHOOL REFORM

For the past two decades, the term *restructuring* has dominated educational discourse about how to change fundamentally the schooling experience for students. Research indicates that restructuring initiatives emerged in several waves (Lusi, 1997). The first wave focused on raising standards. Schools were simply asked "to do more of the same, but just do it better" (Petrie, 1990, p. 14). Petrie (1990) argued that the strategy of asking schools to do more of the same failed to recognize the systemic nature of the educational enterprise. This wave has been characterized as piecemeal and disconnected (Cohen & Spillance, 1992; Smith & O'Day, 1990). Though schools and educators were asked, and in many cases were required, to make significant changes, research suggests that this wave of reform left the fundamental nature of teaching and learning unchanged (Cohen, 1988; Cuban, 1990; Firestone, 1989). The second wave shifted the focus of reform to the redistribution of power (Murphy, 1992). Reformers sought to decentralize control of curriculum, budgets, and staffing to principals, teachers, and parents (Clune & White, 1988). This wave called for school-by-school, locally adapted change that was respectful and sensitive to the local context (Elmore & McLaughlin, 1988). Reforms were designed to "capitalize on the energy and creativity of individuals at the school level" (Murphy, 1992, p. 6). Although this wave produced a number of schools in which teaching and learning were qualitatively different, the number of schools that experienced and sustained fundamental change was not widespread (Lusi, 1997). The third wave of reform represents a fundamental shift in how educators and policy makers view the purpose of education (Murphy, 1992). It seeks to alter the traditional concepts behind school policy. The goal of education is no longer viewed as the maintenance of the organizational infrastructure but rather the development of human resources (Mojkowski & Fleming, 1988). At the high school level, comprehensive school reform has focused primarily on policies and practices aimed at universally improving educational quality in failing schools. For example, the often-cited *Breaking Ranks* report (National Association of Secondary School Principals, 1996) suggests that there are perhaps hundreds of challenges facing high schools and any number of critical goals that could be focused on by a school or district vying for improvement. Yet, several core themes are laid out in *Breaking Ranks* that are deemed to be central to any short list of high school reform initiatives. These themes, or guiding principles, include the following statements:

> High school is, above all else, a learning community and each school must commit itself to expecting demonstrated academic achievement for every student in accord with standards that can stand up to national scrutiny.

High school must function as a transitional experience, getting each student ready for the next stage of life, whatever it may be for that individual, with the understanding that, ultimately, each person needs to earn a living.

High school must be a gateway to multiple options.

High school must prepare each student to be a lifelong learner.

High school must provide an underpinning for good citizenship and for full participation in the life of a democracy.

High school must play a role in the personal development of young people as social beings that have needs beyond those that are strictly academic.

High school must lay a foundation for students to be able to participate comfortably in an increasingly technological society.

High school must equip young people for life in a country and a world in which interdependency will link their destiny to that of others, however different those others may be from them.

High school must be an institution that unabashedly advocates on the behalf of young people.

Each of these statements represents broad ideas or responsible goals for any high school attempting to prepare adolescents for higher education and adult life, apparently, irrespective of the cultural traditions of the students. We cite these excerpts from *Breaking Ranks* not as hard and fast rules for governing high school reform but instead as noteworthy pursuits for reform frequently appearing throughout the research and policy literature.

We underscore the fact that although these guiding principles can be seen as goals of high school reform, no specific reference is made to whether or how racial/ethnic and gender issues influence or alter the implementation process. However, embedded within the policies and practices of many of the current reform strategies is the belief that more students, and we argue particularly African American male students, can be better served educationally when traditional notions of teaching and learning are reconceptualized. Jordan and his colleagues argued that this reconceptualization at the high school level requires the restructuring of three important dimensions of the schooling process: (a) structural reform, (b) curriculum and instruction, and (c) professional development opportunities for teachers (Jordan & Cooper, 2003; Jordan, McPartland, Legters, & Balfanz, 2000). Building on that work, we argue that a fourth dimension also warrants attention: specifically, the norms that guide and direct school policy and practice. Restructuring of the norms that guide policy and practice refers to altering institutional ethos in ways that value and celebrate the unique contributions and learning styles of each student. This involves seeing racial affirmation, cultural history, family background, and native language other than English as assets to the learning process not as barriers to intellectual pursuits.

CHANGING SCHOOL NORMS AND CULTURE

Changing school norms and culture is driven in part by changing beliefs about academic ability and intelligence (Oakes, Lipton, & Jones, 1995). Policies and practices that relate to such issues as the social organization of schools, grouping practices, curriculum choices, and methods of instruction are all rooted in beliefs about how the differences between and among students should be addressed. If the old mantra "all kids can learn" is to be institutionalized in our public school system and guide our policy and practice, educators will have to come to see all students as valuable assets to the educational enterprise. Unfortunately, despite evidence that challenges the deficit model perspective, many educators enter the classroom with perspectives and biases that interfere with their ability to teach all students equally (Lou, 1994). Many educators still use the deficit paradigm to understand and interact with African American males.

The deficit model perspective, which grew out of research in the 1960s (Deutsch & Brown, 1964; John & Goldstein, 1964), focuses on a perceived cultural, psychological, and/or mental deficiency of Black males (Sleeter & Grant, 1994) and blames them for their social and academic failure. Such normative beliefs result in African American boys' being disproportionately mislabeled as mentally retarded, assigned to special education classes, and frequently identified as discipline problems. Thus, if comprehensive school reform is to serve as a vehicle to promote greater academic and social success for African American males, norms about race and culture must be explicitly addressed.

Although many reform initiatives incorporate multicultural education—a construct that has emerged as an umbrella concept to deal with race, culture, language, social class, and disability (Sleeter & Grant, 1994)—there is a widespread philosophy among school reformers that effective education should be culturally neutral. However, many scholars of color disagree with this precedent. There is considerable evidence that issues of race and cultural background do in fact play a key role in the education of African American students (Cooper & Datnow, 2000; Delpit, 1995; Irvine, 1990; Ladson-Billings, 1994; Tatum, 1992). Neglecting the role of culture in educating children and adolescents is defined in Irvine's (1990) notion of "cultural aversion," which she describes as a general reluctance by educators to consider race and race-related issues such as equality, prejudice, discrimination, and social justice. According to Irvine (1990),

This color-blind philosophy is linked to educators' uncomfortableness in discussing race, their lack of knowledge of cultural heritage of their students' peers, and their fears and anxieties that open consideration of differences might incite racial discord or perhaps upset a fragile, often unpredictable, racial harmony. (p. 26)

There is a preference among many educators and policy makers to focus on the broad issues pertaining to school reform and improvement, as if they were devoid of cultural implications. Although the existing educational literature contains a number of policy and practice recommendations for educating African American males, it begs an important question: "What can be done within the context of comprehensive school reform to bolster the overall achievement and scholastic success for African American male students?" Although comprehensive school reform is beginning to take into account various strategies for improving school organization, curriculum, and professional development, the issue of race within the context of comprehensive reform has been largely ignored.

The schism between the discourse on comprehensive school reform and issues of race and culture is particularly salient in relation to teacher quality and recruitment. However, the success of school reform is strongly dependent on the staffing situation at the particular site. Many models of high school reform are asked to assume existing levels of educational staff. Concern is often focused on policies and practices to be implemented, such as building smaller learning communities and using cooperative learning techniques, with less attention paid to the characteristics (both achieved and ascriptive) of the educators implementing the reform. Teacher background characteristics, such as gender and race/ethnicity as well as their education, training, and experience, are critical factors. Several scholars have written about the implications of cultural and social distances between students and teachers (Delpit, 1995; Ladson-Billings, 1994; Rist, 1970). Irvine (1990) suggested that what she calls "cultural synchronization" between students and teachers is a critical component of motivating Black students to achieve. For the current wave of reform initiatives to be most effective in meeting the challenges faced by African American males in public education, comprehensive school reform research and policy must be joined with teacher recruitment research and policy.

TEACHER/STUDENT CULTURAL CONGRUENCE

Aside from sleeping and perhaps playing, there is no other activity that occupies as much of a student's time as attending school. Given this, one could conclude that there is perhaps no single criterion greater than the student/teacher relationship for success in school. Despite the importance of this relationship, many of the students who are training to be educators have little, if any, experience interacting with racially and culturally different students. Although there is no substitute for effective school organization, curriculum, and programs of professional development, the question of who teaches African American boys is as critical to the academic success of these students as what is taught and how it is presented.

Many studies have been conducted focusing on microprocesses and student-teacher interaction within the classroom. Studies addressing issues such as teacher expectancies (Dusek, 1975; Elashoff & Snow, 1971; Entwisle & Hayduk, 1978; Rist, 1970) and cultural synchronization (Irvine, 1990) cast light on the degree to which ascriptive factors such as race/ethnicity, gender, and social class can influence student learning. However, developing strategies for mitigating the effects of low expectancies, cultural ambivalence, or general misunderstandings between teachers and students can be difficult. In fact, success is often fleeting and difficult to sustain. This is primarily because attempts to change expectancies and cultural sensitivities cut to the core of teachers and other school personnel as individuals, as well as the social conditions students face in school and in their community. Therefore, we contend that to advance research and development on the central principles of comprehensive school reform, the role of Black male teachers as successful role models warrants serious consideration. This assertion is based on theories of cultural synchronization coupled with an understanding that overall teacher quality and effectiveness trumps racial congruence between students and teachers. To be more specific, an experienced and effective teacher of any racial background is more preferable for Black male students than an ineffective teacher of African American descent. However, having stated this, Black male teachers perhaps have several important advantages in educating Black boys. These advantages include, for example, modeling appropriate behavior, strategic use of shared knowledge, and in some cases, common social experiences. The rapport that Black male teachers establish with Black male students through their common cultural heritage can be maintained in the face of social class differences. Therefore, in addition to raising the overall quality of the school through comprehensive reform, the value-added dimension of being exposed to good teachers who are Black males might be a factor in raising the success rates of Black male students.

But, merely increasing the number of Black male teachers alone is not the answer. Instead, we suggest that shared cultural knowledge generated by coming from the same racial and gender group can provide a value-added dimension to teaching and learning, holding constant a teacher's ability to teach, his or her educational credentials, and level of experience. Perhaps a wrinkle in this conjecture is that, although Black male teachers and students may share common cultural experiences, teachers are, by definition, middle class. Thus, complete cultural congruence or synchronization is ultimately unachievable in some contexts.

Still, there are many examples of racially isolated schools, which employ many Black teachers, where Black male students consistently fail. Perhaps here the persistent underperformance of Black males can be explained by a combination of factors such as inadequate resources, unstable leadership, overall teacher quality, and a host of student inputs including the intractable conditions brought on by poverty.

FUNDAMENTAL CHANGE REQUIRES AN INTEGRATIVE APPROACH

The primary aim of comprehensive school reform is to effect deep changes in the structure/organization, curriculum and teaching practices, and professional development agenda of schools (Jordan et al., 2000), and we add as well, changes in the norms that guide both policy and practice. To be effective in this endeavor we argue that it requires a four-pronged integrative approach. We contend that these four dimensions of the schooling process, when taken together, are the most critical components of the educational process and greatly shape and influence how students experience school. Moreover, we argue that a synchronicity of these four components is a necessity in the attempt to create an environment that is nurturing to and supportive of the African American male experience in our public schools and in the attempt to break the predictable cycle of failure for this population of America's youth.

Changing of school structures and organization refers to altering the social and/or physical organization of the school. These types of changes include various initiatives such as career academies, smaller learning communities, extended instructional periods, reduced class size, interdisciplinary teacher teams, and block scheduling. Changes such as these provide educators with the flexibility to incorporate more of the cooperative learning exercises and experience that research suggests are particularly effective in increasing the academic success of African American students (Cooper & Slavin, 2001). At the center of the current school restructuring movement is the notion that if we can alter the way in which schools are organized, we can change how teachers teach and how students learn (Elmore, 1996).

How teachers teach and how and what students learn is at the center of this four-pronged integrative approach. Altering curriculum and instruction addresses this concern by attempting to improve both the content and delivery of academic subject matter. This is achieved by developing innovative ways to teach the core subject matters while infusing culturally relevant pedagogy and literature into the courses. As research has clearly demonstrated, making the type of fundamental changes necessary to alter the schooling experience for African American males requires increasing the number of professional development opportunities for teachers and administrators. Not only is there a need to increase the frequency of opportunities for educators to engage in open dialogue about education, but also a need to develop a variety of forums and venues in which these opportunities are presented. Although there is some agreement among researchers that the likelihood of a successful reform increases in cases when all three dimensions are taken into consideration, a persuasive argument can be made that altering school norms and creating a new culture is itself an additional, critical dimension that must be addressed if comprehensive reform is to make a fundamental change in the schooling experience of African American males.

One of the major reasons cited for the lack of engagement of African American males in the schooling process is a sense of isolation and alienation from the institution. For many Black boys, school is viewed as a place of anonymity and failure. However, by breaking a large school down into smaller learning communities or by establishing interdisciplinary teams of teachers with common planning time, new patterns of relationships and normative structures can emerge that will support the educational pursuits of Black boys. For example, when large poorly managed schools, overrun by chaos, are restructured into self-contained, smaller learning communities, expectations for teachers and students can be altered as a result of this structural shift. Because smaller elementary and high schools are easier to manage, chaos becomes order (Lee & Loeb, 2000). One of the reasons for this positive change is that it becomes easier for teachers and administrators in smaller environments not only to learn the names of all the students they interact with during the day but also to know something about what motivates them. One-on-one relationships between educators and students facilitate the creation of a new culture and climate within the school consisting of both a warm and caring environment for students as well as an effective academic process.

SUMMARY AND CONCLUSION

Although there is a general understanding among educators, policy makers, and researchers that at-risk students are culturally and ethnically diverse, as well as disproportionately African American, Latino, and Native American, we have yet to develop adequate policies and practices for taking full advantage of students' cultural histories. Although multicultural education and culturally relevant pedagogy/curricula are slowly penetrating comprehensive school reform, there is little evidence of a significant impact on the achievement and school success of African American males. Furthermore, the overall impact of comprehensive high school reform on closing the gaps between African American males and other adolescent groups has not been thoroughly investigated. Because educational institutions are compulsory through age 16, they absorb a disproportionate responsibility for ameliorating the negative effects of inequality in society. Conventional wisdom suggests that one of the core purposes of the school is to embody egalitarian principles such as democracy and the maintenance of an equal opportunity social structure. Schools should provide a vehicle of social mobility for disadvantaged and minority students while providing middle-class students with the skills to reproduce their social status. However, educational and social mobility is a zero-sum game (Jencks et al., 1972); success for one individual reduces the probability of success for another. Suppose, for example, that school dropout was eliminated and that every high school graduate was suddenly qualified to attend college. Even if this were to happen, we do not have a higher education infrastructure to support such an influx of new students. Therefore, it is difficult to conceive of an educational system that truly leaves no student behind without reconceptualizing broader social, economic, and political structures. In the case of African American males, many reform agendas have missed the mark. African American males are at risk in school just as they are at risk in the larger spheres of society. It is perhaps due, in part, to historical and ongoing inequality and racism. The criminalization of African American males through racial profiling, persistent disparaging media images as challenged by the National Association for the Advancement of Colored People, and the overrepresentation of African American males in state and federal prisons are all elements that contribute to the endangerment and at-risk standing of the African American juvenile and adolescent. The implementation of school reform and positive, culturally synchronic role models aims to counteract the negative influences and images that create the gap between the members of this demographic population and their peers.

REFERENCES

Balfanz, R., & Legters, N. E. (1998). *How many truly awful urban high schools are there? Some early estimates.* Unpublished manuscript, Johns Hopkins University, Baltimore.

Bowles, S., & Gintis, H. (1976). *Schooling in capitalist America.* New York: Basic Books.

Boykin, A. W. (1986). The triple quandary of schooling Afro-American children. In U. Neisser (Ed.), *The school achievement of minority children* (pp. 57–92). Hillsdale, NJ: Lawrence Erlbaum.

Brown v. Board of Education, 347 U.S. 483 (1954).

Clune, W. H., & White, P. A. (1988). *School-based management: Institutional variation, implementation, and issues for further research.* New Brunswick, NJ: Rutgers University, Eagleton Institute of Politics, Center for Policy Research in Education.

Cohen, D. K. (1988). Teaching practice: Plus que ca change. In P. W. Jackson (Ed.), *Contributing to educational change: Perspectives on research and practice* (pp. 27–84). Berkeley, CA: McCutchan.

Cohen, D. K., & Spillance, J. (1992). Policy and practice: The relations between governance and instruction. In G. Grant (Ed.), *The review of research in education* (pp. 3–49). Washington, DC: American Educational Research Association.

Cooper, R. (1996). De-tracking reform in an urban California high school: Improving the schooling experience of African American students. *Journal of Negro Education, 65*(2), 190–208.

Cooper, R. (1999). A promising example of urban school reform: De-tracking in a racially mixed high school. *Journal of Education for Students Placed at Risk, 4*(3), 259–275.

Cooper, R. (2000). Urban school reform from a student of color perspective. *Urban Education, 34*(5), 597–622.

Cooper, R., & Datnow, A. (2000). African-American students' success in independent schools: A model of family, peer, community, and school influences. In M. Sanders (Ed.), *Schooling students placed at risk: Research, policy, and practice in the education of poor and minority adolescents* (pp. 187–206). Hillsdale, NJ: Lawrence Erlbaum.

Cooper, R., & Slavin, R. E. (2001). Cooperative learning programs and multicultural education: Improving intergroup relations. In F. Salili & R. Hoosain (Eds.), *Research on multicultural education and international perspectives* (pp. 15–33). Greenwich, CT: Information Age.

Cuban, L. (1990). Reforming again, again, and again. *Educational Researcher, 19*(1), 3–13.

Darling-Hammond, L. (2000). Teacher quality and student achievement: A review of state policy evidence [Electronic version]. *Education Policy Analysis Archives, 8*(1).

Delpit, L. (1995). *Other people's children: Cultural conflict in the classroom.* New York: New Press.

Deutsch, M., & Brown, B. (1964). Social influences in Negro-White intelligence differences. *Journal of Social Issues, 20,* 24–35.

Dusek, J. B. (1975). Do teachers bias children's learning? *Review of Educational Research, 45*(4), 661–684.

Elashoff, J. D., & Snow, R. E. (1971). *Pygmalion reconsidered.* Worthington, OH: Charles A. Jones.

Elmore, R. E. (1996). Getting to scale with good educational practice. *Harvard Educational Review, 66,* 1–26.

Elmore, R. E., & McLaughlin, M. W. (1988). *Steady work: Policy, practice and the reform of American education.* Santa Monica, CA: RAND.

Entwisle, D. R., & Hayduk, L. A. (1978). *Too great expectations: The academic outlook of young children.* Baltimore: Johns Hopkins University Press.

Epstein, J. L. (1995). School, family, community partnerships: Caring for the children we share. *Phi Delta Kappan, 76,* 701–712.

Firestone, W. A. (1989). Educational policy as an ecology of games. *Educational Researcher, 18*(7), 18–23.

Garibaldi, A. M. (1992). Educating and motivating African American males to succeed. *Journal of Negro Education, 61,* 4–11.

Gibbs, J. T. (Ed.). (1988). *Young, Black, and male in America: An endangered species.* Dover, MA: Auburn House.

Hare, B. R. (1987). Structural inequality and the endangered status of Black youth. *Journal of Negro Education, 56*(1), 100–110.

Harris, W. G., & Duhon, G. M. (1999). *The African American male perspective of barriers to success.* Lewiston, NY: Edwin Mellen Press.

Holland, S. H. (1991). Positive role models for primary-grade Black inner-city males. *Equity and Excellence, 25*(1), 40–44.

Irvine, J. J. (1990). *Black students and school failure: Policies, practices and prescriptions.* New York: Greenwood.

Jencks, C., Smith, M., Acland, H., Bane, M. J., Cohen, D., Gintis, H., et al. (1972). *Inequality: A reassessment of the effect of family and schooling in America.* New York: Basic Books.

John, V., & Goldstein, L. (1964). The social context of language acquisitions. *Merrill Palmer Quarterly, 10,* 265–275.

Johnson, D. W., & Johnson, R. T. (1981). Effects of cooperative and individualistic learning experience on interethnic interaction. *Journal of Educational Psychology, 73,* 444–449.

Jordan, W., & Cooper, R. (2003). High school reform and Black male students: Limits and possibilities of policy and practice. *Urban Education, 38*(2), 196–216.

Jordan, W. J., McPartland, J. M., Legters, N. E., & Balfanz, R. (2000). Creating a comprehensive school reform model: The talent development high school with career academies. *Journal of Education for Students Placed At Risk, 5*(1/2), 159–181.

Kozol, J. (1991). *Savage inequalities: Children in America's schools.* New York: Harper Perennial.

Kunjufu, J. (1986). *Countering the conspiracy to destroy Black boys* (Vol. 2). Chicago: African American Images.

Ladson-Billings, G. (1994). *The dream-keeper: Successful teachers of African American children.* San Francisco: Jossey-Bass.

Lee, V. E., & Loeb, S. (2000). School size in elementary schools: Effects on teacher's attitudes and student achievement. *American Education Research Journal, 37*(1), 3–31.

Lou, R. (1994). Teaching all students equally. In H. Roberts, J. C. Gonzalez, O. Harris, D. Huff, A. M. Johns, R. Lou, & O. Scott (Eds.), *Teaching from a multicultural perspective* (pp. 28–45). Thousand Oaks, CA: Sage.

Lusi, S. (1997). *The role of state departments of education in complex school reform.* New York: Teachers College Press.

Mojkowski, C., & Fleming, D. (1988). *School-site management: Concepts and approaches.* Andover, MA: Regional Laboratory for Educational Improvement of the Northeast and Islands.

Murphy, J. (1992). Restructuring America's schools: An overview. In C. Finn & T. Rebarbert (Eds.), *Education reform in the 1990s* (pp. 3–20). New York: Macmillan.

National Association of Secondary School Principals. (1996). *Breaking ranks: Changing an American institution.* Reston, VA: Author.

Oakes, J. (1985). *Keeping track: How schools structure inequality.* New Haven, CT: Yale University Press.

Oakes, J., Lipton, M., & Jones, M. (1995, April). *Changing minds: Deconstructing intelligence in de-tracking schools.* Paper presented at the annual meeting of the American Educational Research Association, San Francisco.

Peters, M. (1981). Parenting in Black families with young children: A historical perspective. In J. McAdoo (Ed.), *Black children: Social, educational, and parental environments* (pp. 211–224). Beverly Hills, CA: Sage.

Petrie, H. G. (1990). Reflections on the second wave of reform: Restructuring the teaching profession. In S. L. Jacobson & J. A. Conway (Eds.), *Educational leadership in an era of reform* (pp. 14–29). New York: Longman.

Polite, V. C., & Davis, J. E. (1999). *African American males in school and society: Practices and policies for effective education.* New York: Teachers College Press.

Rist, R. C. (1970). Student social class and teacher expectations: The self-fulfilling prophecy in ghetto education. *Harvard Educational Review, 40*(3), 411–451.

Sanders, M. G. (1996). Building family partnerships that last. *Educational Leadership, 54*(3), 61–66.

Sanders, M. G. (1998). The effects of school, family and community support on the academic achievement of African American adolescents. *Urban Education, 33*(3), 385–409.

Sanders, M. G. (2000). *Schooling students placed at risk: Research, policy, and practice in the education of poor and minority adolescents.* Hillsdale, NJ: Lawrence Erlbaum.

Schofield, J. S. (1991). School desegregation and inter-group relations: A review of the literature. In G. Grant (Ed.), *Review of research in education* (Vol. 17, pp. 335–409).Washington, DC: American Educational Research Association.

Sleeter, C., & Grant, C. (1994). *Making choices for multicultural education: Five approaches to race, class and gender.* New York: Macmillan.

Smith, M. S., & O'Day, J. (1990). Systemic school reform. In M. B. Ginsburg (Ed.), *Politics of education association yearbook, 1990* (pp. 233–267). New York: Taylor & Francis.

Tatum, B. (1992). Talking about race, learning about racism: The application of racial identity development theory in the classroom. *Harvard Educational Review, 62*(1), 1–24.

Wang, M. C., & Gordon, E. W. (Eds.). (1994). *Educational resilience in inner-city America: Challenges and prospects.* Hillsdale, NJ: Lawrence Erlbaum.

Winfield, L. F. (1991). Resilience, schooling, and development in African American youth: A conceptual framework. *Educational and Urban Society, 24,* 5–14.

CHAPTER TWO

Developing the Talents of African American Male Students During the Nonschool Hours

Olatokunbo S. Fashola

Johns Hopkins University

Fifty years after the *Brown v. Board of Education* (1954) decision to integrate public schools in an attempt to improve opportunities for all public school students, research shows that African American students continue to score below White students in the areas of science, mathematics, reading, and writing (National Center for Educational Statistics, 1998). This disparity may have decreased slightly during the years, yet recent reports indicate that the achievement gap between White and African American students has remained fairly constant during the past 6 to 8 years (National Assessment of Educational Progress, 1999; National Center for Educational Statistics, 1998). Although there are many African American students who perform well in their individual schools and school districts, national reports show that as a group, African American students are not performing as well as their White counterparts (National

Assessment of Educational Progress, 1999; National Center for Educational Statistics, 1998).

Many children, regardless of socioeconomic status, race, and gender, need additional help in academic work beyond instruction provided during the regular school day. For many families, particularly African American families, the after-school hours are an ideal time for providing students with rich, stimulating experiences to which they would not normally have access during the regular school day (Fashola, 1998a; Posner & Vandell, 1994). Many families, especially low-income African American families, are unable to participate in after-school programs for various reasons, such as lack of access to transportation, inaccessibility to additional funding to pay for after-school programs, and in some cases, time.

This chapter examines strategies for developing the talents of African American students during the nonschool hours and provides examples of some programs that have been successful at eliminating barriers and developing the talents of African Americans in many areas, including education. As we examine these programs, we specifically attempt to focus on success, or potential for success, among African American males.

Why focus on African American males? One of the terms frequently used to describe this population is *endangered species.* African American adult males have some of the highest incarceration and homicide rates in the country, and this has been the case for more than a decade (Clear, 1994). African American males have one of the highest expulsion and dropout rates from high school and college, and statistics show that African American males are also choosing not to enroll in college (Braddock, 1990; National Assessment of Educational Progress, 2003; Owens, 1990). If this is indeed the case, society provides few, if any, opportunities for advancement to young African American males with less than a high school diploma. As a result, the simple ability to remain in the workforce may soon become an unreachable goal for this population. Providing educational after-school programs in a school-based setting provides African American male students with qualified teachers and trained staff who can work with much smaller groups of children to enrich their experiences in the areas of academics, culture, and social interaction with peers.

As educators, our calling is to educate all children, including African American males. As psychologists, our role is to determine internal factors that serve as barriers to and facilitators of these goals.

As sociologists, we are expected to determine societal factors that serve as barriers to and facilitators of the attainment of these goals. However, as educated problem solvers seeking to understand the multiple factors that present risks or threats to the academic achievement of African American male students, we attempt to find and implement solutions that will eliminate or dissolve these barriers. We realize that there is more to the education of the child than just the school classroom, but for many school-aged African American children, the school building is the only place where they receive any form of assistance pertaining to educational matters. As educators, we also realize that there are many other factors that influence children beyond the classroom, such as the family and community, but because we are more capable of addressing obstacles to the success of the children in the classroom, we neglect these additional "external" factors.

This chapter addresses what takes place during the regular school day but also seeks to go beyond this and address the role of the school in the life of African American students, especially African American males. One way to concentrate on developing the talents of African American males during the nonschool hours is to investigate after-school and extended school-day programs that have been successful at attending to the development of African American students, specifically African American males.

Why address after-school programs? Research shows (Braddock, 1990) that many African American males are at risk for dropping out of school at an early age and develop feelings of failure very early in life (Hudley, 1992). Feelings of academic inadequacy combined with feelings of isolation and low self-esteem are a few of the reasons why African American male students tend to fail in, and eventually drop out of, school (Hudley, 1992; Sanders & Herting, 2000). Knowing this, our question becomes, "What can the schools do that will make the experiences more positive so that students will be more motivated to stay in school and succeed academically?" Although many may argue that it is not the role of the school to educate children beyond the walls of the classroom, research shows (Bronfenbrenner, 1986; Epstein, 1995; Rogoff, 1990, 1995, 1996; Vygotsky, 1978) that what takes place outside the school affects the child just as strongly as what takes place inside the school. If the school is able to positively reach out to the children and the other communities that influence them, this could be the beginning of a positive trend of having the school serve as a hub of activity for African American students and the community.

There are already some examples of programs taking place around the country, such as L.A.'s BEST, Empowerment Zone after-school programs in Baltimore and Philadelphia, 21st Century Community Learning Centers, Child First in Baltimore, and many other recent programs that have addressed the need for extended-hour programs. Some after-school programs have focused on cultural issues and athletics, but few, if any, of these have special components of their programs dedicated to addressing the educational advancement of African American students and African American males in particular. The programs to be discussed in this chapter have shown evidence of effectiveness in providing recreational and academic assistance among African American students during the nonschool hours and were developed to serve students who may need additional opportunities to learn beyond those provided in the classroom.

With the U.S. Congress having passed legislation to provide enrichment during the nonschool hours as a means to end social promotion and to improve the academic achievement of students, public schools are in a quandary as to which programs will best suit the needs of their students. Specifically, they are interested in knowing how to design programs and what features the programs should include. Given the precarious position of this topic with respect to African American males, schools should be interested in exploring what they can do to attract and retain African American males so that they can also receive the maximum benefits of the after-school program.

Programs seeking to improve academic achievement of African American males must be sure to research the goals and outcomes of specific programs before choosing to implement them in their schools or centers. Regardless of the type of program being offered to the children, there are some underlying qualities that all programs must have to offer the best services to their youth and families. Examples of these qualities include trained staff, structured programs, flexibility of program choice, positive environments, continuous evaluation of the program toward program goals, and a clear understanding of program goals (Fashola, 1999c; Fashola & Slavin, 1997, 1998b). Research shows that these qualities contribute to positive environments and, in some cases, positive outcomes in after-school care settings (Pierce, Hamm, & Vandell, 1997; Posner & Vandell, 1994; Rosenthal & Vandell, 1996; Vandell & Corasaniti,

1988). The next section briefly distinguishes between programs with goals as safe havens, those with goals as fun centers, and, finally, programs with goals of improving academic achievement using either remedial or enrichment activities. Also, given the various descriptions of nonschool-hour programs, such as day care, after school, and extended school day, it is important to distinguish different types of programs that serve students during the after-school hours by focusing on their goals and structures.

AFTER-SCHOOL PROGRAMS

After-school programs are generally likely to involve school-age children only (ages 5 to 18) and emphasize academic, as well as nonacademic, activities. These programs seek to help children make creative use of their free time and usually, when compared with day care programs, are more likely to provide transportation, offer a wider variety of recreational programs, and have increased child-to-adult ratios. These programs are typically more affordable than child care programs. Some after-school programs offer specialized activities, using professionals or qualified persons and volunteers to provide instruction in cultural enrichment areas such as ballet, tap dancing, music, karate, and chess. Examples of some community-based after-school programs include Boys and Girls Clubs, the YMCA, Big Brothers/Big Sisters, some 4-H programs, ASPIRA, church programs, and various municipal parks and recreational programs. Academic achievement, attendance, or other school-related outcomes may or may not be the primary or secondary goal of these programs.

SCHOOL-BASED ACADEMIC EXTENDED-DAY PROGRAMS

School-based academic extended-day programs also take place during the after-school hours, but differ from community-based after-school programs in that they are directly connected to the academic school day. Although community-based after-school programs may or may not take place on the school grounds, the school-based academic extended-day programs typically take place at the school, providing a mixture of academic, recreational, and cultural programs. Regular school-day teachers and paraprofessionals are usually paid to stay at the school site during the after-school hours or to participate in or to supervise such programs.

As noted, this type of model has a main academic focus, and the goals, outcomes, and methods of academic instruction are directly related to and aligned with the core daytime academic curriculum. Teachers conduct small group tutorials or teach remedial classes, supervise homework clubs, and teach study skills and advanced-level or enrichment courses (e.g., foreign language or computer science). In addition, paraprofessionals and/or community volunteers may provide cultural and recreational programs. Teachers may also supervise and train volunteers or paraprofessionals to provide academic or nonacademic services. Extended school-day programs can be schoolwide or districtwide. They are rarely mandatory but may provide inducements for children to attend.

Some school-based initiatives invite community members to their program planning sessions and include them as teachers for some of the classes and activities. These individuals may be associated, for example, with churches, private and public corporations, law enforcement agencies, parent groups (e.g., parent-teacher associations), businesses, and members of the armed forces. In some cases, school and program personnel make the after-school program a hub of community activity, and with time, the program and the school may begin to collaborate and to have a broad impact on the community.

One trend in some extended school-day and after-school programs is the development of curricula tied to district, state, and national goals yet designed for after-school education. Such programs may involve well-designed curricula, teacher training, and student assessments. These programs provide students with complete and well-tested approaches, resources, and trainers, reducing the need for every school to create its own extended school-day or after-school curriculum. Some seem promising, have been widely used, and have at least anecdotal indications of effectiveness in individual schools. However, many have not been used with at-risk students, and although they may have been assessed for implementation fidelity and student enjoyment, few have been evaluated or examined for their impact on achievement using methods that would pass even the most minimal evaluation standards.

In cases where schools are not equipped to create their own programs, or if schools have the funding to select currently existing programs, the following section provides examples of programs created for after-school use that were either designed for after-school purposes, have been used in such settings, or have been evaluated for use in after-school settings. For a more in-depth description of such programs, see Fashola (1998a, 2001).

The first group of programs includes academically based after-school and extended school-day programs with evidence of effectiveness among African American male students. Four such programs are included in this chapter. The second section of this chapter provides information about features of patterns of success among programs that have been beneficial to the talent development of African American students. The third section provides information about barriers to success among after-school programs serving African American males.

CRITERIA FOR INCLUSION

There are numerous after-school and extended school-day programs in operation across the country. However, to be included in this first section that focuses mainly on academics, the programs described herein had to meet certain criteria. These criteria included evidence of having an after-school focus, having an academic focus, wide replication, evaluation and evidence of effectiveness in after-school settings, and evidence of effectiveness among African American students. These criteria were then divided into three categories and evaluated on the basis of the available evidence. The next section provides information about these categories.

Effectiveness

Evidence of effectiveness was determined by the research design used, evaluation or assessment measures used, and power of the results. Research designs that yielded evidence of effectiveness used pre- and postassessments, with the students either randomly assigned to experimental and control conditions, or evenly matched, based on key demographic and/or dependent measures. Assessment measures were considered fair or appropriate measures if they were externally developed, preferably standardized tests. Finally, the power of the results was determined using effect sizes. The effect size is computed as the difference between the experimental and control group means, divided by the control group's standard deviation (Glass, McGaw, & Smith, 1981). Fashola and Slavin (1997) described an effect size of 1.0 as equivalent to 100 points on the SAT scale, two stanines, 15 points of IQ, or about 21 National Curve Equivalents (NCEs). For the purposes of educational programs, an effect size of +0.25 is considered educationally significant as is an NCE gain above 8 points.

Replicability

Replicability is seen as the ability of the program to duplicate itself and its results beyond the original implementation site. Replicability of a program and its results helps to determine the potential generalizability for new institutions considering the adoption of the program. All of the programs reviewed in this chapter have evidence of extensive replicability.

Evidence of Evaluation or Application With African American Male Students

Although there are many after-school programs serving African American students on a day-to-day basis, there are very few specifically serving this population with evidence of effectiveness. The four academic programs reviewed in this chapter fulfill this criterion.

The next section provides a brief description of the academically based programs reviewed in this chapter. It mainly consists of programs designed to provide assistance to students experiencing academic difficulties or programs designed to provide enriching opportunities for students in the areas of language arts and reading.

EFFECTIVE ACADEMICALLY ORIENTED AFTER-SCHOOL AND EXTENDED SCHOOL-DAY PROGRAMS FOR AFRICAN AMERICAN STUDENTS

Howard Street Tutoring Program (HSTP)

The Howard Street Tutoring Program (HSTP) is an academically oriented remedial program created specifically to improve the academic outcomes of low-achieving students during the after-school hours (Morris, 1990; Morris, Shaw, & Perney, 1990). This program was patterned after an existing program with evidence of effectiveness in reading achievement but was created to provide a cost-efficient program for families needing academic enrichment for their children. It was specifically designed for students in Grades 2 and 3 who are reading at levels significantly below grade level. When after-school programs implement the HSTP, a reading specialist or reading teacher becomes the on-site coordinator of the program. The coordinator is responsible for writing appropriate lesson plans and training and coordinating the activities of a staff of volunteers. As this is a volunteer program, the staff consists of nonpaid adults and college students who must go through a training program before they become tutors. Classroom teachers use an informal reading inventory to assess potential student participants prior to determining their eligibility for the program. Students performing significantly below grade level are placed in the program. Once enrolled, every week the students engage in daily 1-hour individual tutoring sessions with volunteer tutors.

The HSTP has been evaluated on a small scale. In two Chicago evaluations (Morris, 1990; Morris et al., 1990), the participating students outperformed randomly assigned comparison groups in word recognition, spelling, and basal passage reading (Harris & Jacobson, 1980; Schlagal, 1989). Effect size results showed that students in the treatment group outscored the students in the control groups on all of the study measures and in all of the areas: word recognition (+0.56), basal word recognition (+0.59), spelling (+0.56), and basal passages (+0.99). The HSTP still exists around the country, but its creator has since moved on to another institution (Appalachian State University in North Carolina) where he has begun a similar program (Early Steps) for first-grade students encountering similar difficulties in reading. Partially because of its potential success among African American males, the HSTP was used to train tutors by a community after-school reading program that hoped to attract more African American males to attend.

Help One Student to Succeed (HOSTS)

Help One Student to Succeed (HOSTS) (Gallegos, 1995; HOSTS Corporation, 1994; Wilbur, 1995) is a model that helps schools create tutoring programs for at-risk students using a mentoring approach. HOSTS schools feature one-to-one, after-school tutorial services to Title I students in elementary through high school who are performing below the 30th percentile. Volunteers from businesses and the community, as well as peers and cross-age mentors, are trained by HOSTS staff to serve as tutors for the program. When schools implement HOSTS, the program helps school staff to choose from a comprehensive database of learning materials that are not only especially tailored to the individual needs of children receiving services but also coordinated with what is being taught in the regular classroom. The mentor or tutor follows a carefully designed lesson plan generated by the Title I teacher from a comprehensive database that aligns the curriculum of the schools to local objectives or state frameworks.

Whereas HOSTS evaluations have not included pre-, post-, or experimental-control group comparisons, student success has been measured by examining NCE scores and gains and determining the number of participants who pass at grade level in reading. In a multi-state study of HOSTS conducted for the purpose of obtaining national Title I validation (HOSTS, 1994), participating students in Grades 1, 2, and 3 made substantial NCE spring-to-spring gains (15, 25, and 25, respectively); and students in other grades also made significant NCE gains. These NCE gains exceeded those of the school and the state.

Since its inception in Vancouver, Washington, in 1972, HOSTS has involved more than 150,000 students and 100,000 mentors in more than 4,000 programs nationwide, many of which are after-school programs.

Extended School-Day Tutoring
Program in the Memphis City Schools

In 1995, the Center for Research in Educational Policy (CREP) at the University of Memphis, Tennessee, developed an extended school-day tutoring program for use in the Memphis school system (Ross, Smith, Casey, & Slavin, 1996). The goal of the program, which was piloted in the Memphis public schools during the 1st year, was to use group tutoring during after-school hours to improve the reading performance of students in Grades 2, 3, and 4. The CREP program used an academic language arts curriculum that featured materials adapted from the Success for All reading program (Slavin, Madden, Dolan, & Wasik, 1996) as well as other reading strategies.

Teachers were trained in how to tutor students in reading using Success for All's Story Telling and Retelling method and the Scott

Foresman reading series. However, it should be noted that only some of the schools involved in the program used the Success for All curriculum during the regular school day. Students were selected into the program based on their need for additional instruction. They were taught how to read and retell the assigned stories and to use additional follow-up activities and strategies, such as partner reading. Students enrolled in the program attended the extended school-day tutoring program from 1 to 4 hours each week. After their language arts lessons, they had opportunities to engage in cultural, recreational, and other academic enrichment programs such as book clubs, computer skill-building activities, and test-taking strategies.

The evaluation of the CREP program was both formative and summative. Formative measures consisted of a teacher survey and observation forms that measured the level of implementation of the tutoring program. The summative part of the evaluation measured Tennessee Comprehensive Assessment Program scores at the end of the session. The participants in the study included 656 Title I students in Grades 2, 3, and 4. Half of the students participated in the program and half did not. Students were randomly selected into each group, but they were matched on the basis of standardized test scores, attitude, behavior, grade, and age. The two groups were compared prior to the intervention in various ways using prereading Tennessee Comprehensive Assessment Program test scores, and no significant differences were found. Overall, the greater the attendance rates, the more likely participating students were to perform better than their counterparts, with effect sizes ranging from +0.11 to +0.23. The program was found to be particularly effective for third graders. Students in third grade who attended 80% or more of the CREP sessions not only significantly outperformed their counterparts in the control group, but also outperformed treatment and control groups in Grades 2 and 4. The total increase in the number of NCE points for students in third grade was 8.5. This total increase was lower for students in other grades.

Two issues that plague evaluations of nonmandatory after-school programs are attendance and selection of a control group; both were factors in this study. The average attendance rate for the after-school tutoring program was 75%. The treatment group consisted of students who attended the program at least 50% of the time for some of the analyses and at least 80% for others. The students who did not attend or who had low attendance were added to the control group. Difficulties in finding an appropriate control group also affected this study. For example, 11 of the 13 schools showed correlations of +0.94 or higher on the pretests between the control- and treatment-group students, whereas 1 school showed a moderate correlation (+0.47) and another school showed a negative correlation (−0.10). These data suggest that the control groups and the experimental groups were not well matched. The initial analyses described above included the outlier groups. Despite these limitations, the overall conclusion was that the CREP program enhanced the academic skills of the students who were exposed to it, the majority of whom were African American.

Exemplary Center for Reading Instruction (ECRI)

The goal of the Exemplary Center for Reading Instruction (ECRI) (Reid, 1989) is to improve the reading achievement of elementary school students. This program emphasizes such reading-related skills as word recognition, spelling, penmanship, proofing, and writing leading to improvement in decoding, comprehension, and vocabulary study skills. ECRI has been developed and evaluated as a regular school-day and an after-school program.

Although ECRI has been used mostly as an in-school language arts program, it has also been frequently used as an after-school remedial tutoring program (Fashola, 1999b). The ECRI after-school program began as a remedial tutoring program at Brigham Young University in Utah, with goals of improving the reading skills of special education students and high school students who were behind in reading. The program currently exists as a reading clinic in which future and current teachers are trained to help students with reading difficulties using the ECRI method.

The lessons for ECRI are scripted and incorporate multisensory and sequential methods and strategies of teaching. In a typical lesson, teachers introduce new concepts using at least seven methods of instruction, teaching at least one comprehension skill, one study skill, and one grammar or creative writing skill. Initially, students are prompted for answers by teachers. As the students begin to master the information presented, fewer and fewer prompts are provided until students can perform independently.

The main evaluation of ECRI as an after-school program used volunteers to tutor two groups of randomly assigned students who were experiencing reading difficulties. The experimental group was taught by parents who had been trained to use ECRI, whereas the control group was taught using a generic reading intervention. ECRI students received lessons in reading, writing, and spelling. At the end of the school year, students were tested using a standardized test (Durrell Analysis of Reading Difficulty), which showed that ECRI students had made significantly greater gains than the control group (effect size = +1.21). The ECRI-tutored group also outscored control students on each of the Durrell test scores (Muir, 1974). Another study included students from Grades 2 through 12. Prior to ECRI, remedial students had a shockingly low achievement gain of only 3 months (0.3) for each year in school. Once ECRI was implemented, schools saw gains of 17 months in the Gates-MacGinite test of oral and silent reading and gains of 25 months in oral reading, comprehension, and spelling (Reid, 1989). Yet another study of the use of ECRI as a remedial tutoring program showed the results of students in Grades 1 to 6. The study included 114 students who were not reading at grade level. At the end of the school year, after approximately 45 hours of ECRI instruction, results showed NCE gains in all grades ranging from 11 to 19.88 NCE scores (Muir, 1974).

BEYOND ACADEMICS: DEVELOPING CULTURALLY AND RECREATIONALLY ENRICHING PROGRAMS

There are some after-school programs designed to develop the talents of African American students during the nonschool hours through cultural and educational enrichment. Such programs seek to enrich the life experiences of African American students by introducing them to experiences that they would otherwise not be exposed to on a daily basis. But exposing the students to one-time positive experiences is not enough of an encounter to develop specific talents academically, recreationally, or culturally.

To develop their talents fully, additional hands-on encounters in areas of nonacademic enrichment should be given to the children on a regular basis. For example, an urban youth who has expressed an interest in outdoor life could be invited to participate in an outdoor hiking event sponsored by a club or by an individual who has taken an interest in exposing youth to such events. Although exposing this child to the event may have been an enriching and stimulating experience, an isolated encounter will not necessarily develop the talents or interests that the student may possess for hiking. Although a singular opportunity may foster a child's interest in a particular activity, further experiences must be available in order for the student to explore in depth his or her interest.

After-school or extended school-day programs provide talent-development activities and additional opportunities by creating clubs, scheduled classes, and activities that foster expert-novice activities that would afford African American students these opportunities. Creating clubs that allow opportunities for talent development is an endeavor that would be beneficial to youth in African American communities, especially if they are well developed, goal oriented, and have been evaluated for evidence of effectiveness. Some organizations that offer such opportunities include Boy Scouts of America, Girl Scouts of America, YMCAs, YWCAs, 4-H clubs, Campfire Boys & Girls, and Boys and Girls Clubs of America. Such organizations provide opportunities for young children to be introduced to new skills and to develop new talents. Programs such as 4-H, Scouting, and Campfire Boys and Girls have various levels of skill/talent development that are tailored developmentally to the age levels of participants. The goals of such programs are to enrich and expand the opportunities of all children by exposing them to a variety of activities. If these programs are implemented in schools and communities during the nonschool hours, the fees for implementing them are low, and some programs will usually provide ongoing training for all participants. Fashola (1998a) provided a listing and extensive review of additional programs that serve these purposes and show promise.

THREE PROMISING COMMUNITY-BASED PROGRAMS

Three particularly interesting community-based programs that show promise are the Big Brothers/Big Sisters program, the Boys and Girls Clubs of America, and the Coca-Cola Valued Youth Program.

Big Brothers/Big Sisters Program

In this volume on the education of African American males, several of the authors have discussed a need for more positive African American male role models in the lives of school-aged youth. The

Big Brothers/Big Sisters program is an organization designed to do just this.

Big Brothers/Big Sisters of America was created specifically to provide young children from single-parent families with adult mentors. The organization is mainly funded by the U.S. Department of Justice. The goal of this program is to provide young children (especially inner-city children and children from single-parent homes) with role models in their everyday lives who will provide them with positive experiences, teach them to make healthy decisions, and help them to strive for the best in life.

Children participate in the Big Brothers/Big Sisters program by connecting with local agencies. If the slots are full, the agencies create a waiting list. Adults who sign up to be Big Brothers/Big Sisters are screened. If selected, they are trained and asked to spend at least 4 to 6 hours every month with their little brothers or sisters.

A randomized evaluation study of the Big Brothers/Big Sisters program was performed to investigate the effects on youth who had access to the services compared to youth who had not been provided with such services (Tierney, Grossman, & Resch, 1995). In this study, 959 children (ages 10 to 16) who had applied to be a part of the Big Brothers/Big Sisters program were randomly assigned to a treatment group or a waiting list, which served as a control group (472 participants), for 18 months. Results showed that students in the treatment group were significantly less likely to start using drugs and alcohol or to engage in aggressive activities and more likely to improve their peer relationships. Evaluations of the study have shown that both the adults and the children have enjoyed participating in the program. In the mid-1990s, the U.S. Department of Justice granted agencies across the country additional funding based on evidence that such programs had reduced violence, teen pregnancy, and undesirable behaviors among inner-city youth.

Although this program was not specifically designed to serve African American males exclusively, it can certainly be noted that the goals and outcomes of this program should be emulated by other organizations intending to improve social and behavioral skills of African American males. The research design for the study and the evaluation, using random assignment, suggests that the outcomes can definitely be attributed to the effects of the programs. Outcomes such as reduced aggressive behavior, improved peer relationships, increased school attendance rates, and improved school performance ought to be goals for any program intending to develop the talents of African American males. Community-based programs seeking to mentor African American males should consider meeting with and becoming a part of the Big Brothers/Big Sisters programs.

Boys and Girls Clubs of America

Boys and Girls Clubs of America comprise a national network of more than 2,000 neighborhood-based facilities, serving from 2 to 8 million young people annually, primarily from disadvantaged communities. Known as "the positive place for kids," the clubs provide guidance-oriented character development programs on a daily basis for 6- to 18-year-old children, conducted by a full-time, trained professional staff. Boys and Girls Clubs programs emphasize educational achievement, career exploration, drug and alcohol prevention and avoidance, health and fitness, gang and violence prevention, cultural enrichment, leadership development, and community service.

Boys and Girls Clubs programs were also developed to provide youth with safe havens during the nonschool hours. In addition, the programs provide fairly structured environments in which young children receive homework help, some academic classes, opportunities to use computers, and other recreational opportunities. Boys and Girls Clubs also allow children to develop cultural and recreational skills through instruction in drama, dance, and club sports such as basketball, volleyball, football, and soccer. Boys and Girls Clubs exist throughout the county in both rural and urban neighborhoods.

In recent years, Boys and Girls Clubs have begun to place more emphasis on providing the students with academic assistance, particularly homework help. Schinke, Cole, and Poulin (2000) conducted a study of the effects of a homework-help program, titled *Project Learn,* on homework completion and academic achievement of attendees of Boys and Girls Clubs. Results showed that students involved in Project Learn completed significantly more homework than did students in the comparison group. Although the research design was not as rigorous as the Big Brothers/Big Sisters of America design and results were not as strong, they can still be seen as promising. The Boys and Girls Clubs of America have since created a national educational advisory committee and are currently working on better ways to serve students and evaluate these services. For example, the programs are attempting to create more formal relationships with schools in an effort to "tighten up" their academic programs. If the academic programs are solidified, Boys and Girls Clubs may become exemplary models of programs that serve African American youth, particularly males.

Coca-Cola Valued Youth Program (VYP)

Another program of particular interest in the area of mentoring and community enhancements is the Coca-Cola Valued Youth Program (VYP). This is a cross-age program that actually strives to serve two groups of participants. The first group involves students in junior high, middle, or high school who may be at risk for dropping out. The second group consists of lower grade elementary school students in need of academic remediation. The Coca-Cola VYP recruits older students who are at risk for dropping out of school, trains and pays them to become tutors, and then pairs them up with elementary school students in need of academic remediation. The next section provides a brief description of the Coca-Cola VYP and its evaluation results.

The VYP is a cross-age tutoring program designed to increase the self-esteem and school success of at-risk middle and high school students by placing them in positions of responsibility as tutors of younger elementary school students. The Intercultural Development Research Association in San Antonio, Texas, originally developed the VYP. The original implementation of the program involved a collaboration with five school districts in San Antonio between 1984 and 1988, with approximately 525 high school tutors and 1,575 elementary tutees.

The main goal of the VYP program is to reduce the dropout rate of at-risk students by improving their self-concept and academic skills. Making them tutors and providing assistance with basic academic skills accomplishes this goal. The program also emphasizes elimination of nonacademic and disciplinary factors that contribute to dropping out. For example, the program attempts to develop students' senses of self-control, decrease student truancy, and reduce disciplinary referrals. It also seeks to form home/school partnerships to increase the level of support available to students.

When students agree to serve as tutors, they are required to enroll in a special tutoring class that allows them to improve their own basic academic skills, as well as their tutoring skills. The students involved as tutors are paid a minimum-wage stipend. Each tutor works with three elementary school students at a time for a total of about 4 hours per week. They are taught to develop self-awareness and pride, which is expected to make them less likely to exhibit disciplinary problems. Functions are held to honor and recognize the tutors as role models. They receive T-shirts, caps, and certificates of merit for their efforts.

The main evaluation of the Coca-Cola VYP compared 63 VYP tutors to 70 students in a comparison group (Cardenas, Montecel, Supik, & Harris, 1992). The students in four San Antonio schools were matched on the basis of age, ethnicity, free lunch eligibility, percentage of students retained in grade, scores on reading tests, quality of school, and self-concept. They were selected (not randomly) for participation into the program based on scheduling and availability, and the remaining students were placed into the comparison group. Nearly all the students in both groups were Latino and limited in English language proficiency. The control students were somewhat less likely to qualify for free lunch or to have been retained in grade.

Two years after the program began, 12% of the comparison students, but only 1% of the VYP students, had dropped out of school. Reading grades were significantly higher for the VYP group, as were scores on a self-esteem measure and on a measure of attitude toward school.

The VYP has been widely replicated throughout the Southwest and elsewhere. In 1990, the Coca-Cola Company provided additional funding for sites in California, Florida, New York, and Texas, and the program is now being extended into schools in Idaho, Oregon, Montana, and other states. The Coca-Cola VYP has also been used in after-school settings.

PATTERNS OF SUCCESS AMONG THE PROGRAMS

Addressing the Source of the Problem

While developing well-rounded programs that will help to improve the lives of African American males, it is unwise to assume that the availability of funds and the presence of trained professionals will ensure success by virtue of their presence. Similarly, although the resources are present and the programs are affordable, we should be careful not to assume that students will attend the programs simply because they exist. This is an important point to consider, especially if the goal is to reach out to all African American males, including those experiencing feelings of inadequacy in school. If African American male students do not experience success during the regular school day, it is highly unlikely that they will be motivated to remain in school for another 2 to 3 hours unless they can be ensured that their negative experiences during the regular school day will not be replicated and that they will benefit from this extra enrichment during the after-school hours.

If we seek to help a specific population, it is important to understand the needs and wants of the population being served. From a psychological perspective, the first step involves understanding the individual feelings of the African American male child and the factors that foster feelings of failure and isolation. The second step is to identify factors in the school setting that may or may not create these feelings and the ensuing behavioral results of these factors. The third step is to find alternatives that will bring together the targeted populations and the service providers and create situations that will change the dynamics of this relationship and make it more positive for both groups. Keeping in mind that the ultimate outcome is academic success, it is logical to select the school as the hub of this activity.

During the past few years, the federal government has allocated millions of dollars to a source of funding named 21st Century Community Learning Centers. The goals of these programs have been to provide after-school funding to public schools across the country with the goals of improving academic, recreational, cultural, social, community, and other aspects of the lives of school-aged children. These programs operate in school buildings and, thus, should make attendance easy and eliminate problems often associated with after-school programs such as transportation, affordability, and access to the program.

The research of Hudley (1992) addressed the first step: finding the causes of feelings of academic inadequacy and feelings of success in African American males. Hudley studied the causes of pride, anger, and guilt among school-aged males aged 16 to 19. Interestingly, she found that individual success in situations outside school prevailed over school or academic success as a source of pride. She also found that experiences of being successful in situations that placed them in positions of responsibility also elicited success.

An example of this is demonstrated in a study by Tanksley (1995), who implemented an after-school reading program, titled Reading Is Fundamental, in an attempt to increase the academic performances of low-performing students. During the 1st year of the program, the staff realized that the rate of African American male enrollment was extremely low. One reason for this was that the African American male students were not successful in school and, thus, were not motivated to attend after-school programs that might expose them to a similar experience. A second reason was that although the after-school programs augmented their academic components with recreational and cultural activities for the children such as dance and cooking, these activities were not really appealing to this population. The program coordinators decided that this was a problem that needed to be rectified by finding additional programs and classes that would increase African American male participation in the program. They engaged in extensive research and identified three main reasons why the students were not participating in the program.

The first factor that influenced participation in the program was the level of the involvement of parents and primary caretakers. The more parents and primary caretakers were involved, the more likely the students were to believe that involvement in the program was important and relevant. With the population in this study, fewer of the African American males had parents or primary caretakers who participated in the study, and this factor contributed to their lack of participation.

The second factor influencing participation was the lack of available adult African American male role models on the staff of the program. Many of the young African American male student participants came from single-parent homes mostly headed by females and did not have access to African American males who would encourage and motivate them to succeed academically. The schools that the students attended also provided few such role models, as the percentages of African American male instructors were extremely low, both at the elementary and secondary school levels. Third, the enrichment and recreational activities designated as "fun" activities did not attract the male populations. Many of the activities such as arts and crafts, ballet, jazz, and singing did not appeal to the majority of African American males.

The Reading Is Fundamental program rectified these factors by providing the following solutions. First, they reached out to the parents and encouraged them to become more involved in the after-school opportunities of the students. Parents were invited to participate in focus groups, invited to serve as chaperones on field trips, and were asked to be responsible for transporting the children to various required programmatic events. Second, the program hired more male staff to serve as role models to the African American males and also to tutor the children on a weekly basis. Additional male staff included substance abuse coordinators, guest speakers, and van drivers. Third, because many of the African American male students enjoyed sports as a form of recreation, the coordinators of the program created participatory sports programs for the children. They also contacted a local basketball team whose speakers encouraged the participants to succeed in school and served as role models.

As a result of these efforts, African American males increased their attendance in the Reading Is Fundamental program. More of the students attended and participated in the culturally relevant programs, and finally, more of the African American male students attended the tutorial sessions than in the previous year.

Looking at some of the programs discussed in this chapter, we may discern common trends in those programs considered to be successful.

Specific Program Goals. First, the programs that achieved success among the African American male students were created, or adapted from other programs, in response to a problem that existed specifically among students of this population. The programs saw a certain need to improve academic achievement and assessed the reason why this problem existed. With this goal in mind, they focused on creating possible solutions: academically oriented after-school programs that would provide the target population with increased opportunities to learn, thus eliminating the original obstacles to academic success. The basic structure may not have necessarily been designed only for the targeted African American children or males, but based on the experiences within the communities, adaptations or modifications were developed to best serve each community.

Professional Development and Training. Second, once the target programs were created, another factor that ensured success and effectiveness was the training of the staff. For the academic programs reviewed in this chapter, academic success was measured by improvement of the academic grades of the students and academic programs were programs created specifically to improve education in specific fields, such as reading, math, writing, and language arts. The academically oriented programs discussed in this chapter all hired credentialled staff that practiced teaching in the target areas. Even the community-based programs of the Boys and Girls Clubs, Big Brothers/Big Sisters, and the Coca-Cola VYP included training components for their staffs.

Although volunteers may be instructors, an accredited instructor is usually hired in a supervisory role with the goal to oversee the academic implementation of the programs. An additional key role for the accredited academic staff member is that this person is responsible for training the staff that implements the academic work with the students. In some cases, the accredited staff member actually teaches the students. Regardless, all of the programs placed teachers with credentials specializing in the areas of improvement in charge of the academic components of the program.

All of the programs have implementation training and procedural manuals that must be used by the service deliverers. The training includes a specific number of professional or paraprofessional hours at the beginning stages of the program and continuous assessment toward these goals as the program progresses. Teachers, instructors, and volunteers who do not complete the training program do not work with the students. These programs also have manuals that provide curriculum material contents to be used in the academic programs.

Evaluation. A third feature that these academic programs share is that they have all been evaluated for evidence of effectiveness using pre-, post-, and experimental-control or quasi-experimental designs. This feature establishes confidence in the programs' effectiveness and replicability for future communities that may choose to implement them. Educators, parents, and administrators should expect positive results when after-school programs are developed and implemented with a rigorous evaluation framework.

Because after-school programs are seldom mandated for all children in a school, and in light of some of the prevalent barriers to implementing successful after-school programs, there is always some uncontrolled factor that influences why some children attend these programs and others do not. Assuming that after-school programs cannot serve all applicants, there are methods such as random sampling, matching the treatment and the control groups on important basic demographics, or possibly comparing students who sign up for the program first to those who sign up later. Random sampling, matched groups, and waiting lists are some of the ways to conduct rigorous evaluations of after-school programs.

INVESTMENT IN THE POPULATIONS SERVED

Barriers to Participation in After-School Programs

In some cases, even when programs may have all of the components required to run effectively, they may still have problems recruiting the target population. Despite outlining clear goals for the program, providing professional development for staff, and building a rigorous evaluation mechanism into the after-school programs, such well-planned efforts sometimes do not address certain barriers to participation. This section addresses some common barriers to participation in after-school programs among African American male students.

Transportation. In a survey conducted (Fashola, 1998b) in public schools (Title I) across the country, teachers were asked to state the top obstacles or barriers to participation in after-school programs. The schools reported that the most frequent obstacle was transportation. There is a strong relationship between the availability of transportation and the extent to which a program can successfully serve its target population. It is important to find creative ways to address the issue of transportation. Busing alternatives are some of the solutions adopted by certain programs (Jones, 1995), whereas others have created programs within the neighborhoods of the clientele that they serve. Sometimes though, transportation problems may occur even when the program operates in the community. For example, some of the children may be too young to walk home at the end of the day, even if the program is located in the neighborhood. In other cases, for instance during the winter months, parents may not wish to have their children walking home in the dark. Thus they may opt not to enroll their children in after-school programs. In still other cases, students' transportation "passes" may expire prior to the end of the after-school program, making it difficult for students to use affordable transportation.

It is crucial to find creative ways to address this if programs are to affect students placed at risk.

Cost. Affordability is another issue. Effective programs cost money, and this tends to be a significant barrier to participation in the program for many families. Sometimes students in the programs have siblings who could benefit from the programs, but providing these families with discounts in enrollment still will not necessarily facilitate access to the program. After-school service providers must be sure to research the communities of their targeted populations and explore ways to make the program more accessible and available to the population. Some of the programs researched in this chapter have minimal or no costs attached to them.

The issue of cost also affects the staff. Usually, well-trained and qualified staffs draw higher salaries. The more academically specialized the program, the more the program should expect to pay the staff. The cost factor also indirectly influences the attendance of these students because to pay the teachers a competitive salary, programs may have to charge for participants.

Siblings. This barrier to after-school participation is also very real. Programs attempting to cater to older students would be more likely to experience this threat than would programs catering to younger children. In this case, many older students who do not have siblings enrolled in the program will eventually be lost because they are responsible for taking care of those younger siblings who are not enrolled in the program. The extent to which programs are able to serve siblings who are also in need of after-school services will determine the extent to which the after-school programs can serve their targeted populations.

DISCUSSION

Although Piaget (1952; Inhelder & Piaget, 1958) and Vygotsky (1978) discussed cognitive development from different perspectives, they both addressed an important and critical issue: the necessity and relevance of external stimulation via cognitively stimulating experiences (Confrey, 1991). They both expressed the necessity of a cognitively stimulating environment in order for the child to improve and enhance current and future cognitive functioning. The quality of the interactions that the child has with a stimulating environment and a more capable adult depends on two things. First, it is dependent on the extent to which the adult has adequate knowledge of child development and cognition. Second, it depends on the extent to which the adult has the knowledge, through training or otherwise, on how to scaffold, mentor, and communicate with the child. After-school programs seeking to develop the talents of African American male students should possess or acquire a deep understanding of the population that they work with and also understand effective ways to stimulate the students cognitively, emotionally, and behaviorally. If we intend to use after-school programs and interventions to develop the talents of African American male students, then we should be ready to train the teachers, provide the materials to teachers and students, and believe in the students' ability to succeed.

Factors such as positive staff regard, positive peer interactions, and structured programs (with less flexibility) also have a positive impact on African American male adjustment and performance during the regular school day socially, mentally, and academically. Pierce et al. (1997), for instance, provided evidence suggesting that after-school programs can have significantly positive effects on social adjustment, social skills, and academic achievement during the regular school day. To yield such positive results though, issues of the population's need, structure, staff training, program goals, and cost must be taken into consideration.

Posner and Vandell (1994) conducted one of the most well-known studies evaluating the effects of structured academic after-school programs on low-income African American students. In this study, four different types of after-school settings were evaluated: maternal care, informal adult supervision, self-care, and formal after-school programs. Almost 60% of the students in the program qualified for free and reduced lunches, 50% of the students were from single-parent families, and none of the parents of these students had completed college. The students involved in the after-school programs were in one of three different settings.

First, there were child care programs staffed by child care providers. Second, there was an academic program primarily staffed by teachers from the children's school-day programs and specifically focused on academic remediation and enrichment programs. Third, there was a program involved mainly in recreational and cultural activities, with some homework assistance. The students involved in the program had the same curriculum during the day. The outcome measures used included ratings of the children's behavior by the parents and children, academic ratings of the children's success, report card grades, and standardized test scores.

The results of an analysis of the effects of this program showed that African American students who had been involved in the program performed better academically at the end of the year in mathematics, reading, and other subjects ($p < .01$) and had better conduct ratings than children who were either in mother care or in other informal arrangements. Additional improvements included better work habits, better emotional adjustment, and better peer relations than those experienced by students in the other settings. The students who were involved in the third program spent significantly more time on academics and enrichment lessons and less time watching television.

Research shows that these qualities contribute to positive environments and, in some cases, positive outcomes in after-school care settings (Pierce et al., 1997; Posner & Vandell, 1994; Rosenthal & Vandell, 1996; Vandell & Corasaniti, 1988). Regardless of the type of program being offered to the children or the reasons for offering the program, there are some underlying qualities that all programs must have to offer the best services to youth and their families. Examples of these qualities include trained staff, structured programs, flexibility of program choice, positive environments, continuous evaluation of the program toward program goals, and a clear understanding of program goals (Fashola, 1999c; Fashola & Slavin, 1998a).

CONCLUSION

This chapter has presented four existing, effective models that have been successful in improving the academic achievement of African American male students. We also present additional programs that demonstrate success at developing the talents of African American students (including males) through mentoring programs. There are undoubtedly many programs in existence in our communities that attempt to develop the talents of African American male students, but there are also many barriers to the success of these programs achieving their goals. Among programs intended to increase academic achievement, those that provide greater structure, a stronger link to the school-day curriculum, well-qualified and well-trained staff, and opportunities for one-to-one tutoring seem particularly promising (Fashola, 1999a; Wasik & Slavin, 1993). Programs of all types, whether academic, recreational, or cultural in focus, appear to benefit from consistent structure, active community involvement, extensive training for staff and volunteers, and responsiveness to participants' needs and interests.

The programs reviewed in this chapter have in some way overcome these barriers and, thus, have proven successful. This is not to say that these are the only programs that have ever benefited African American male students. Rather, this chapter shows that the programs in existence could possibly identify some of the specific factors that have made these programs successful and implement them themselves.

We need much more research on the effects of all types of after-school programs, especially those intended to enhance achievement of African American male students. There is a particular need for development and evaluation of replicable, well-designed programs capable of being used across a wide range of circumstances. This chapter describes a few programs that are being used or are capable of being used during the nonschool hours. Educators and policy makers should see these programs as interesting alternatives that offer practical ideas and some indications for how after-school programs might be structured.

As educators, sociologists, and psychologists continue to seek interventions to close the Black-White and gender gaps in educational achievement, we must be sensitive to the needs of the particular populations that we seek to serve. In this chapter, the population of concern is that of African American school-aged males. Rather than simply stating the plight of this "endangered population," this chapter has attempted to provide readers with examples of programs that have successfully worked with this population and achieved results. The academic programs such as ECRI and HSTP were specifically designed with African American males in mind and have produced the desired results. Programs such as Reading Is Fundamental and the Boys and Girls Clubs of America, although they may not have been created for this population, are sensitive to the needs of their African American male participants and try to find ways to improve the attendance and services provided to the students. Principals, teachers, administrators, and community members intending to address the needs of African American males during the non-school hours should use this chapter as a resource to help them to build on existing initiatives or to select the components of the program that best fit their needs when designing an after-school program. If all of the suggested factors are considered and implemented, it is hoped that the possibilities facing African American males will not be as grim as those presented in the beginning of this chapter, and academic and social success will no longer elude our school-aged African American males.

REFERENCES

Braddock, J. H. (1990). *Hearing on the Office of Educational Research and Improvement.* Washington, DC: Government Printing Office.

Bronfenbrenner, U. (1986). Alienation and the four worlds of childhood. *Phi Delta Kappan, 67*(6), 430, 432–436.

Brown v. Board of Education, 347 U.S. 483 (1954).

Cardenas, J. A., Montecel, M. R., Supik, J. D., & Harris, R. J. (1992). The Coca-Cola Valued Youth Program: Dropout prevention strategies for at-risk students. *Texas Researcher, 3,* 111–130.

Clear, T. R. (1994). *Hearing on the federal prison population: Present and future trends.* Washington, DC: Government Printing Office.

Confrey, J. (1991). Steering a course between Vygotsky and Piaget. *Educational Researcher, 20*(8), 28–32.

Epstein, J. L. (1995). School/family/community partnerships: Caring for the children we share. *Phi Delta Kappan, 76*(9), 701–712.

Fashola, O. S. (1998a). *Review of extended school-day programs and their effectiveness* (Center for the Education of Students Placed at Risk Tech. Rep. No. 24). Baltimore: Johns Hopkins University, Center for Social Organization of Schools.

Fashola, O. S. (1998b, April). *What Title I schools have to say about their after-school programs.* Paper presented at the annual convention of the American Educational Research Association, San Diego, CA.

Fashola, O. S. (1999a). *The Child First Authority after-school program: A descriptive evaluation* (Center for the Education of Students Placed at Risk Tech. Rep. No. 38). Baltimore: Johns Hopkins University, Center for Social Organization of Schools.

Fashola, O. S. (1999b). *Five promising remedial reading intervention programs.* Washington, DC: American Federation of Teachers.

Fashola, O. S. (1999c). Here's how: Implementing effective after-school programs. *National Association of Elementary School Principals Newsletter, 17*(3), 1–4.

Fashola, O. S. (2001). *Building effective after-school programs.* Thousand Oaks, CA: Corwin Press.

Fashola, O. S., & Slavin, R. E. (1997). Promising programs for elementary and middle schools: Evidence of effectiveness and replicability. *Journal of Education for Students Placed at Risk, 2*(3), 251–307.

Fashola, O. S., & Slavin, R. E. (1998a). Effective dropout prevention and college attendance programs. *Journal on the Education of Students Placed at Risk, 3*(2), 159–183.

Fashola, O. S., & Slavin, R. E. (1998b). Schoolwide reform programs: What works? *Phi Delta Kappan, 79*(5), 370–379.

Gallegos, G. (1995). *Investing in the future: HOSTS evaluation for the Pasadena Independent School District.* Vancouver, WA: HOSTS Corporation.

Glass, G. V., McGaw, B., & Smith, M. L. (1981). *Meta-analysis in social research.* Beverly Hills, CA: Sage.

Harris, A. J., & Jacobson, M. D. (1980). A comparison of the Fry, Spache, and Harris-Jacobson readability formulas for primary grades. *Reading Teacher, 33*(8), 920–924.

HOSTS Corporation. (1994). *Independent evaluations of the HOSTS structured mentoring program in language arts.* Vancouver, WA: Author.

Hudley, C. A. (1992). Attributions for pride, anger, and guilt among incarcerated adolescents. *Criminal Justice and Behavior, 19*(2), 189–205.

Inhelder, B., & Piaget, J. (1958). *The growth of logical thinking from childhood to adolescence: An essay on the construction of formal operational structures.* New York: Basic Books.

Jones, J. H. (1995). Extending school hours: A capital idea. *Educational Leadership, 53*(3), 44–46.

Morris, D. (1990). *The Howard Street tutoring manual: Case studies in teaching beginning readers.* Boone, NC: Appalachian State University Reading Clinic.

Morris, D., Shaw, B., & Perney, J. (1990). Helping low readers in grades 2 and 3: An after-school volunteer tutoring program. *Elementary School Journal, 91,* 132–150.

Muir, R. I. (1974). *An analysis of a parent tutorial program for children with reading disabilities.* Unpublished master's thesis, Brigham Young University, Provo, UT.

National Assessment of Educational Progress. (1999). *Reading report card for the nation and states.* Washington, DC: Department of Education.

National Center for Educational Statistics. (1998). *The condition of education, 1994.* Washington, DC: Department of Education.

Owens, M. R. (1990). *Hearing on the Office of Educational Research and Improvement.* Washington, DC: Government Printing Office.

Piaget, J. (1952). *The origins of intelligence in children.* New York: International Universities Press.

Pierce, K. M., Hamm, J. V., & Vandell, D. L. (1997). *Experiences in after-school programs and children's adjustment.* Madison: University of Wisconsin, Wisconsin Center for Educational Research.

Posner, J. K., & Vandell, D. L. (1994). Low-income children's after-school care: Are there beneficial effects of after-school programs? *Child Development, 65*(2), 440–456.

Reid, E. M. (1989). *Exemplary Center for Reading Instruction: Submission to the program effectiveness panel of the U.S. Department of Education.* Washington, DC: Department of Education.

Rogoff, B. (1990). *Apprenticeship in thinking: Cognitive development in social context.* New York: Oxford University Press.

Rogoff, B. (1995). Observing sociocultural activity on three planes: Participatory appropriation, guided participation, apprenticeship. In J. V. Wertsch, P. del Rio, & A. Alvarez (Eds.), *Sociocultural studies of mind* (pp. 139–164). New York: Cambridge University Press.

Rogoff, B. (1996). Developing understanding of the idea of communities of learners. *Mind, Culture, and Activity, 1,* 209–229.

Rosenthal, R., & Vandell, D. (1996). Quality of care at school-aged child-care programs: Regulatable features, observed experiences, child perspectives, and parent perspectives. *Child Development, 67*(5), 2434–2445.

Ross, S. M., Smith, L. J., Casey, J., & Slavin, R. E. (1996). *Evaluation of the extended day tutoring program in Memphis City Schools.* Baltimore: Johns Hopkins University, Center for Research on the Education of Students Placed at Risk.

Sanders, M. G., & Herting, J. R. (2000). Gender and the effects of school, family, and church support on the academic achievement of African-American urban adolescents. In M. G. Sanders (Ed.), *Schooling students placed at risk: Research, policy, and practice in the education of poor and adolescent minorities* (pp. 141–162). Mahwah, NJ: Lawrence Erlbaum.

Schinke, S. P., Cole, K. C., & Poulin, S. R. (2000). Enhancing the educational achievement of at-risk youth. *Prevention Science, 1*(1), 51–60.

Schlagal, R. C. (1989). Constancy and change in spelling development. *Reading Psychology, 10*(3), 207–232.

Slavin, R. E., Madden, N. A., Dolan, L. J., & Wasik, B. A. (1996). *Every child, every school: Success for all.* Thousand Oaks, CA: Corwin Press.

Tanksley, M. D. (1995). *Improving the attendance rate for African-American male students in an after-school reading program through parental involvement, positive male role models, and tutorial instruction* (Ed.D. Practicum). Ft. Lauderdale, FL: Nova Southeastern University, Fischler Graduate School of Education and Human Services.

Tierney, J. P., Grossman, J. B., & Resch, N. L. (1995). *Making a difference: An impact study of Big Brothers/Big Sisters.* Philadelphia: Public/ Private Ventures.

Vandell, D. L., & Corasaniti, M. A. (1988). The relationship between third graders' after-school care and social, academic, and emotional functioning. *Child Development, 59*(4), 868–875.

Vygotsky, L. S. (1978). *Mind in society: The development of higher mental process.* Cambridge, MA: Harvard University Press.

Wasik, B. A., & Slavin, R. E. (1993). Preventing early reading failure with one-to-one tutoring: A review of five programs. *Reading Research Quarterly, 28*(2), 178–200.

Wilbur, J. (1995). A gift of time: HOSTS, Help One Student to Succeed. *Partnerships in Education Journal, 9*(3), 1–5.

CHAPTER THREE

The Trouble With Black Boys

The Role and Influence of Environmental and Cultural Factors on the Academic Performance of African American Males

Pedro A. Noguera

Harvard University

All of the most important quality-of-life indicators suggest that African American males are in deep trouble. They lead the nation in homicides, both as victims and perpetrators (Skolnick & Currie, 1994), and in what observers regard as an alarming trend, they now have the fastest growing rate for suicide (National Research Council, 1989; Poussaint & Alexander, 2000). For the past several years, Black males have been contracting HIV and AIDS at a faster rate than any other segment of the population (Auerbach, Krimgold, & Lefkowitz, 2000; Centers for Disease Control, 1988; Kaplan, Johnson, Bailey, & Simon, 1987), and their incarceration, conviction, and arrest rates have been at the top of the charts in most states

SOURCE: This chapter originally appeared in the *Harvard Journal of African American Public Policy, 7* (Summer, 2001) and is reprinted by permission of the Harvard Journal of African American Public Policy, Cambridge, Massachusetts.

for some time (Roper, 1991; Skolnick & Currie, 1994). Even as babies, Black males have the highest probability of dying in the 1st year of life (Auerbach et al., 2000; National Research Council, 1989), and as they grow older they face the unfortunate reality of being the only group in the United States experiencing a decline in life expectancy (Spivak, Prothrow-Stith, & Hausman, 1988). In the labor market, they are the least likely to be hired and in many cities, the most likely to be unemployed (Feagin & Sikes, 1994; Hacker, 1992; Massey & Denton, 1993; Moss & Tilly, 1995; Wilson, 1987).

Beset with such an ominous array of social and economic hardships, it is hardly surprising that the experience of Black males in education, with respect to attainment and most indicators of academic performance, also shows signs of trouble and distress. In many school districts throughout the United States, Black males are more likely than any other group to be suspended and expelled from school (Meier, Stewart, & England, 1989). From 1973 to 1977 there was a steady increase in African American enrollment in college. However, since 1977 there has been a sharp and continuous decline, especially among males (Carnoy, 1994; National Research Council, 1989). Black males are more likely to be classified as mentally retarded or suffering from a learning disability, more likely to be placed in special education (Milofsky, 1974), and more likely to be absent from advanced-placement and honors courses (Oakes, 1985; Pollard, 1993). In contrast to most other groups where males commonly perform at higher levels, such as in math- and science-related courses, the reverse is true for Black males (Pollard, 1993). Even class privilege and the material benefits that accompany it fail to inoculate Black males from low academic performance. When compared with their White peers, middle-class African American males lag significantly behind in both grade point average and on standardized tests (Jencks & Phillips, 1998).

It is not surprising that there is a connection between the educational performance of African American males and the hardships they endure within the larger society (Coleman et al., 1966). In fact, it would be more surprising if Black males were doing well academically in spite of the broad array of difficulties that confronts them. Scholars and researchers commonly understand that environmental and cultural factors have a profound influence on human behaviors, including academic performance (Brookover & Erickson, 1969; Morrow & Torres, 1995). What is less understood is how environmental and cultural forces influence the way in which Black males come to perceive schooling and how those perceptions influence their behavior and performance in school. There is considerable evidence that the ethnic and socioeconomic backgrounds of students have bearing on how students are perceived and treated by the adults who work with them within schools (Brookover & Erickson, 1969; Morrow & Torres, 1995). However, we know less about the specific nature of the perceptions and expectations that are held toward Black males and how these may in turn affect their performance within schools. More to the point, there is considerable confusion regarding why being Black and male causes this segment of the population to stand out in the most negative and alarming ways, both in school and in the larger society.

This chapter is rooted in the notion that it is possible to educate all children, including Black males, at high levels. This idea is not an articulation of faith but rather a conclusion drawn from a vast body of research on human development and from research on the learning styles of Black children (Lee, 2000). Therefore, it is possible for schools to take actions that can reverse the patterns of low achievement among African American males. The fact that some schools and programs manage to do so already is further evidence that there exists a possibility of altering these trends (Edmonds, 1979). To the degree that we accept the idea that human beings have the capacity to resist submission to cultural patterns, demographic trends, environmental pressures and constraints, bringing greater clarity to the actions that can be taken by schools and community organizations to support the academic achievement of African American males could be the key to changing academic outcomes and altering the direction of negative trends for this segment of the population (Freire, 1972).

This chapter explores the possibility that the academic performance of African American males can be improved by devising strategies that counter the effects of harmful environmental and cultural forces. Drawing on research from a variety of disciplines, the chapter begins with an analysis of the factors that place certain individuals (i.e., African American males) at greater risk than others. This is followed by an analysis of the ways in which environmental and cultural forces interact and influence academic outcomes and how these factors shape the relationship between identity, particularly related to race and gender, and school performance. Finally, strategies for countering harmful environmental and cultural influences, both the diffuse and the direct, are explored with particular attention paid to recommendations for educators, parents, and youth service providers who seek to support young African American males.

THE NATURE OF THE "RISK"

The good news is that not all Black males are at risk. I was reminded of this fact on my way to work one morning. Before driving to San Francisco with a colleague, another Black male academic, we stopped to pick up a commuter so that we could make the trip across the Bay Bridge in the faster carpool lane during the middle of the rush hour. As it turned out, the first carpooler to approach our car was another Black male. As we drove across the bridge, we made small talk, going from basketball to the merits of living in the Bay Area, until finally we approached the subject of our careers. The rider informed us that he managed a highly profitable telecommunications firm, and if his plans progressed as he hoped, he would be retiring on a very lucrative pension in Hawaii before the age of 50. Contemplating his financial good fortune and that of my colleague and myself (although the two of us had no plans for early retirement), I posed the question, "What explains why we are doing so well and so many brothers like us are not?"

The answer was not obvious. All three of us were raised in working-class families, had grown up in tough neighborhoods, had close friends and family members who had been killed while they were young, and knew others who were serving time in prison. What made our lives, with our promising careers and growing families, so fortunate and so different? All three of us were raised by both of our parents, but further exploration revealed that none of us had regular contact with our fathers. We all attended public schools, but each of us felt that we had succeeded in spite of, and not because of, the schools we attended. With time running out as we approached our rider's stop, we threw out the possibility that the only thing that spared us the fate of so many of our brethren was luck, not getting caught for past indiscretions and not being in the wrong place at the wrong time.

Viewed in the context of the negative social patterns cited previously, the explanation for our apparent good luck does not seem mysterious. Although it is true that many Black males are confronted with a vast array of risks, obstacles, and social pressures, the majority manages to navigate these with some degree of success. The good news is that most Black males are not in prison, do not commit suicide, and have not contracted HIV/AIDS. These facts do not negate the significance of the problems that confront Black males, but they do help to keep the problems in perspective. Understanding how and why many Black males avoid the pitfalls and hardships that beset others may help us to devise ways to protect and provide support for more of them.

The effects of growing up in poverty, particularly for children raised in socially isolated, economically depressed urban areas, warrants greater concern, especially given that one out of every three Black children is raised in a poor household (Carnoy, 1994). Here the evidence is clear that the risks faced by children, particularly African American males, in terms of health, welfare, and education are substantially greater (Gibbs, 1988). A longitudinal study on the development of children whose mothers used drugs (particularly crack cocaine) during pregnancy found that when compared with children residing in similar neighborhoods from similar socio-economic backgrounds, the children in the sample showed no greater evidence of long-term negative effects. This is not because the incidence of physical and cognitive problems among the sample was not high, but because it was equally high for the control group. The stunned researchers, who fully expected to observe noticeable differences between the two groups, were compelled to conclude that the harmful effects of living within an impoverished inner-city environment outweighed the damage inflicted by early exposure to drugs (Jackson, 1998).

A vast body of research on children in poverty shows that impoverished conditions greatly increase the multiplier effect on risk variables (e.g., single-parent household, low birth weight, low educational attainment of parents; Gabarino, 1999). Poor children generally receive inferior services from schools and agencies that are located in the inner city, and poor children often have many unmet basic needs. This combination of risk factors means it is nearly impossible to establish cause and effect relationships among them. For example, research has shown that a disproportionate number of poor children suffer from a variety of sight disorders (Harry, Klingner, & Moore, 2000). However, the disabilities experienced by children are often related to poverty rather than a biological disorder. For example, because poor children often lack access to preventive health care, their untreated vision problems are inaccurately diagnosed as reading problems, and as a consequence, large numbers are placed in remedial and special education programs (Harry et al., 2000). Throughout the country, Black children are overrepresented in special education programs. Those most likely to be placed in such programs are overwhelmingly Black, male, and poor (Harry et al., 2000).

The situation in special education mirrors a larger trend in education for African Americans generally and males in particular. Rather than serving as a source of hope and opportunity, some schools are sites where Black males are marginalized and stigmatized (Meier et al., 1989). In school, Black males are more likely to be labeled with behavior problems and as less intelligent even while they are still very young (Hilliard, 1991). Black males are also more likely to be punished with severity, even for minor offenses, for violating school rules (Sandler, Wilcox, & Everson, 1985) and often without regard for their welfare. They are more likely to be excluded from rigorous classes and prevented from accessing educational opportunities that might otherwise support and encourage them (Oakes, 1985). Consistently, schools that serve Black males fail to nurture, support, or protect them.

However, changing academic outcomes and countering the risks experienced by Black males are not simply a matter of developing programs to provide support or bringing an end to unfair educational policies and practices. Black males often adopt behaviors that make them complicit in their own failure. It is not just that they are more likely to be punished or placed in remedial classes; it is also that they are more likely to act out in the classroom and to avoid challenging themselves academically. Recognizing that Black males are not merely passive victims but may also be active agents in their own failure means that interventions designed to help them must take this into account. Changing policies, creating new programs, and opening new opportunities will accomplish little if such efforts are not accompanied by strategies to actively engage Black males and their families in taking responsibility to improve their circumstances. Institutionally, this may require programmatic interventions aimed at buffering and offsetting the various risks to which Black males are particularly vulnerable. However, to be effective such initiatives must also involve efforts to counter and transform cultural patterns and what Ogbu (1987) has called the "oppositional identities" adopted by Black males that undermine the importance they attach to education.

As I will illustrate, one of the best ways to learn how this can be done is to study those schools and programs that have proven successful in accomplishing this goal. In addition, it is important for such work to be anchored in a theoretical understanding of how the pressures exerted on Black males in American society can be contested. Without such an intellectual underpinning, it is unlikely that new interventions and initiatives will succeed at countering the hazardous direction of trends for African American males.

STRUCTURAL VERSUS CULTURAL EXPLANATIONS

Epidemiologists and psychologists have identified a number of risk factors within the social environment that, when combined, are thought to have a multiplier effect on risk behavior. Lack of access to health care, adequate nutrition, and decent housing, growing up poor and in a single-parent household, being exposed to substance abuse at a young age, and living in a crime-ridden neighborhood are some of the variables most commonly cited (Earls, 1991). Similarly, anthropologists and sociologists have documented ways in which certain cultural influences can lower the aspirations of Black males and contribute to the adoption of self-destructive behavior. Ogbu (1987) argued that community-based "folk theories" that suggest that because of the history of discrimination against Black people, even those who work hard will never reap rewards equivalent to Whites, could contribute to self-defeating behaviors. There is also evidence that many Black males view sports or music as more promising routes to upward mobility than academic pursuits (Hoberman, 1997). Finally, some researchers have found that for some African American students, doing well in school is perceived as a sign that one has "sold out" or opted to "act White" for the sake of individual gain (Fordham, 1996; Ogbu, 1990).

Despite their importance and relevance to academic performance, risk variables and cultural pressures cannot explain individual behavior. Confronted with a variety of obstacles and challenges, some Black males still find ways to survive and, in some cases, to excel. Interestingly, we know much less about resilience, perseverance, and the coping strategies employed by individuals whose lives are surrounded by hardships than we know about those who succumb and become victims of their environment. Deepening our understanding of how individuals cope with, and respond to, their social and cultural environments is an important part of finding ways to assist Black males with living healthy and productive lives.

In the social sciences, explanations of human behavior, especially that of the poor, have been the subject of considerable debate. Most often, the debate centers on those who favor structural explanations of behavior and those who prefer cultural explanations of behavior. Structuralists generally focus on political economy, the availability of jobs and economic opportunities, class structure, and social geography (Massey & Denton, 1993; Tabb, 1970; Wilson, 1978, 1987). From this perspective, individuals are viewed as products of their environment, and changes in individual behavior are made possible by changes in the structure of opportunity. From this theoretical perspective, holding an individual responsible for their behavior makes little sense because behavior is shaped by forces beyond the control of any particular individual. Drug abuse, crime, and dropping out of school are largely seen as social consequences of inequality. According to this view, the most effective way to reduce objectionable behavior is to reduce the degree and extent of inequality in society.

In contrast, culturalists downplay the significance of environmental factors and treat human behavior as a product of beliefs, values, norms, and socialization. Cultural explanations of behavior focus on the moral codes that operate within particular families, communities, or groups (Anderson, 1990). For example, the idea that poor people are trapped within a "culture of poverty," which has the effect of legitimizing criminal and immoral behavior, has dominated the culturalists' perspective of poverty (Glazer & Moynihan, 1963; Lewis, 1966). For the culturalists, change in behavior can only be brought about through cultural change. Hence, providing more money to inner-city schools or busing inner-city children to affluent suburban schools will do little to improve their academic performance because their attitudes toward school are shaped by the culture they brought from home and the neighborhood in which they live (Murray, 1984). According to this view, culture provides the rationale and motivation for behavior, and cultural change cannot be brought about through changes in governmental policy or by expanding opportunities.

A growing number of researchers are trying to find ways to work between the two sides of the debate. Dissatisfied with the determinism of the structuralists, which renders individuals as passive objects of larger forces, and with the "blame the victim" perspective of the culturalists, which views individuals as hopelessly trapped within a particular social/cultural milieu (Ryan, 1976), some researchers have sought to synthesize important elements from both perspectives while simultaneously paying greater attention to the importance of individual choice and agency (McLeod, 1987). From this perspective, the importance of both structure and culture is acknowledged, but so too is the understanding that individuals have the capacity to act and make choices that cannot be explained through the reductionism inherent in either framework (Morrow & Torres, 1995). The choices made by an individual may be shaped by both the available opportunities and the norms present within the cultural milieu in which they are situated. However, culture is not static and individual responses to their environment cannot be easily predicted. Both structural and cultural forces influence choices and actions, but neither has the power to act as the sole determinant of behavior because human beings also have the ability to produce cultural forms that can counter these pressures (Levinson, Foley, & Holland, 1996; Willis, 1977).

This is not to suggest that because individuals have the capacity to counter these forces, many will choose or be able to do so. The effects of poverty can be so debilitating that a child's life chances can literally be determined by a number of environmental and cultural factors such as the quality of prenatal care, housing, and food available to their mothers that are simply beyond the control of an individual or even of concerted community action. It would be naive and erroneous to conclude that strength of character and the possibility of individual agency can enable one to avoid the perils present within the environment or that it is easy for individuals to choose to act outside the cultural milieu in which they were raised. Even as we recognize that individuals make choices that influence the character of their lives, we must also recognize that the range of choices available is profoundly constrained and shaped by external forces. For this reason, efforts to counter behaviors that are viewed as injurious—whether dropping out of school, selling drugs, or engaging in violent behavior—must include efforts to comprehend the logic and motivations behind the behavior. Given the importance of agency and choice, the only way to change behavioral outcomes is to understand the cognitive processes that influence how individuals adapt, cope, and respond.

In a comprehensive study of teen pregnancy, Kristen Luker (1996) demonstrated the possibility for synthesizing the two perspectives—structural and cultural explanations of human behaviors that traditionally have been seen as irreconcilable. Teen pregnancy, which for years has been much more prevalent among low-income females than middle-class White females, has traditionally been explained as either the product of welfare dependency and permissive sexual mores (the culturalists) or the unfortunate result of inadequate access to birth control and economic opportunities (the structuralists). Through detailed interviews with a diverse sample of teen mothers, Luker put forward a different explanation that draws from both the cultural and the structural perspectives and acknowledges the role and importance of individual choice. She pointed out that although both middle-class and lower-class girls engage in premarital sex and sometimes become pregnant, middle-class girls are less likely to have babies during adolescence because they have a clear sense that it will harm their chance for future success. In contrast, when confronted with an unexpected pregnancy, poor girls are more likely to have babies; they do not perceive it as negatively affecting their future because college and a good job are already perceived as being out of reach. In fact, many girls in this situation actually believe that having a baby during adolescence will help them to settle down because they will now be responsible for another life (Luker, 1996).

Given the importance of individual "choice" to this particular behavior, any effort to reduce teen pregnancy that does not take into account the reasoning that guides decision making is unlikely to succeed. Similarly, efforts to improve the academic performance of African American males must begin by understanding the attitudes that influence how they perceive schooling and academic pursuits. To the extent that this does not happen, attempts to help Black males based primarily on the sensibilities of those who initiate them are unlikely to be effective and may be no more successful than campaigns that attempt to reduce drug use or violence by urging kids to "just say no" (Skolnick & Currie, 1994).

Investigations into the academic orientation of Black male students must focus on the ways in which the subjective and objective dimensions of identity related to race and gender are constructed within schools and how these influence academic performance. Although psychologists have generally conceived of identity construction as a natural feature of human development (Cross, Parnham, & Helms, 1991; Erickson, 1968), sociologists have long recognized that identities, like social roles, are imposed on individuals through various socialization processes (Goffman, 1959). The processes and influences involved in the construction of Black male identity should be at the center of analyses of school performance because it is on the basis of their identities that Black males are presumed to be at risk, marginal, and endangered in school and throughout American society (Anderson, 1990; Gibbs, 1988; Kunjufu, 1985).

Structural and cultural forces combine in complex ways to influence the formation of individual and collective identities, even as individuals may resist, actively or passively, the various processes involved in the molding of the "self." The fact that individuals can resist, subvert, and react against the cultural and structural forces that shape social identities compels us to recognize that individual choice, or what many scholars refer to as agency, also plays a major role in the way identities are constructed and formed (Giroux, 1983). For this reason, research on identity must pay careful attention to the attitudes and styles of behavior that African American males adopt and produce in reaction to the social environment and how these influence how they are seen and how they see themselves within the context of school. Writing on the general importance of identity to studies of schooling, Levinson et al. (1996) argued that "student identity formation within school is a kind of social practice and cultural production which both responds to, and simultaneously constitutes, movements, structures, and discourses beyond school" (p. 12).

Students can be unfairly victimized by the labeling and sorting processes that occur within school in addition to being harmed by the attitudes and behavior they adopt in reaction to these processes. For this reason, it is important to understand the factors that may enable them to resist these pressures and respond positively to various forms of assistance that may be provided within school or in the communities where they reside. By linking a focus on identity construction to an analysis of cultural production, it is the goal of this chapter to gain greater insight into how schools can be changed and how support programs can be designed to positively alter academic outcomes for African American males.

IDENTITY AND ACADEMIC PERFORMANCE

It has long been recognized that schools are important sites of socialization. Schools are places where children learn how to follow instructions and obey rules, how to interact with others, and how to deal with authority (Apple, 1982; Spring, 1994). Schools are important sites for gender role socialization (Thorne, 1993), and in most societies, they are primary sites for instruction about the values and norms associated with citizenship (Loewen, 1995; Spring, 1994).

For many children, schools are also places where they learn about the meaning of race. Although this may occur through lesson plans adopted by teachers, it is even more likely that children learn about race through the hidden or informal curriculum (Apple, 1982) and through nonstructured school activities such as recess (Dyson, 1994). Even when teachers do not speak explicitly about race and racial issues with children, children become aware of physical differences related to race quite early (Tronyna & Carington, 1990). However, children do not become aware of the significance attached to these physical differences until they start to understand the ideological dimensions of race and become cognizant of differential treatment that appears to be based on race (Miles, 1989). Name-calling, including the use of racial epithets, serves as one way of establishing racial boundaries even when children do not fully understand the meaning of the words that are used (Tronyna & Carington, 1990). Similarly, school practices that isolate and separate children on the basis of race and gender also send children important messages about the significance of race and racial differences (Dyson, 1994; Thorne, 1993). Schools certainly are not the only places where children formulate views about race, but because schools are often sites where children are more likely to encounter persons of another race or ethnic group, they play a central role in influencing the character of race relations in communities and the larger society (Peshkin, 1991).

As young people enter into adolescence and develop a stronger sense of their individual identities (Erickson, 1968), the meaning and significance of race also change. Where it was once an ambiguous concept based largely on differences in physical appearance, language, and styles of behavior, race becomes a more rigid identity construct as children learn the historical, ideological, and cultural dimensions associated with racial group membership (Cross et al., 1991; Tatum, 1992). Even children who once played and interacted freely across racial lines when they were younger often experience a tightening of racial boundaries and racial identities as they get older and begin following patterns of interaction modeled by adults (Metz, 1978; Peshkin, 1991). Peer groups play a powerful role in shaping identity because the desire to be accepted by one's peers and "fit in" with one's peers often becomes a paramount concern for most adolescents. Research has shown that in secondary school, peer groups assume a great influence over the orientation young people adopt toward achievement (Phelan, Davidson, & Ya, 1998), and they profoundly shape the way identities are constituted in school settings (Steinberg, 1996). As adolescents become clearer about the nature of their racial and gender identities, they begin to play a more active role in maintaining and policing these identities. Peer groups are also likely to impose negative sanctions on those who violate what are perceived as established norms of behavior and who attempt to construct identities that deviate significantly from prevailing conceptions of racial and gender identity (Peshkin, 1991).

Despite the importance that several researchers have placed on the role of peer groups in the socialization process, peer groups are by no means the only forces that shape the social construction of identity within schools (Fordham, 1996; Ogbu, 1987; Solomon, 1992; Steinberg, 1996). The structure and culture of school plays a major role in reinforcing and maintaining racial categories and the stereotypes associated with them. As schools sort children by perceived measures of their ability and as they single out certain children for discipline, implicit and explicit messages about racial and gender identities are conveyed. To the degree that White or Asian children are disproportionately placed in gifted and honors classes, the idea that such children are inherently smarter may be inadvertently reinforced. Similarly, when African American and Latino children are overrepresented in remedial classes, special education programs, or on the lists for suspension or expulsion, the idea that these children are not as smart or as well behaved is also reinforced (Ferguson, 2000). Such messages are conveyed even when responsible adults attempt to be as fair as possible in their handling of sorting and disciplinary activities. Because the outcomes of such practices often closely resemble larger patterns of success and failure that correspond with racial differences in American society, they invariably have the effect of reinforcing existing attitudes and beliefs about the nature and significance of race.

For African American males, who are more likely than any other group to be subjected to negative forms of treatment in school, the message is clear: Individuals of their race and gender may excel in sports, but not in math or history. The location of Black males within school, in remedial classes or waiting for punishment outside the principal's office, and the roles they perform within school suggest that they are good at playing basketball or rapping, but debating, writing for the school newspaper, or participating in the science club are strictly out of bounds. Such activities are out of bounds not just because Black males may perceive them as being inconsistent with who they think they are but also because there simply are not enough examples of individuals who manage to participate in such activities without compromising their sense of self. Even when there are small numbers of Black males who do engage in activities that violate established norms, their deviation from established patterns often places them under considerable scrutiny from their peers who are likely to regard their transgression of group norms as a sign of "selling out."

Researchers such as Ogbu and Fordham have attributed the marginality of Black students to oppositional behavior (Fordham, 1996; Ogbu, 1987). They argue that Black students hold themselves back out of fear that they will be ostracized by their peers. Yet, what these researchers do not acknowledge is the dynamic that occurs between Black students, males in particular, and the culture that is operative within schools. Black males may engage in behaviors that contribute to their underachievement and marginality, but they are also more likely to be channeled into marginal roles and to be discouraged from challenging themselves by adults who are supposed to help them. Finally, and most important, Ogbu and Fordham fail to take into account the fact that some Black students, including males, find ways to overcome the pressures exerted on them and manage to avoid choosing between their racial and gender identity and academic success. Even if few in number, there are students who manage to maintain their identities and achieve academically without being ostracized by their peers. Understanding how such students navigate this difficult terrain may be the key to figuring out how to support the achievement of larger numbers of Black students.

An experience at a high school in the Bay Area illustrates how the interplay of these two socializing forces, peer groups and school sorting practices, can play out for individual students. I was approached by a Black male student who needed assistance with a paper on *Huckleberry Finn* that he was writing for his 11th-grade English class. After reading what he had written, I asked why he had not discussed the plight of Jim, the runaway slave who is one of the central characters of the novel. The student informed me that his teacher had instructed the class to focus on the plot and not to get into issues about race because, according to the teacher, that was not the main point of the story. He explained that two students in the class, both Black males, had objected to the use of the word "nigger" throughout the novel and had been told by the teacher that if they insisted on making it an issue they would have to leave the course. Both of these students opted to leave the course even though it meant that they would have to take another course that did not meet the college preparatory requirements. The student I was helping explained that because he needed the class he would just "tell the teacher what she wanted to hear." After our meeting, I looked into the issue further and discovered that one student, a Black female, had chosen a third option: She stayed in the class but wrote a paper focused on race and racial injustice, even though she knew it might result in her being penalized by the teacher.

This example reveals a number of important lessons about the intersection of identity, school practices, and academic performance. Confronted by organizational practices, which disproportionately place Black students in marginal roles and groupings, and pressure from peers, which may undermine the importance attached to academic achievement, it will take considerable confidence and courage for Black students to succeed. The four Black students in this English class were already removed from their Black peers by their placement in this honors course. In such a context, one seemed to adopt what Fordham (1996) described as a "raceless" persona (the student I was assisting) to satisfy the demands of the teacher, but this is only one of many available options. Two others responded by choosing to leave for a lower level class where they would be reunited with their peers with their identities intact but with diminished academic prospects. The option exercised by the female student in the class is perhaps the most enlightening yet difficult to enact. She challenged her teacher's instructions, choosing to write about race and racism, even though she knew she would be penalized for doing so. Yet she also had no intention of leaving the class, despite the isolation she experienced, to seek out the support of her peers.

This case reveals just some of the ways Black students may respond to the social pressures that are inherent in school experiences. Some actively resist succumbing to stereotypes or the pressure of peers, whereas others give in to these pressures in search of affirmation of their social identity. For those who seek to help Black students and males in particular, the challenge is to find ways to support their resistance to negative stereotypes and school sorting practices and to make choosing failure a less likely option for them. The teacher mentioned in the case just described may or may not have even realized how her actions in relation to the curriculum led her Black students to make choices that would profoundly influence their education. As the following section will illustrate, when educators are aware of the social and cultural pressures exerted on students, the need to choose between one's identity and academic success can be eliminated.

LEARNING FROM STUDENTS AND THE SCHOOLS THAT SERVE THEM WELL

Fortunately, there is considerable evidence that the vast majority of Black students, including males, would like to do well in school (Anderson, 1990; Kao & Tienda, 1998). In addition, there are schools where academic success for Black students is the norm and not the exception (Edmonds, 1979; Sizemore, 1988). Both of these facts provide a basis for hope that achievement patterns can be reversed if there is a willingness to provide the resources and support to create the conditions that nurture academic success.

In my own research at high schools in northern California, I have obtained consistent evidence that most Black students value education and would like to succeed in school. In response to a survey about their experiences in school, nearly 90% of the Black male respondents ($N = 147$) responded "agree" or "strongly agree" to the questions "I think education is important" and "I want to go to college." However, in response to the questions "I work hard to achieve good grades" and "My teachers treat me fairly," less than a quarter of the respondents, 22% and 18% respectively, responded affirmatively. An analysis of just these responses to the survey suggests a disturbing discrepancy between what students claim they feel about the importance of education, the effort they expend, and the support they receive from teachers (Noguera, 2001). Similar results were obtained from a survey of 537 seniors at an academic magnet high school. African American males were least likely to indicate that they agreed or strongly agreed with the statement "My teachers support me and care about my success in their class" (see Table 3.1).

Table 3.1   "My Teachers Support Me and Care About My Success in Their Class" (in percentages) ($N = 537$)

	Black Male	Black Female	Asian Male	Asian Female	White Male	White Female
Strongly agree	8	12	24	36	33	44
Agree	12	16	42	33	21	27
Disagree	38	45	16	15	18	11
Strongly disagree	42	27	18	16	28	18

Rosalind Mickelson (1990) found similar discrepancies between expressed support for education and a commitment to hard work. Her research findings led her to conclude that some Black students experience what she referred to as an "attitude-achievement paradox." For Mickelson, the reason for the discrepancy is that although many Black students say they value education, such an expression is little more than an "abstract" articulation of belief. However, when pressed to state whether they believe that education will actually lead to a better life for them, the Black students in Mickelson's study expressed the "concrete" belief that it would not. Mickelson concluded that the contradiction between abstract and concrete beliefs toward education explains why there is a discrepancy between the attitudes expressed by Black students and their academic outcomes.

Although Mickelson's (1990) findings seem plausible, I think it is also important to consider how the experiences of Black students in schools, especially males, may result in a leveling of aspirations. If students do not believe that their teachers care about them and are actively concerned about their academic performance, the likelihood that they will succeed is greatly reduced. In MetLife's annual survey on teaching, 39% of students surveyed ($N = 3,961$) indicated that they trust their teachers "only a little or not at all"; when the data from the survey were disaggregated by race and class, minority and poor students indicated significantly higher levels of distrust (47% of minorities and 53% of poor students stated that they trusted their teachers only a little or not at all) (MetLife, 2000). Though it is still possible that some students will succeed even if they do not trust or feel supported by their teachers, research on teacher expectations suggests that these feelings have a powerful effect on student performance (Weinstein, Madison, & Kuklinski, 1995). Moreover, there is research that suggests that the performance of African Americans, more so than other students, is influenced to a large degree by the social support and encouragement that they receive from teachers (Foster, 1997; Ladson-Billings, 1994; Lee, 2000). To the extent that this is true, and if the nature of interactions between many Black male students and their teachers tends to be negative, it is unlikely that it will be possible to elevate their achievement without changing the ways in which they are treated by teachers and the ways in which they respond to those who try to help them.

However, there are schools where African American male students do well and where high levels of achievement are common. For example, an analysis of the academic performance indicators of public schools in California revealed that there are 22 schools in the state where Black students comprise 50% or more of the student population and have aggregate test scores of 750 or greater (1,000 is the highest possible score) (Foster, 2001). Most significantly, when the test score data for these schools were disaggregated on the basis of race and gender, there was no evidence of an achievement gap. Though schools such as these are few in number, given the fact that there are more than 2,000 public schools in California, the fact that they exist suggests that similar results should be possible elsewhere.

Researchers who have studied effective schools have found that such schools possess the following characteristics: (a) a clear sense of purpose, (b) core standards within a rigorous curriculum, (c) high expectations, (d) a commitment to educate all students, (e) a safe and orderly learning environment, (f) strong partnerships with parents, and (g) a problem-solving attitude (Murphy & Hallinger, 1985; Sizemore, 1988). Though the criteria used to determine effectiveness rely almost exclusively on data from standardized tests and ignore other criteria, there is no disagreement that such schools consistently produce high levels of academic achievement among minority students. Researchers on effective schools for low-income African American students also cite the supportive relations that exist between teachers and students and the ethos of caring and accountability that pervade such schools as other essential ingredients of their success (Sizemore, 1988). Educational reformers and researchers must do more to investigate ways to adopt strategies that have proven successful at schools where achievement is less likely. As Ron Edmonds (1979), formerly one of the leading researchers on effective schools, stated, "We already know more than enough to successfully educate all students" (p. 26). The challenge before educators and policy makers is to find ways to build on existing models of success.

Unfortunately, most African American children are not enrolled in effective schools that nurture and support them while simultaneously providing high-quality instruction. Even as pressure is exerted to improve the quality of public education so that the supply of good schools is increased, other strategies must be devised at the community level to provide Black children with support. For example, there are long-standing traditions within Jewish and many Asian communities to provide children with religious and cultural instruction outside of school. In several communities throughout the United States, Black parents are turning to churches and community organizations as one possible source of such support (McPartland & Nettles, 1991). In northern California, organizations such as Simba and the Omega Boys Club (both community-based mentoring programs) provide African American males with academic support and adult mentors outside of school (Watson & Smitherman, 1996). Organizations such as these affirm the identities of Black males by providing them with knowledge and information about African and African American history and culture and by instilling a sense of social responsibility toward their families and communities (Ampim, 1993; Myers, 1988). Unfortunately, these organizations are small and are largely unable to serve the vast numbers of young people in need. Moreover, it is unlikely that such organizations can completely counter the harmful effects of attendance in unsupportive and even hostile schools because they are designed to complement learning that is supposed to take place in school. Still, the model they provide demonstrates that it is possible to work outside of schools to have a positive influence on the academic performance of African American youth. Given their relative success but small size, it would be advisable to find ways to replicate them elsewhere.

Drawing from the research on mentoring and student resilience that has identified strategies that are effective in supporting the academic achievement of African American students, community organizations and churches can attempt to compensate for the failings of schools. Through after-school and summer school programs, these groups can provide young people with access to positive role models and social support that can help buffer young people from the pressures within their schools and communities (Boykin, 1983). Although such activities should not be seen as a substitute for making public schools more responsive to the communities that they serve, they do represent a tangible action that can be taken immediately to respond to the needs of Black youth, particularly males, who often face the greatest perils.

Conclusion: The Need for Further Research

Although this chapter made reference to the cultural norms, attitudes, and styles of behavior African American males may adopt and produce that can diminish the importance they attach to academic achievement, the emphasis of this chapter has been on the ways in which schools disserve and underserve this population of students. Such an emphasis is necessary because research on effective schools has shown that when optimal conditions for teaching and learning are provided, high levels of academic success for students, including African American males, can be achieved. Put differently, if we can find ways to increase the supply of effective schools, it may be possible to mitigate some of the risks confronting Black males. This does not mean the question of how to influence the attitudes, behaviors, and stances of Black males toward school and education generally does not need to be addressed or that it does not require further investigation. To the extent that we recognize that all students are active participants in their own education and not passive objects whose behavior can be manipulated by adults and reform measures, then the importance of understanding how to influence behavior cannot be understated. Learning how to influence the attitudes and behaviors of African American males must begin with an understanding of the ways in which structural and cultural forces shape their experiences in school and influence the construction of their identities. In this regard, it is especially important that future research be directed toward a greater understanding of youth culture and the processes related to cultural production.

Like popular culture, youth culture—and all of the styles and symbols associated with it—is dynamic and constantly changing. This is particularly true for inner-city African American youth, whose speech, dress, music, and tastes often establish trends for young people across America. For many adults, this culture is also impenetrable and often incomprehensible. Yet despite the difficulty of understanding and interpreting youth culture, it is imperative that efforts to help Black youth be guided by ongoing attempts at understanding the cultural forms they produce and the ways in which they respond and adapt to their social and cultural environment. Without such an understanding, efforts to influence the attitudes and behaviors of African American males will most likely fail to capture their imaginations and be ignored.

The importance of understanding youth culture became clear when embarking on research on how the popular media influence the attitudes of young people toward violence. Part of this research attempted to study how young people react to violent imagery in films by watching segments of popular movies with groups of middle school students and discussing their interpretations and responses to the ways violence was depicted. Following a series of discussions of their moral and ethical judgments of the violence conveyed in the films, the students asked to watch the film *Menace to Society* as part of the research exercise. Surprisingly, several of the students owned copies of the film and many had seen the film so many times that they had memorized parts of the dialogue. The film, which tells the story of a young man growing up in south central Los Angeles, is filled with graphic images of violence. After viewing, it became apparent that there might be some truth to the idea that violent films do condition young people to rationalize violent behavior as a legitimate and appropriate way for resolving conflicts and getting what they want. However, when discussing the film, it became clear that most were repulsed by the violence even though they were entertained by it, and rather than identifying with perpetrators of violence in the film, they identified most strongly with those characters who sought to avoid it (Noguera, 1995).

This experience and others like it made me realize how easy it is for adults to misinterpret and misunderstand the attitudes and behavior of young people. Generational differences, especially when compounded by differences in race and class, often make it difficult for adults to communicate effectively with youth. Many adults are aware of the chasm that separates them from young people, yet adults typically take actions intended to benefit young people without ever investigating whether the interventions meet the needs or concerns of youth. There is a need to consult with young people on how the structure and culture of schools contribute to low academic achievement and to enlist their input when interventions to improve student performance are being designed and implemented.

In addition to research on youth culture, there is a pressing need for further research on how identities—especially related to the intersection of race, class, and gender—are constructed within schools and how these identities affect students' attitudes and dispositions toward school, learning, and life in general. Presently such an analysis is largely absent from the policies and measures that are pursued to reform schools and improve classroom practice. Consistently, the focus of reform is on what adults and schools should do to improve student achievement, with students treated as passive subjects who can easily be molded to conform to our expectations. To devise a policy that will enable successes achieved in a particular program, classroom, or school to be replicated elsewhere, we must be equipped with an understanding of the process through which identities are shaped and formed within schools. There is also a need for further research on peer groups and their role in influencing the academic orientation of students.

Much of what I know about the plight of African American males comes from my personal experience growing up as a Black male and raising two sons. I have an intuitive sense that the way we are socialized to enact our masculinity, especially during adolescence, is a major piece of the problem. Researchers such as Geneva Smitherman (1977) and others have argued that Black children, and males in particular, often behave in ways that are perceived as hostile and insubordinate by adults. Others suggest that males generally, and Black males especially, have particularly fragile egos and are susceptible to treating even minor slights and transgressions as an affront to their dignity and sense of self-respect (Kunjufu, 1985; Madhubuti, 1990; Majors & Billson, 1992; West, 1993). Such interpretations resonate with my own experience, but it is still not clear how such knowledge can be used to intervene effectively on behalf of African American males.

I recall that as a young man, I often felt a form of anger and hostility that I could not attribute to a particular incident or cause. As a teacher, I have observed similar forms of hostility among Black male students, and for the past 3 years, I have witnessed my eldest son exhibit the same kinds of attitudes and behavior. Undoubtedly, some of this can be explained as a coping strategy: Black males learn at an early age that by presenting a tough exterior it is easier to avoid threats or attacks (Anderson, 1990). It may also be true, and this is clearly speculation, that the various ways in which Black males are targeted and singled out for harsh treatment (at school or on the streets by hostile peers or by the police) elicit postures of aggression and ferocity toward the world.

Given the range and extent of the hardships that beset this segment of the population, there is no doubt that there are some legitimate reasons for young Black males to be angry. Yet it is also clear that this thinly veiled rage and readiness for conflict can be self-defeating and harmful to their well-being. One of the consequences of this hostility and anger may be that such attitudes and behaviors have a negative effect on their academic performance. Adults, especially women, may be less willing to assist a young male who appears angry or aggressive. A colleague of mine has argued that what some refer to as the "fourth grade syndrome," the tendency for the academic performance of Black males to take a decisive downward turn at the age of 9 or 10, may be explained by the fact that this is the age when Black boys start to look like young men (Hilliard, 1991; Kunjufu, 1985). Ferguson (2000) found in his research in Shaker Heights, Ohio, that Black students were more likely than White students to cite "toughness" as a trait they admired in others. If these researchers are correct, and if the toughness admired by Black males evokes feelings of fear among some of their teachers, it is not surprising that trouble in school would be common. Gaining a clearer understanding of this phenomenon may be one important part of the process needed for altering academic trends among Black males.

Still, it would be a mistake to conclude that until we find ways to change the attitudes and behaviors of Black males, nothing can be done to improve their academic performance. There is no doubt that if schools were to become more nurturing and supportive, students would be more likely to perceive schools as a source of help and opportunity rather than an inhospitable place that one should seek to escape and actively avoid. Changing the culture and structure of schools such that African American male students come to regard them as sources of support for their aspirations and identities will undoubtedly be the most important step that can be taken to make high levels of academic achievement the norm rather than the exception.

REFERENCES

Ampim, M. (1993). *Towards an understanding of Black community development.* Oakland, CA: Advancing the Research.

Anderson, E. (1990). *Streetwise: Race, class, and change in an urban community.* Chicago: University of Chicago Press.

Apple, M. (1982). *Education and power.* Boston: ARK.

Auerbach, J. A., Krimgold, B. K., & Lefkowitz, B. (2000). *Improving health: It doesn't take a revolution. Health and social inequality.* Washington, DC: Kellogg Foundation.

Boykin, W. (1983). On the academic task performance and African American children. In J. Spencer (Ed.), *Achievement and achievement motives* (pp. 16–36). Boston: Freeman.

Brookover, W. B., & Erickson, E. L. (1969). *Society, schools, and learning.* Boston: Allyn & Bacon.

Carnoy, M. (1994). *Faded dreams: The politics and economics of race in America.* New York: Cambridge University Press.

Centers for Disease Control. (1988). Distribution of AIDS cases by racial/ethnic group and exposure category: United States (June 1, 1981, to July 4, 1988). *Morbidity and Mortality Weekly Report, 55,* 1–10.

Coleman, J., Campbell, E., Hobson, C., McPartland, J., Mood, A., Weinfeld, F., et al. (1966). *Equality of educational opportunity.* Washington, DC: Government Printing Office.

Cross, W., Parnham, T., & Helms, J. (1991). *Shades of Black: Diversity in African American identity.* Philadelphia: Temple University Press.

Dyson, A. H. (1994). The Ninjas, the X-Men, and the Ladies: Playing with power and identity in an urban primary school. *Teachers College Record, 96*(2), 219–239.

Earls, F. (1991). Not fear, nor quarantine, but science: Preparation for a decade of research to advance knowledge about causes and control of violence in youths. *Journal of Adolescent Health, 12,* 619–629.

Edmonds, R. (1979). Effective schools for the urban poor. *Educational Leadership, 37*(1), 15–27.

Erickson, E. (1968). *Identity: Youth and crisis.* New York: Norton.

Feagin, J. R., & Sikes, M. P. (1994). *Living with racism: The Black middle class experience.* Boston: Beacon.

Ferguson, R. (2000). *A diagnostic analysis of Black-White GPA disparities in Shaker Heights, Ohio.* Washington, DC: Brookings Institution.

Fordham, S. (1996). *Blacked out: Dilemmas of race, identity, and success at Capital High.* Chicago: University of Chicago Press.

Foster, M. (1997). *Black teachers on teaching.* New York: New Press.

Foster, M. (2001). *University of California report of Black student achievement.* Unpublished manuscript, University of California, Santa Barbara.

Freire, P. (1972). *Pedagogy of the oppressed.* New York: Continuum Publishing.

Gabarino, J. (1999). *Lost boys: Why our sons turn to violence and how to save them.* New York: Free Press.

Gibbs, J. T. (1988). *Young, Black, and male in America: An endangered species.* New York: Auburn House.

Giroux, H. (1983). *Theory and resistance in education.* New York: Bergin & Harvey.

Glazer, N., & Moynihan, D. (1963). *Beyond the melting pot.* Cambridge, MA: MIT Press.

Goffman, E. (1959). *The presentation of self in everyday life.* Garden City, NY: Doubleday.

Hacker, A. (1992). *Two nations: Black, White, separate, hostile, unequal.* New York: Scribner.

Harry, B., Klingner, J., & Moore, R. (2000, November). *Of rocks and soft places: Using qualitative methods to investigate the processes that result in disproportionality.* Paper presented at the Minority Issues in Special Education Symposium, Harvard University, Cambridge, MA.

Hilliard, A. (1991). Do we have the will to educate all children? *Educational Leadership, 49*(1), 31–36.

Hoberman, J. (1997). *Darwin's athletes.* New York: Houghton Mifflin.

Jackson, J. (1998). The myth of the crack baby. *Family Watch Library, September/October,* 4–12.

Jencks, C., & Phillips, M. (Eds.). (1998). *The Black-White test score gap.* Washington, DC: Brookings Institution.

Kao, G., & Tienda, M. (1998). Educational aspirations among minority youth. *American Journal of Education, 106,* 349–384.

Kaplan, H., Johnson, R., Bailey, C., & Simon, W. (1987). The sociological study of AIDS: A critical review of the literature and suggested research agenda. *Journal of Health and Social Science Behavior, 28,* 140–157.

Kunjufu, J. (1985). *Countering the conspiracy to destroy Black boys.* Chicago: African American Images.

Ladson-Billings, G. (1994). *The dreamkeepers: Successful teachers of African American children.* San Francisco: Jossey-Bass.

Lee, C. (2000). *The state of knowledge about the education of African Americans.* Washington, DC: American Educational Research Association, Commission on Black Education.

Levinson, B., Foley, D., & Holland, D. (1996). *The cultural production of the educated person.* Albany: SUNY Press.

Lewis, O. (1966). *La vida: A Puerto Rican family in the culture of poverty—San Juan and New York.* New York: Random House.

Loewen, J. (1995). *Lies my teacher told me.* New York: New Press.

Luker, K. (1996). *Dubious conceptions: The politics of teenage pregnancy.* Cambridge, MA: Harvard University Press.

Madhubuti, H. R. (1990). *Black men, obsolete, single, dangerous? The Afrikan American family in transition: Essays in discovery, solution, and hope.* Chicago: Third World Press.

Majors, R., & Billson, M. (1992). *Cool pose: Dilemmas of Black manhood in America.* New York: Simon & Schuster.

Massey, D., & Denton, N. (1993). *American apartheid.* Cambridge, MA: Harvard University Press.

McLeod, J. (1987). *Ain't no makin' it.* Boulder, CO: Westview.

McPartland, J., & Nettles, S. (1991). Using community adults as advocates or mentors for at-risk middle school students: A two-year evaluation of Project RAISE. *American Journal of Education, 99*(4), 568–586.

Meier, K., Stewart, J., & England, R. (1989). *Race, class and education: The politics of second generation discrimination.* Madison: University of Wisconsin Press.

MetLife. (2000). *The MetLife survey of the American teacher, 2000: Are we preparing students for the 21st century?* New York: Author.

Metz, M. (1978). *Classrooms and corridors.* Berkeley: University of California Press.

Mickelson, R. (1990). The attitude achievement paradox among Black adolescents. *Sociology of Education, 63*(1), 37–62.

Miles, R. (1989). *Racism.* London: Routledge Kegan Paul.

Milofsky, C. (1974). Why special education isn't special. *Harvard Educational Review, 44*(4), 437–458.

Morrow, R. A., & Torres, C. A. (1995). *Social theory and education: A critique of theories of social and cultural reproduction.* Albany: SUNY Press.

Moss, P., & Tilly, C. (1995). *Raised hurdles for Black men: Evidence from interviews with employers* (Working paper). New York: Russell Sage.

Murphy, J., & Hallinger, P. (1985). Effective high schools: What are the common characteristics? *NASSP Bulletin, 69*(477), 18–22.

Murray, C. A. (1984). *Losing ground: American social policy, 1950–1980.* New York: Basic Books.

Myers, L. J. (1988). *Understanding an Afrocentric worldview: Introduction to an optimal psychology.* Dubuque, IA: Kendall/Hunt.

National Research Council. (1989). *A common destiny: Blacks and American society.* Washington, DC: National Academy Press.

Noguera, P. (1995). Reducing and preventing youth violence: An analysis of causes and an assessment of successful programs. In California Wellness Foundation (Ed.), *1995 Wellness Lectures* (pp. 25–43). Oakland: California Wellness Foundation and the University of California, Berkeley.

Noguera, P. (2001). Racial politics and the elusive quest for equity and excellence in education. *Education and Urban Society, 34*(1), 27–42.

Oakes, J. (1985). *Keeping track: How schools structure inequality.* New Haven, CT: Yale University Press.

Ogbu, J. (1987). Opportunity structure, cultural boundaries, and literacy. In J. Langer (Ed.), *In language, literacy and culture: Issues of society and schooling* (pp. 42–57). Norwood, NJ: Ablex.

Ogbu, J. (1990). Literacy and schooling in subordinate cultures: The case of Black Americans. In K. Lomotey (Ed.), *Going to school* (pp. 3–21). Albany: SUNY Press.

Peshkin, A. (1991). *The color of strangers, the color of friends.* Chicago: University of Chicago Press.

Phelan, P. A., Davidson, H., & Ya, C. (1998). *Adolescent worlds.* Albany: SUNY Press.

Pollard, D. S. (1993). Gender, achievement and African American students' perceptions of their school experience. *Educational Psychologist, 28*(4), 294–303.

Poussaint, A., & Alexander, A. (2000). *Lay my burden down: Unraveling suicide and the mental health crisis among African Americans.* Boston: Beacon.

Roper, W. L. (1991). The prevention of minority youth violence must begin despite risks and imperfect understanding. *Public Health Reports, 106*(3), 229–231.

Ryan, W. (1976). *Blaming the victim.* New York: Vintage.

Sandler, D. P., Wilcox, A. J., & Everson, R. B. (1985). Cumulative effects of lifetime passive smoking on cancer risks. *Lancet, 1*(24), 312–315.

Sizemore, B. (1988). The Madison School: A turnaround case. *Journal of Negro Education, 57*(3), 243–266.

Skolnick, J. H., & Currie, E. (Eds.). (1994). *Crisis in American institutions* (9th ed.). New York: HarperCollins.

Smitherman, G. (1977). *Talkin' and testifyin': The language of Black America.* Boston: Houghton Mifflin.

Solomon, P. (1992). *Black resistance in high school.* Albany: SUNY press.

Spivak, H., Prothrow-Stith, D., & Hausman, A. (1988). Dying is no accident: Adolescents, violence, and intentional injury. *Pediatric Clinics of North America, 35*(6), 1339–1347.

Spring, J. (1994). *American education.* New York: McGraw-Hill.

Steinberg, L. (1996). *Beyond the classroom.* New York: Simon & Schuster.

Tabb, W. (1970). *The political economy of the Black ghetto.* New York: Norton.

Tatum, B. D. (1992). Talking about race, learning about racism: The application of racial identity development theory in the classroom. *Harvard Educational Review, 62*(1), 1–24.

Thorne, B. (1993). *Gender play.* New Brunswick, NJ: Rutgers University Press.

Tronyna, B., & Carington, B. (1990). *Education, racism and reform.* London: Routledge Kegan Paul.

Watson, C., & Smitherman, G. (1996). *Educating African American males: Detroit's Malcom X Academy.* Chicago: Third World Press.

Weinstein, R. S., Madison, S., & Kuklinski, M. (1995). Raising expectations in schooling: Obstacles and opportunities for change. *American Educational Research Journal, 32*(1), 121–159.

West, C. (1993). *Race matters.* Boston: Beacon.

Willis, P. (1977). *Learning to labor.* New York: Columbia University Press.

Wilson, W. (1978). *The declining significance of race.* Chicago: University of Chicago Press.

Wilson, W. (1987). *The truly disadvantaged.* Chicago: University of Chicago Press.

CHAPTER FOUR

Teachers' Perceptions and Expectations and the Black-White Test Score Gap

Ronald F. Ferguson

Harvard University

A frican American children arrive at kindergarten with fewer reading skills than Whites, even when their parents have equal years of schooling (Phillips, Crouse, & Ralph, 1998, chapter 5). In an ideal world, schools would reduce these disparities. Unfortunately, national data show that, at best, the Black-White test score gap is roughly constant (in standard deviations) from the primary through the secondary grades.[1] At worst, the gap widens.[2] Among Blacks and Whites with equal current scores, Blacks tend to make less future

SOURCE: This chapter originally appeared in *The Black-White Test Score Gap*, edited by C. Jencks and M. Phillips (Washington, D.C.: Brookings Institution Press). It also appeared in *Urban Education, Volume 38, Number 4*. It is reprinted by permission of the Brookings Institution.

AUTHOR'S NOTE: Thanks to Karl Alexander, Bill Dickens, James Flynn, Christopher Jencks, Meredith Phillips, and Jason Snipes for helpful discussions and comments on earlier drafts. I am also grateful to Lee Jussim and Meredith Phillips for calculations that they conducted at my request for this chapter. Jason Snipes provided able research assistance.

progress. This chapter addresses some of the ways that schools might affect this story. It examines evidence for the proposition that teachers' perceptions, expectations, and behaviors interact with students' beliefs, behaviors, and work habits in ways that help to perpetuate the Black-White test score gap.[3]

No matter what material resources are available, no matter what strategies districts use to allocate children to schools, and no matter how children are grouped for instruction, children spend their days in social interaction with teachers and other students. As students and teachers immerse themselves in the routines of schooling, both perceptions and expectations reflect and determine the goals that both students and teachers set for achievement, the strategies they use to pursue the goals, the skills, energy, and other resources they use to implement the strategies, and the rewards they expect from making the effort. These should affect standardized scores as well as other measures of achievement.

This chapter examines the controversial but common assumption that teachers' perceptions, expectations, and behaviors are biased by racial stereotypes. The literature is full of seeming contradictions. For example, Sara Lawrence Lightfoot (1978) wrote,

> Teachers, like all of us, use the dimensions of class, race, sex, ethnicity to bring order to their perception of the classroom environment. Rather than teachers gaining more in-depth and holistic understanding of the child, with the passage of time teachers' perceptions become increasingly stereotyped and children become hardened caricatures of an initially discriminatory vision. (pp. 85–86)

Similarly, Baron, Tom, and Cooper (1985) wrote,

> The race or class of a particular student may cue the teacher to apply the generalized expectations, therefore making it difficult for the teacher to develop specific expectations tailored to individual students. In this manner, the race or class distinction among students is perpetuated. The familiar operation of stereotypes takes place in that it becomes difficult for minority or disadvantaged students to distinguish themselves from the generalized expectation. (p. 251)

Conversely, doubting that bias is important, Brophy (1985) wrote, "Few teachers can sustain grossly inaccurate expectations for many of their students in the face of daily feedback that contradicts those expectations" (p. 304). In addition, Haller (1985) observed,

> Undoubtedly there are some racially biased people who are teachers. . . . However, . . . the problem does not seem to be of that nature. Conceiving it so is to confuse the issue, to do a serious injustice to the vast majority of teachers, and ultimately to visit an even more serious one on minority pupils. After all, . . . children's reading skills are not much improved by subtly (and not so subtly) labeling their teachers racists. (p. 481)[4]

Some aspects of this debate are substantive, but others are semantic. This chapter begins by distinguishing among alternative definitions of racial bias and reviewing evidence on teachers' perceptions and expectations. Later sections address ways that teachers' and students' behaviors might be both causes and consequences of racially disparate perceptions and expectations regarding achievement and, therefore, contribute to perpetuating the Black-White test score gap.

Bias in Teachers' Perceptions and Expectations

Expectations, perceptions, and behaviors that look biased if judged by one criterion often look unbiased if judged by another. However, writers on racial bias seldom evaluate their findings by more than a single standard. The discourse that results can be quite perplexing, as one body of literature alleges bias and another denies it. Much of this disagreement is really about what we mean by *bias*. At least three different conceptions of bias appear in this debate.

Bias is deviation from some benchmark that defines neutrality (or lack of bias). One type of benchmark is "unconditionally" race neutral. By this criterion, teachers who are unbiased expect the same on average of Blacks and Whites. A second type of benchmark is "conditionally" race neutral—conditioned on observable, measurable criteria. For example, teachers should expect the same of Black and White students on the condition that they have the same past grades and test scores. A third type of benchmark is conditioned not on past performance but instead on unobserved potential. It requires neutrality among—for example, equal expectations and aspirations for—Blacks and Whites who have equal "potential." Unfortunately, insofar as "potential" differs from past performance, it is difficult to prove. Assuming that Black and White children have the same potential at birth, which seems a fair assumption, then there is no distinction at birth between unconditional race neutrality and neutrality conditioned on unobserved potential. However, as children grow older, disparities in potential may develop if experience alters potential (e.g., consider recent literature on brain development). Thus, as children grow older, unconditional race neutrality may or may not remain the best approximation to neutrality conditioned on unobserved potential.

UNCONDITIONAL RACIAL NEUTRALITY

Unconditional race neutrality requires that perceptions, expectations, and behaviors be uncorrelated with race. By this definition, an unbiased perception, expectation, or treatment has the same average value for all racial groups. This benchmark for racial bias is the standard in experimental studies. The typical finding in such studies is that teachers are racially biased.

Researchers in experimental studies fabricate information about students. The information includes race in addition to other characteristics, but the sample is selected to avoid any correlation of these other characteristics with race.[5] In a typical experiment, teachers receive information about students via written descriptions, photographs, videotapes, or occasionally real children who act as the experimenter's confederates. Teachers then predict one or more measures of ability or academic performance for each student. If the experiment is run well, teachers do not discern that race is a variable in the experiment or that the real purpose is to assess their racial biases.

Baron et al. (1985) conducted a meta-analysis of experimental studies that focused on teachers' expectations, 16 of which dealt with race. Teachers had higher expectations for White students in 9 of the studies and for Blacks in 1 of the studies. Six studies in which the differences were statistically insignificant did not report which group was favored. Of the 5 studies with statistically significant differences, all favored Whites. In the meta-analysis, the hypothesis of identical expectations for Black and White students is clearly rejected ($p < .002$).[6]

The meta-analysis of Baron et al. (1985) missed one interesting study by DeMeis and Turner (1978) that makes no reference to teachers' expectations, attitudes, or biases in its title.[7] Nevertheless, it supports the same conclusion. In the DeMeis and Turner study, the participants were 68 White, female, elementary schoolteachers drawn from summer school classes at a university in Kentucky during the 1970s. Their teaching experience averaged 7 years. The students in the study were a pool of fifth-grade males responding to the question, "What happened on your favorite TV show the last time you watched it?" Each tape was accompanied by a picture of a Black or White student. DeMeis and Turner asked teachers to rate the taped responses for personality, quality of response, current academic abilities, and future academic abilities. The race of the student in the picture was a statistically significant predictor ($p < .0001$) for each of the four outcomes.[8]

If the benchmark is unconditional racial neutrality, teachers hold racially biased expectations. What should we make of this pervasive racial bias? Consider people who learn from real life that the odds of getting heads are 60:40 when flipping coins. Place these people in an experimental situation where, unknown to them, the odds have been set at 50:50. If each person is given only one toss of the coin in the experimental situation, what will he or she predict? Will their predictions be unbiased? If, as in the experiments discussed above, the benchmark for declaring expectations unbiased is unconditional racial neutrality, then biased expectations are what one should expect in an environment where real differences in performance between Blacks and Whites are the norm.[9] For the same reasons, bias of this type is also pervasive in naturalistic studies (i.e., studies in real classrooms without experimental controls).

Experimental research of this kind establishes that teachers believe certain stereotypes and use the stereotypes in one-time encounters with experimental targets. But it does not establish that the stereotypes would be biased estimates of the average if they were applied in real classrooms outside the experimental setting. Nor does it prove that teachers in real classrooms treat students inappropriately or that their stereotypes prevent them from forming accurate perceptions about individual students.

EVIDENCE OF ACCURACY

For more than two decades, scholars in education have emphasized that teachers' contemporaneous perceptions of students' performance as well as their expectations for students' future performance are generally accurate (e.g., see Egan & Archer, 1985; Good, 1987; Hoge & Butcher, 1984; Mitman, 1985; Monk, 1983; Pedulla, Airasian, & Madaus, 1980). For example, first-grade teachers can learn enough about children in the first few weeks of school to predict with some accuracy the students' rank order on exams held at the beginning of second grade (Brophy & Good, 1974, Table 6.1). Once set, teachers' expectations do not change a great deal. This may be because even early impressions of students' proficiencies are accurate, and the actual rank order does not change much.

There could be several reasons for stability in rank orderings. First, teachers' perceptions and expectations might be relatively inflexible. Self-fulfilling expectation effects, discussed below, will typically be strongest for teachers whose expectations are the least flexible.[10] For these teachers, correlations between beginning-of-year and end-of-year assessments should be among the highest.[11] A second reason for stability of class-rank orderings might be that few students try hard to change their positions. A third reason might be that the pace and style of standard teaching offer few effective opportunities for students who are behind to catch up.[12] Most evidence about the accuracy of teachers' perceptions comes from correlations between teachers' predictions and actual test scores, which typically range between .50 and .90 (Brophy & Good, 1974; Egan & Archer, 1985; Evertson, Brophy, & Good, 1972; Irvine, 1985; Willis, 1972). At least in the low end of this range, one could also focus on the inaccuracy of the predictions in "glass half empty" fashion.

I found only three studies that reported separate correlations for Blacks and Whites. Haller (1985) found that teachers' subjective assessments of fourth, fifth, and sixth graders' reading proficiency correlated .73 with the Comprehensive Test of Basic Skills for White students and .74 for Blacks.[13] Irvine (1990) had teachers rank 213 fifth, sixth, and seventh graders on general academic ability during the second, tenth, and final weeks of the 1983 to 1984 school year.[14] Correlations between these ratings and scores on the California Achievement Test (CAT) were similar for Blacks and Whites.[15] Gaines (1990) also found that teachers' predictions of students' performances on the Iowa Test of Basic Skills were as accurate for Blacks as for Whites.

This similarity in correlations for Blacks and Whites means that the rank order of achievement among Blacks is as stable as that among Whites and that teachers achieve similar accuracy in assessing both racial groups. It does not, however, imply that teachers' perceptions or expectations have the same impact on Blacks and Whites.[16] Neither does it mean that teachers are racially unbiased. Here, accuracy is not always the opposite of bias. If self-fulfilling prophecy always worked perfectly, for example, each student's performance would be exactly what the teacher expected. If expectations were biased, outcomes would be perfectly predicted but biased.

RACIAL NEUTRALITY
CONDITIONED ON OBSERVABLES

Racial neutrality conditioned on observables is a second type of benchmark for measuring bias. Instead of unconditional racial neutrality, as discussed above, the benchmark here assumes that a teacher's perceptions or expectations are unbiased if they are based only on legitimate observable predictors of performance, such as the student's past grades, test scores, attitudes about school, and beliefs about personal ability. Most people would agree that these are reasonable and "legitimate" things on which to base a prediction of performance. The benchmark in this case is only conditionally race neutral: If past performance is correlated with race, the benchmark will be too. Bias is the difference between the actual perception or expectation and the benchmark.

This type of bias can be identified by regressing the teacher's perception or expectation on both race and the other explanatory variables that we regard as "legitimate" determinants of teachers' perceptions or expectations. The coefficient of student race then measures the average racial bias among teachers in the sample. This benchmark is probably more appropriate than unconditional race neutrality when considering, for example, whether teachers are biased in the judgments that they use in nominating students for particular curriculum tracks or ability groups. As we shall see, it might also be more appropriate for use in analyses of whether teachers' biases produce self-fulfilling prophecies of poor performance for Black students. However, it is not sufficient to distinguish conditional from unconditional neutrality; the existing literature often makes a further distinction between past performance and future potential.

RACIAL NEUTRALITY CONDITIONED ON POTENTIAL

A third type of benchmark that may or may not equate with either of the two discussed above is the level of performance that the student could reach at his or her full potential. Here, the bias is in perception or estimation of a person's full potential. The full-potential benchmark equals demonstrated plus latent potential. The alleged racial bias is that people underestimate latent potential more for Blacks than for Whites.

A major concern of African Americans is that teachers underestimate Black students' potential, not necessarily their performance. As an illustration of this concern, consider the following passage from a report by the Committee on Policy for Racial Justice, titled *Visions of a Better Way: A Black Appraisal of American Public Schooling,* published by the Joint Center for Political and Economic Studies in 1989 (as cited in Miller, 1995):

> We hold this truth to be self-evident: all Black children are capable of learning and achieving. Others who have hesitated, equivocated, or denied this fact have assumed that black children could not master their school-work or have cautioned that blacks were not "academically oriented." As a result, they have perpetuated a myth of intellectual inferiority, perhaps genetically based. These falsehoods prop up an inequitable social hierarchy with blacks disproportionately represented at the bottom, and they absolve schools of their fundamental responsibility to educate all children, no matter how deprived. (p. 203)[17]

The passage that follows clearly alleges bias, judged by a "future potential" benchmark:

> In the middle class white school, student inattention was taken as an indication of teacher need to arouse student interest, but the same behavior in a lower class black school was rationalized as boredom due to limited student attention span. In general, the teachers in the lower class black school were characterized by low expectations for the children and low respect for their ability to learn. (from Leacock as cited in Brophy & Good, 1974, p. 10)

If perceptions of children's intellectual potential affect goal setting in both homes and classrooms, which surely they must, then teachers and parents who underestimate children's potential will tend to set goals that are too low.[18] Underestimation of potential is undoubtedly a major problem, irrespective of race. It is a major waste of human potential and a social injustice that we do not give teachers the incentives and supports they need to set, believe in, and skillfully pursue higher goals for all students, but especially for African Americans and other stigmatized minorities. Because we underestimate potential, the payoff to searching more aggressively for ways of helping children would surely be higher than most people imagine.

Bias related to future potential is impossible to estimate reliably because there is no clear basis on which to estimate human potential.[19] Surveys find that expressed beliefs in the intellectual inferiority of Blacks have moderated over the years.[20] For example, the percentage of Whites responding to the General Social Survey that Blacks have less "in-born ability to learn" fell from 27% in 1977 to 10% in 1996 (Jencks & Phillips, 1998, introduction; Kluegel, 1990, pp. 514–515, 517). There is no way to know the degree to which this reduction is due to changes in beliefs or changes in social norms. For example, Tom Smith (as cited in Miller, 1995) discussed how the same General Social Survey found that when respondents were not constrained to attribute differences to genetic factors, 53% agreed that Blacks and Hispanics are less intelligent than Whites; further, 30% of Blacks and 35% of Hispanics agreed (p. 183).[21]

Many experts also think that genetic differences are at least partially to blame for existing Black-White differences in academic achievement. Snyderman and Rothman (as cited in Miller, 1995) discussed a 1984 survey that questioned 1,020 experts on intelligence, most of whom were professors and university-based researchers who study testing, psychology, and education. As Miller (1995) reported, almost half (46%) expressed the opinion that Black-White differences in intelligence are at least partially genetic. Of the others, 15% said that only environment was responsible, 24% regarded the available evidence as insufficient, and 14% did not answer the question (Miller, 1995, pp. 186–187). In other words, only 15% clearly disagreed. With expert opinion slanted so strongly in favor of the genetic hypothesis and widespread media attention to books such as *The Bell Curve,* there is little prospect that "rumors of inferiority" will cease or that racial differences in estimated potential will disappear.[22]

Finally, writers concerned with bias in estimating potential often claim that it leads to self-fulfilling prophecies. Their point is that children would achieve more if teachers and other adults expected that they could. In most cases, a more appropriate terminology than "self-fulfilling" might be to say that bias of this type produces expectations that are "sustaining" of past trends.[23] A sustaining expectation is likely to block the absorption of new information into a decision process and thereby to sustain the trend that existed before the new information arrived.

TYPE II BIAS AND SELF-FULFILLING PROPHECY

A self-fulfilling prophecy is one that makes a bias in a teacher's expectation regarding a student's performance affect the student's performance. Self-fulfilling prophecies can be associated with any of the three conceptions of bias discussed above, but only those associated with the second type (where the benchmark is conditioned on observables) can be well measured. Although the basic idea was introduced into social science by Merton (1948), Rosenthal and Jacobson's (1968) work sparked a small industry of such studies during the 1970s and early 1980s. The effect shows up (and also fails to show up) in a wide range of experimental studies for both animal and human subjects (Rosenthal, 1994). Experimental studies in education typically involve random assignment of students to groups that have been labeled as high or low performing.

Successful instigation of self-fulfilling prophecies by researchers requires that (a) teachers believe false information given to them about students, (b) teachers act on the information in ways that students can perceive, and (c) students respond in ways that confirm the expectation. The effect can fail to appear, which it often does, if any of these conditions fail.[24]

In experiments that confirm the effect, groups labeled as high performing outperform those labeled as low performing. A meta-analysis by Smith (1980) identified 44 effect-size estimates for reading scores, with an average effect size of 0.48 standard deviations, distinguishing students with high and low labels.[25] The average across 17 effects for math, reported in the same paper, was much smaller at 0.18. Why effects should be smaller for math than for reading is unclear. Perhaps math instruction is less flexible and therefore less affected by teacher perceptions.

Brophy (1985), a leader in the field since the early 1970s, asserted that, on average, teacher expectations in real classrooms probably make only a small difference in student achievement (p. 304).[26] He added the caveat, however, that teachers who hold rigid expectations and permit these to guide interactions with their students can produce effects that are larger. It is plausible, but not established in any literature that I have seen, that expectations might be more rigid regarding Black students than Whites. Moreover, expectation effects might accumulate from year to year. Surprisingly, there appears to be no good evidence on the degree to which expectation effects accumulate. If small effects accumulate, they could make a larger difference with the passage of time. In the short run, even a small difference due to expectations could push a score across the boundary between two grade levels and, thereby, become consequential.

In naturalistic studies, the magnitude of self-fulfilling prophecy can be estimated as the coefficient on a teacher's expectation measure in an equation where the dependent variable is the student's actual performance at the end of a school year.[27] Assuming that the estimated effect of the teacher's expectation is not simply a stand-in for omitted variables, the idiosyncratic contribution of the teacher's expectation is the consequence of bias. When teacher biases exist but do not affect actual scores or grades, it can be because teachers do not act on their biases or because student performance does not respond to the biased actions that teachers take. Finally, it is also important to note that a teacher's perception of current performance and his or her expectation for future performance can differ with one showing bias and the other not.[28]

TESTING FOR RACIAL DIFFERENCES IN EXPECTANCY EFFECTS

Jussim, Eccles, and Madon (1996) are the only researchers who have tested for racial differences in impacts of teachers' perceptions on test scores (pp. 350–351).[29] Teachers' perceptions of 1,664 sixth graders' current performance, talent, and effort in math were collected in October of the 1982 to 1983 school year.[30] Jussim et al. then tested for what they called "racial stereotype bias" (whether student race predicts teachers' October perceptions after controlling for previous grades, previous test scores, self-concept of math ability, self-reported level of effort, and self-reported time spent on homework). This type of bias uses the second type of benchmark defined above—racial neutrality conditioned on observables, including past performance. Jussim et al. found no evidence of racial stereotype bias in teachers' perceptions of *current* performance, talent, or effort for this sample of sixth graders.[31] The coefficient on student race was small and statistically insignificant.[32]

If past performance and attitudes explain racial differences in teachers' *current* perceptions, then these perceptions can be an important source of the *future* Black-White test score gap only if teachers' perceptions affect Blacks and Whites differently. This is precisely what Jussim et al. (1996) found. They analyzed the effects of teachers' perceptions of performance, talent, and effort in October on both math grades and scores on the math section of the Michigan Educational Assessment Program for May of the spring semester of the 1982 to 1983 school year.[33]

For both grades and scores, Jussim et al. (1996) found that the estimated impact of teacher perceptions was almost 3 times as great for African Americans as for Whites.[34] Effects were also larger for girls and for children from low-income families. Furthermore, the effect was cumulative across disadvantages or stigmas: Black children from low-income backgrounds experienced the effects of both race and income. Teachers' perceptions of student effort do not affect Michigan Educational Assessment Program scores, but they do affect grades, even though they are not strongly correlated with students' self-reports of effort.[35]

What might explain racial differences in the consequences of teachers' perceptions? One possibility is that the result is simply a statistical artifact due to omitted variable bias. This seems unlikely.[36] A more likely explanation is that teachers are less flexible in their expectations for Blacks, females, and students from low-income households. Or as Weinstein (1985) speculated,

> Minority status may play a role in the vulnerability with which students respond to teacher expectations. Differences in cultural values (family compared to school) may serve to immunize some children from the impact of teacher views of their performance or alternately to heighten their susceptibility to the dominant viewpoint. (p. 344)

Perhaps the behaviors of both teachers and students are affected by the *combination* of the student's race and the teacher's perception of performance. Two sections below address these possibilities.

Table 4.1   Spring Standardized Grades and Test Scores in Mathematics and Fall Performance Ratings, Sixth Grade, 1982–83[a]

Measure and Race	Fall Performance Rating				
	1	2	3	4	5
Predicted spring grades					
Blacks	−1.00	−0.57	−0.14	0.28	0.71
Whites	−0.43	−0.25	−0.07	0.11	0.28
Difference	−0.57	−0.32	−0.07	0.18	0.43
Predicted spring scores					
Blacks	−0.79	−0.46	−0.13	0.20	0.53
Whites	−0.30	−0.17	−0.04	0.09	0.21
Difference	−0.50	−0.29	−0.09	0.11	0.31

SOURCE: Author's calculations based on data from Jussim, Eccles, and Madon (1996, pp. 308–311).

a. All other student characteristics are held constant. Grades and test scores relate to the mathematics section of the Michigan Educational Assessment Program. Fall ratings are such that 1 denotes the lowest level of current performance and 5 denotes the highest level. The overall mean is zero, and the standard deviation is one.

Table 4.1 shows simulated math scores and grades (in standard deviation units) cross-tabulated with teachers' performance ratings for students, holding all other student characteristics constant. For both Blacks and Whites, there is a positive relationship between the teacher's October performance rating and the student's grades and scores in May. However, the effect is stronger for Blacks. Blacks who receive performance ratings in the top category (e.g., Category 5) in October are predicted to outperform Whites who receive the same rating (again, assuming equal values for control variables). Conversely, Blacks who receive the lowest October performance ratings lag an estimated half standard deviation behind Whites who got the same ratings.

If teachers tend to be accurate in their current perceptions and in their expectations for future progress, then the findings of Jussim et al. (1996) require that teachers should expect the pattern shown in Table 4.1.[37] This would be stereotype bias for expected progress, even if there is no such bias in the evaluation of October performance. The accuracy of the stereotype might reflect a self-fulfilling prophecy of the teacher's expectation, or it might not. Evidence that teacher perceptions affect subsequent performance more for Blacks than for Whites suggests either that Black students respond differently than Whites to similar treatment from teachers or that teachers treat Black and White students differently, or both. The next two sections address these possibilities.

DO BLACK AND WHITE CHILDREN RESPOND TO TEACHERS DIFFERENTLY?

The finding that Black students respond more strongly to teachers' beliefs has not been replicated, but it is consistent with findings from several other studies that ask related questions. A study by Casteel (1997) asked eighth and ninth graders whom they want most to please with their class work.[38] "Teachers" was the answer for 81% of Black females, 62% of Black males, 28% of White females, and 32% of White males. Whites were more concerned with pleasing parents. Entwisle and Alexander (1988) found that teachers' ratings of maturity for first graders have larger effects for Blacks than for Whites on both verbal and arithmetic scores on the CAT. Kleinfeld (1972) found that high school students' concept of their ability is more correlated with perceived teacher ratings of ability for Blacks but more correlated with perceived parent ratings for Whites. Irvine (1990) reached similar conclusions.[39]

Jussim et al. (1996) suggested, and I agree, that Claude Steele's (e.g., Steele & Aronson, 1998) work offers one reason why Black and White students might respond differently faced with identical classroom conditions.[40] What Steele called "stereotype threat" and the resulting "stereotype anxiety" can operate for members of any stigmatized group. When the stereotype concerns ability, individuals fear performing in ways that might corroborate the stereotype. They fear that the stereotype might become the basis of others' pejorative judgments, as well as their own self-perceptions.

One effect of the anxiety is "a disruptive apprehension" that can interfere with performance. Under stressful test conditions, Steele found that women and Blacks perform worse when they are primed to be conscious of their race or gender. Steele theorized that when the anxiety is sufficiently chronic, the response can be disidentification with the task at hand or with the general category of tasks.

Students decide not to weigh performance in the particular domain as important to personal goals or self-perceptions.

Steele tested this idea only at the college level, and even there, his findings were only for high-achieving students at highly selective colleges. The degree to which stereotype threat and anxiety might apply for students in primary and secondary schools remains to be investigated. The findings of Jussim et al. (1996) were for sixth graders. Are children this young aware enough of stereotypes to be susceptible to stereotype threat or anxiety?

Perhaps.[41] Gross (1993) studied math performance for students in a racially integrated suburb of Washington, DC, during the 1985 to 1986 school year. In the fourth grade, 92% of Blacks and 86% of Whites who were above grade level on the number of math competencies that they had mastered scored in the 8th and 9th stanines (i.e., ninths) of the CAT. By sixth grade, 82% of Whites who were above grade level in completion of competencies were still in the 8th and 9th stanines on the CAT. For Blacks, however, the figure was only 68%.[42] Gross pointed out that this pattern of performance on the CAT for sixth graders was inconsistent with students' in-school performance, and she used it to caution against basing ability group placements only on test scores.

Gross (1993) and her team also conducted focus groups with middle and high school students. She reported "a deep commitment on the part of high-achieving Black students to do well in mathematics so that they could move on to good colleges and professional careers" (p. 283). But the same students felt

deep frustration at the incidents of racism they had experienced in the lower expectations they had perceived from teachers and other students. . . . This was particularly true regarding the honors-level Black students who reported that each year they had to prove they were capable of doing honors work. (p. 283)

Although the focus groups were for middle and high school students, Gross (personal communication, February 1998) reported that it was common knowledge that children in upper elementary grades felt the same types of pressures. If the CAT for sixth graders was regarded as a test of ability, which it may well have been, then Steele's (Steele & Aronson, 1998) theory could be an important reason why Black sixth graders who were above grade level on competencies got lower CAT scores than White peers with the same level of classroom competence.[43]

Gross (1993) also reported what appears to be the type of disengagement that Steele hypothesized—a type that could help explain the larger negative impact on Black students that Jussim et al. (1996) found when performance was perceived to be low. Gross (1993) reported that teachers said Black students were overrepresented among students who were least studious and least well prepared for class: They "did not come to their classes prepared to work or in the proper frame of mind to attend fully to instruction" (p. 281).

In addition, both teachers and administrators reported that Black parents were less supportive of the school's mission than White parents. Meanwhile, Black parents, when convened in focus groups, were the most supportive of the idea that their children should strive for the higher-level math classes, even if that meant lower grades. White parents were more prone to say that their children should stay in the top sections only if they were likely to do well. Were Black parents sending the mixed message, "Shoot for the top, but if you don't do as well as the White kids, we'll understand"? Could this have contributed to the ambivalence that their children's work habits appeared to express? (See Figure 4.1 on page 97 regarding racial comparisons of work habits and other attitudes.) If Black children sense more ambivalence from their parents than White children do, then teachers' opinions might take on a special significance, as the statistical evidence discussed above appears to show.

In a study inspired by the work of John Ogbu (1978, 1983, 1987; Fordham & Ogbu, 1986), Mickelson (1990) distinguished "abstract" from "concrete" attitudes. Mickelson found that concrete attitudes predict cumulative high school grade point average but abstract attitudes do not.[44] Her measure of abstract attitudes reflects mainstream ideology—standard optimistic rhetoric about education and the American dream. In contrast, her measure of concrete attitudes includes questions that illicit doubt and ambivalence about education as a route to success in mainstream society.[45] Students might acquire concrete attitudes from routine, informal, personal interaction with friends, parents, other adults, and the broader society. Mickelson found that Blacks agreed to an even greater degree than Whites with the optimistic but abstract beliefs about success and the American dream. However, Blacks' concrete attitudes were less hopeful than Whites.' Table 4.2 summarizes the pattern.[46] It suggests a possible

Table 4.2   Mean Scores on Measures of "Abstract" and "Concrete"
Beliefs About the Importance of Education for Success,
by Race and Class Background for 12th Graders in Eight
Los Angeles High Schools, Spring 1983

	Black Male	White Male	Effect Size	Black Female	White Female	Effect Size
For children of white-collar parents						
Abstract score	5.50	5.06	0.58	5.27	5.09	0.24
Concrete score	4.38	4.90	−0.53	4.43	5.00	−0.58
Sample size	56	224		84	241	
For children of blue-collar parents						
Abstract score	5.28	4.99	0.38	5.34	5.21	0.17
Concrete score	4.19	4.54	−0.36	4.19	4.81	−0.63
Sample size	138	100		140	93	

SOURCE: Mickelson (1990).

NOTE: Full sample standard deviations: abstract scores ($SD = .76$); concrete scores ($SD = .98$). Racial differences in abstract scores, $p < .05$; class differences in concrete scores, $p < .0005$; racial differences in concrete scores, $p < .0001$.

reason why surveys usually find that Blacks subscribe to mainstream values as much as Whites do but then behave in ways that show less commitment to mainstream success.

Do Teachers Treat Black and White Students Differently?

I found only four experimental studies dealing with teachers' treatment of Black and White students. All date from the 1970s and early 1980s (Coates, 1972; Feldman & Orchowsky, 1979; Rubovits & Maehr, 1973; Taylor, 1979).[47] These studies control differences between students (or "virtual" or "phantom" students) by matching or random assignment. As with most of the experimental literature already discussed, the experiments are contrived one-time encounters. All four experiments found that teachers were less supportive of Black than White students.

Taylor (1979) conducted an experiment in which a 6-year-old student was said to be watching from behind a screen as the participants, college students in teacher training, taught a prescribed lesson.[48] Taylor found that when these phantom students were Black, they received briefer feedback after mistakes (standardized effect size = 0.613), less positive feedback after correct responses (effect size = 0.423), and fewer "helpful slips of the tongue" (i.e., unauthorized coaching) (effect size = 0.536). Each of the experimental studies suggests that some teachers may be helping Whites more than Blacks and that the differences may be large enough to have nontrivial effects on performance.

Studies of real classrooms confirm this hypothesis. These studies sometimes find no racial differences but more frequently have found differences favoring Whites.[49] Of course, studies finding differences are probably more likely to be published. Nonetheless, if our benchmark is unconditional racial neutrality, there is strong evidence of racial bias in how teachers treat students. It is nearly impossible in naturalistic studies to determine whether teachers would appear racially biased if we controlled racial differences in students' behaviors, work habits, and social skills. But because students and parents cannot read a teacher's mind, they may *think* that differences in treatment reflect unjustified and unfair favoritism. When teachers appear biased, trust may be eroded and relationships spoiled (see below).

EVIDENCE ON POSSIBLE
REASONS FOR DIFFERENTIAL TREATMENT

Typically, we have no way of knowing whether teachers' perceptions of students' attitudes and behaviors are accurate. The finding of Jussim et al. (1996) that teacher perceptions of effort predicted grades but not standardized test scores calls attention to the possibility that perceptions are inaccurate; so does the finding of Jussim et al. that teachers' perceptions of effort were only moderately correlated with students' own self-reports.

In 1990, the *Prospects* survey asked a national sample of teachers to rate specific students in their classes on, "Cares about doing well," "Gets along with teachers," and "Works hard at school" (for more on the *Prospects* survey, see Puma, Jones, Rock, & Fernandez, 1993). The response categories ranged from "very

Figure 4.1   Teachers' Perceptions of Students' Levels of Effort*

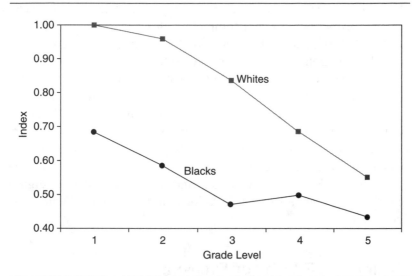

SOURCE: Author's calculations based on data collected in the early 1990s for the *Prospects* study of educational growth and opportunity; see Puma et al. (1993).

NOTE: Teachers rated students on the following criteria: cares about doing well, gets along with teachers, and works hard at school. Data for first graders represent one cohort (1,979 black; 5,333 white); third and fifth graders represent a second cohort (1,276 black; 4,045 white); seventh and ninth graders represent a third cohort (393 black; 2,424 white). Numbers are weighted to be nationally representative. Chi-square tests on each item for each grade show that through the seventh grade, all Black-White differences are statistically significant at the 0.01 level or better. For the ninth grade, the differences are not statistically significant, but the black sample is quite small.

* Composite index for black and white students in first through ninth grades, constructed such that white first graders are equal to 1 and higher index values are better; see text for details.

much" to "not at all." Teachers rated Black children lower than Whites on all three items.[50] To measure racial differences in these ratings, I subtracted for each racial group, the percentage with the lowest ranking (i.e., "not at all") from the percentage with the highest ranking (i.e., "very much") in each grade, and then summed the results for the three questions. Higher values of the index are therefore better. The index is standardized to equal 1 for White first graders. Figure 4.1 shows the means for Blacks and Whites by grade level.

Figure 4.1 shows that teachers perceived the greatest Black-White difference in the early elementary years. After the fifth grade, the gap narrows but does not completely close. The similarity in how Blacks and Whites relate to school by ninth grade is consistent with data on eighth graders from the National Longitudinal Survey (NELS88). Several authors, including Cook and Ludwig in this volume, have remarked on the similarity of Black and White attitudes in NELS88 (see also Miller, 1995; Solorzano, 1992). Because NELS88 did not reach students earlier in their school careers (and also because it does not ask the right questions), it may lead people to underestimate the degree to which Black-White differences in work habits, behavior, and attitudes prior to eighth grade affect teacher-student relations and the Black-White test score gap.

RECIPROCAL EFFECTS OF STUDENT BEHAVIOR AND TEACHER PERFORMANCE

Teachers' judgments about how much they enjoy teaching students inevitably affect teachers' behaviors. This can apply to entire classrooms and to individual students. Teachers may respond to difficult students by withdrawing support (Brophy & Good, 1974).[51] This could help account for the finding of Jussim et al. (1996) that teachers' beginning-of-year perceptions, although initially unbiased, are stronger predictors of end-of-year performance for Blacks. Specifically, between equally low-performing Black and White students, Black students might be perceived as more difficult (and therefore receive less teacher support than Whites), and between equally high-performing Black and White students, Black students might be perceived as less difficult (and therefore receive more teacher support than Whites).[52] I found no quantitative research in naturalistic settings that controlled for initial student performance and then systematically measured racial differences in how much positive reinforcement teachers provided. However, Black *students* on average may give *teachers* less positive reinforcement than White students with the similar beginning-of-year performance.

For example, Willis and Brophy (1974) asked 28 first-grade teachers to nominate three children to each of four groups. The groups, along with Willis and Brophy's summary of teachers' responses, were as follows:

Attachment group: If you could keep one student another year for the sheer joy of it, whom would you pick?

Regarding boys in the *attachment groups,* the teachers made more positive comments about their clothing, . . . more often assigned them as leaders or classroom helpers, . . . high ability [student] who is well-adjusted to the school situation, conforms to the teacher's rules and "rewards" the teacher by being somewhat dependent upon her and by doing well in his schoolwork.

Indifference group: If a parent were to drop in unannounced for a conference, whose child would you be least prepared to talk about?

Boys in the *indifference group* were described as more likely to . . . have a "blank" eye expression, . . . to have a disinterested or uncooperative parent, . . . to have failed to live up to the teachers' initial expectations. . . . Nevertheless, the Metropolitan Readiness Test scores of these boys did not differ significantly from those of their classmates.

Concern group: If you could devote all your attention to a child who concerned you a great deal, whom would you pick?

Boys in the *concern group* were especially likely to be described as . . . having a speech impediment . . . being active and vivacious, seeking teacher attention, . . . needing readiness work, having generally poor oral and verbal skills, . . . and having generally low abilities. . . . [These children were] perceived as making legitimate demands because they generally conform to classroom rules but are in need of help due to low ability.

Rejection group: If your class was to be reduced by one child, whom would you be relieved to have removed?

Boys in the *rejection group* were described as being more likely to be non-White than White, coming from intact families in which both parents were living, as being immature and not well-adjusted, as being independent, as being loud or disruptive in the classroom, as being rarely inactive or not vivacious, . . . as needing extra help because of generally low ability, as needing readiness work. . . . These children did not differ significantly from their classmates on the Metropolitan Readiness Test scores despite the teachers' comments about low ability.

The rejection group was the only one in which non-White boys were overrepresented in teachers' remarks. Clearly, much more was involved in shaping the teacher-to-student relationship than simply the child's initial ability or academic performance, at least in first grade. Children's work habits and behaviors (and sometimes even their parents' behaviors) affected teacher preferences. We know from Figure 4.1 that teachers in the 1990s perceived that Blacks rate lower than Whites on attitudes, effort, and behavior. Based on these patterns, my guess is that *on average,* teachers probably prefer to teach Whites, and *on average,* they probably give Whites more plentiful and unambiguous support.

Mismatches of teachers' and students' races do not appear to be the central problem. Even Black teachers need help in learning to cope with some of the special demands that Black children from disadvantaged backgrounds can present.[53] The following is a quote from a young Black teacher, Paula:

> The first thing I knew was that they were just BADD. I know part of the problem was myself because I was saying things that I probably shouldn't have said because they got me so upset and I wasn't able to handle it. . . . I felt that being black I would automatically know more, and so forth, and in ways I think I do, but [the training program she attended] has helped me to understand things from many perspectives. . . . Black teachers who have been in different programs . . . haven't got this cultural awareness and I know that because they're so negative. . . . Alot of them aren't culturally sensitive to their own culture. (Cabello & Burstein, 1995, pp. 289–290)

It remains an open question how much difference such feelings make for children's outcomes. Many "burned out" teachers in difficult schools may simply be going through the motions, waiting for retirement. Also, it is unclear to what degree this pattern is racially distinct. In many classrooms, teachers and students are embroiled in conflicts and confusion for which they lack the skills and external supports to resolve. Paula was enrolled in a program to help teachers understand, manage, and teach difficult students. Research analyzing the effectiveness and replicability of such programs should be a priority if we are to improve the schooling of Black children in settings where behavior is a problem.

Teachers also need to communicate more clearly about the quality of children's performance in classrooms where achievement correlates closely with race. Signals about performance have racial overtones in such classrooms. This can interfere with teacher-student relations and learning. In focus group discussions with 9- to 19-year-old Black males in a midwestern city in 1996, students had no explanation for their disappointing grades other than teacher prejudice. The students usually spoke of a feeling of prejudice from teachers; teachers who expected more and offered encouragement were the exception.

Teachers in integrated schools can be "biased" in ways as simple as reinforcing a propensity of White children to speak more often in class (e.g., see Katz as cited in Brophy & Good, 1974; Irvine, 1990). Black students may assume that this means teachers think Whites are "smarter" or like the White students more. Ways that teachers communicate about academic ability, especially in integrated schools where the performance of Whites is superior, can affect the degree to which Black students disengage from the pursuit of excellence or stay engaged and aim for mastery.[54]

RESPONSIVE TEACHING

The average Black child arrives at kindergarten with fewer academic skills than the average White child. Schools may then simply push children along in ways that sustain or add to racial disparities, validating the expectation that Black-White differences in achievement are normal or perhaps even inevitable. But if instruction is appropriately stimulating and responsive to children's progress, teachers' expectations may not be either self-fulfilling or sustaining. The more inviting and responsive instruction is to children's efforts to improve, the less teachers' initial perceptions and expectations will predict later success.

Research that measures how instructional methods affect the accuracy of teacher expectations is rare. One relevant set of studies deals with "wait time" or how long a teacher waits for students to raise their hands, to begin talking, and to continue talking after a pause. Minority students in integrated classrooms participate more when wait time is longer; this improves their performance relative to Whites and changes teacher expectations (Rowe, 1986).[56]

Corrective feedback is probably more important than wait time.[57] In a study where race was not mentioned, Guskey (1982) studied 44 intermediate and high school teachers who taught various subjects in two metropolitan school systems. Each teacher taught two matched classes after receiving training in a particular approach to mastery learning. The teacher taught one class using his or her standard methods and another using a "feedback and corrective" process learned in the training.[58] Both classes used the same final exam and grading standards. Guskey compared teacher ratings of "probable achievement" from early in the semester with final grades and exam scores and with ratings of "achievement potential" that teachers gave at the end of the term. For 10 teachers, the training made no difference to their students' performance. However, for 34 other teachers (called the "positive change" group) the experimental classes did better than the control classes on both grades and scores. Among these 34, the improved techniques for feedback and correction made teachers' early expectations less predictive of later achievement. Specifically, correlations between teachers' initial ratings of probable achievement and the students' final grades and exam scores were markedly lower for experimental classes than for classes using customary methods; teachers in the "no-change" group had high correlations in both classes (see Table 4.3). It seems likely that better feedback and corrective methods could also affect the rank order of performance by race, but Guskey did not investigate this issue.

It is worth noting that "responsive" teaching can take negative as well as positive forms. For example, some teachers may give incentives and assistance to students who want to improve their positions in the class and penalize students who do not. Brattesani, Weinstein, and Marshall (1984), in an often-cited study, compared fourth-, fifth-, and sixth-grade classes where student surveys showed high and low levels of differential treatment.[59] In classrooms with more differential treatment, more students with below-average scores at the beginning of the year made unusually large gains, but fewer students with above-average scores made gains.[60]

The Great Expectations (GE) Initiative

The Great Expectations (GE) initiative is a public-private partnership created in 1989 to bring Marva Collins's ideas about teaching into Oklahoma schools.[61] By ending with the GE story, my purpose is to show real people struggling, with some success, to change

Table 4.3   Median Correlations Between Teachers' Initial Ratings of Students, Final Ratings, Students' Course Grades, and Students' Course Examination Scores

| | Correlation Between Initial Rating and | | | | | |
| | Final Rating | | Course Grade | | Final Exam Score | |
	Experi-mental	Control	Experi-mental	Control	Experi-mental	Control
Positive change (N = 34)	.53	.83	.51	.80	.31	.50
No change (N = 10)	.92	.90	.77	.79	.69	.75

SOURCE: Guskey (1982).

NOTE: Of the 44 teachers in the sample, 34 were labeled the "positive change" group because their experimental classes had higher final exam scores and course grades than their control classes. For the 10 teachers in the "no change" group, either grades or scores on the final exam were higher in the control class. Both Guskey (1982) and Brattesani et al. (1984) showed that greater responsiveness to individual children can weaken the link between past and future performance, perhaps also altering trajectories. Both were silent about race and ethnicity. However, studies that deal directly with race do not investigate whether teaching practices can change the rank order of performance among students.

teaching practices and, in the process, teachers' expectations for disadvantaged, mostly minority children. GE includes a range of techniques that Collins developed. It aims to nurture in *every* student, not only the most talented, the expectation that they are destined to be important people if they do their best in school to prepare well for the future. Misbehaving students should be reminded regularly that the teacher cares and refuses to give up on them. Methods combine high challenge for students with forms of feedback from teachers *and* *peers* that make learning fun and emphasize its importance for happy and effective lives. Progress is celebrated so that every student can earn the opportunity for positive recognition from teachers, peers, and parents. In addition to more standard materials for core subjects, the curriculum includes uplifting, forward-looking poetry that students memorize to discuss and recite at school and at home.

The incentive for schools to participate in the GE initiative was a threat of takeover by the state if test scores for third graders persisted below the 25th percentile for 3 consecutive years on the Iowa

Test of Basic Skills. Educators in schools that joined GE had heard of Collins. Many had seen her on CBS's *60 Minutes* and knew of her reputation for working wonders with children in inner-city Chicago. Collins's school had never been independently evaluated, but she appeared to be effective with the types of children that schools in Oklahoma were failing. Administrators were not certain that Collins's methods were transferable from Chicago to Oklahoma, but they judged it worth a try. The first training took place at Collins's Westside Preparatory School in Chicago for two teachers from each of 25 pilot schools. In Chicago, they had a "seeing is believing" experience concerning what children from disadvantaged backgrounds could achieve. Thus confronted, they became students of Collins's methods.

Nevertheless, as the initiative spread through the 25 schools, there was substantial resistance from other teachers who had not gone to Chicago. The resistance came in three basic forms:

Time: "I just don't have the time to try this. It's too much. I just can't do it."

Satisfaction with current practices: "I just don't see the need for doing things differently from what I already do."

Hopeless students: "You don't know my kids. You couldn't do that with my kids. All that positive stuff is treating kids like babies; discipline has to be tough—you can't mix it with being nice."

The head mentor teacher told me that virtually all of the resistance she encountered combined one or more of these three perspectives. Her responses to the excuses were sometimes successful, sometimes not.[62]

Some teachers were insecure. Their low expectations for students were partly the consequence of low expectations for themselves as teachers.[63] At the other extreme were people who thrived using Collins's ideas and felt professionally rejuvenated. A baseline survey that I administered at a summer institute in July 1993 asked respondents who had prior GE training to describe the changes in their classrooms since they began using GE methods. The questions were worded as follows: "Because of Great Expectations, the improvement in the [aspect of classroom performance] of my students has been: 1 = *More than I thought was possible*, 2 = *A lot*, 3 = *Some*, 4 = *None*." The percentage giving each answer for each of the four aspects of classroom performance is shown in Table 4.4.

Table 4.4   Teachers' Assessments of Student Progress Due to the
Great Expectations Program in Oklahoma ($N = 76$)

Teachers' Assessment	Academic Performance	Attitudes	Behaviors	Teachers' Job Satisfaction
More than I thought was possible	22.37	31.59	25.00	35.53
A lot	55.26	46.05	44.74	48.68
Some	22.37	19.74	28.95	13.16
None	0.00	2.63	1.32	2.16

SOURCE: Tabulations from a survey that I conducted at the Summer Institute for Great Expectations in July 1993. The summer institute was targeted primarily at teachers who had no prior training. This sample of 76 teachers represents close to a 100% response rate from the previously trained teachers who attended during the week that the survey was administered.

The following two teachers are "existence proofs" of the proposition that teaching practices and expectations can change dramatically, even among experienced teachers. At the same time, both teachers expressed reservations.[64]

Greg Robarts, Fourth-Grade Teacher, Beehive Elementary School

Robarts's classroom is an almost even mix of Black, White, Chicano, and Native American children, almost all of whom are from very poor families. Before GE, Robarts had taught for 17 years and believed himself to be a good teacher. But seeing what children at Westside Preparatory School in Chicago could do gave him pause. He said, "I didn't really know how to teach reading. After one workshop in phonics I feel that I know more today than I learned in 17 years teaching." He described seeing Westside Preparatory School as "an awakening":

I saw something I'd never seen before; I actually saw education taking place. I saw children interested in learning. After seeing her approach, and seeing that it worked, I thought, "What I'm doing now isn't working. At best it's just kind of passing. . . ." I had to rededicate myself.

Collins's basic philosophy resonated with Robarts's beliefs about teaching, but he had to unlearn old habits: sitting at his desk and saying, "Open the book to page 34, here are the instructions. . . ." Even his own principal described Robarts as a "desk sitter" before he changed to the GE way of running his classroom: "Teach on your feet, not in your seat." Before GE,

> I was secure with all the books and things. A lot of teachers are where I was. They're embarrassed to say "I don't know." It's that fear of judgment . . . teachers are hesitant to ask. . . . Teaching independently, . . . instead of from the book, those are the kinds of things that I wasn't courageous enough to try.

> [Question: How long was it before you felt comfortable with this new style?]

> Oh, I think after about the first day. And I made some horrible mistakes. But my kids just hugged me and said, "Oh, Mr. Robarts, you're so different from when you left!" And they would just say, "Oh, you're doing well." And when I would start kind of maybe, "Well maybe I need to sit down now; I've kind of done the Marva Collins stuff now, so maybe I need to sit down," the kids would say, "Mr. Robarts, we sense that you're being average again." And so I said, "Okay." So I always asked them to encourage me when they sensed that I was being average or substandard.

People only vaguely familiar with the GE approach often say it overemphasizes memorization and underemphasizes higher-order thinking. Robarts disagreed. He said memorization and higher-order thinking are complements, not substitutes. Memory is the foundation for higher-order thinking. He found that many children cannot remember a dictated sentence long enough to write it on their papers. After a few weeks of memorizing poetry and other things, he said, the change is remarkable. He thinks people who dismiss memory work as outmoded are simply uninformed concerning how children learn, not only because memory supports higher-order thinking but also because children can memorize things that are worth knowing. In addition, recitation by children of what they have memorized builds self-confidence and motivation. Robarts said,

If you had told me 2 years ago that I would have a class of fourth graders that would know all the states and capitals and would know geographically where things are located, that could spell words, that could read, that could do . . . I would have said, "Well, maybe if you're in Quail Creek—which is a very affluent area of Oklahoma City—perhaps. But in this area, no, it wouldn't happen."

You know, maybe rote memory is not positive in some aspects, but I think that when a child has experienced total failure all through school it can be a major first step.

Much of the memory work in GE classrooms is memorization of poetry that contains rules for healthy and productive living— messages worth remembering.

Robarts reported exciting results from his efforts: "Absenteeism is almost nil, refusal to do homework is almost nil, test scores are substantially up." Also, he had a "miracle turn-around student" during his first semester using Collins's methods. The student's disciplinary folder was a "blizzard of suspensions." He was diagnosed as learning disabled, Robarts said, a "throw-away child":

He was not supposed to be able to do anything. He came very hostile . . . a tough cracker to break. I didn't understand when Collins said, "You can look in the eyes of the children when they come, and there's a dullness." I know what she means now. Children like Jerry have been so programmed to believe that the school is nothing. That *they* are nothing, that the only guarantee they have in school is failure. And it's so exciting to see their eyes brighten and to see the *child* say that they *can* do.

When Jerry transferred to a new school the next year, his classmates teased him for speaking standard English. Jerry persisted, with support from his new teacher. On returning to visit Robarts, Jerry reported that his new classmates began to change to be more like him because of the positive responses he was getting from the teacher.

Robarts realizes that he is not typical. Other teachers need more ongoing support. I first interviewed Robarts in December of 1991. This was after the first summer institute but 9 months before mentor teachers began working in teachers' classrooms. At that time, Robarts was sober in his comments about the value of a 4-hour demonstration that he was scheduled to give the next week, with his class, for teachers who had not gone to the previous summer institute:

> We'll get them excited. They'll go back to their classrooms, they'll meet with the same failures that they've had. They'll struggle. They'll crash. They'll burn. They'll say, "To hell with it. It's just another thing that they're doing." And that will be the end of it. If there is no follow-through, no support person, no person to be supportive and say, "Well now, this is a possibility," it will all come to naught.

Robarts was among the teachers who pushed for establishment of the summer institutes and the use of mentor teachers for ongoing technical assistance. Both were instituted and remain in place, complemented now by an academy for principals that has been in place for the past few years.

Mrs. Gloria Chavers, Third-Grade Teacher, Lafayette Elementary School

Chavers recalled not thinking much about GE at the time that her school applied to participate. However, she noted that when the first two teachers came back from Chicago, "They were excited. There was no doubt about that." The principal asked other teachers to visit the classrooms of the trained teachers to observe.

> So we went to Mrs. Sherrin's room. But this excitement that she had, I couldn't pick up on it. Because, and I talked at length with the principal about it at the time, I hadn't experienced what they had experienced. And for them to sit and tell me about what a 5-year-old, and they would call these little children's names, you know, they could recite all this. I'd never been around any children who could do this, so it was hard for me to envision.

Chavers also recalled that she saw changes that she did not like in Sherrin's students. As a second-grade teacher, she had taught some of the same children whom Sherrin was teaching in the third grade. Now, the children were calling themselves "college bound." Chavers said her view at the time was that "in this school system, college is not for everyone. We have a lot of lower socioeconomic people. College is the exception, not the rule."

Finally, the opportunity came to attend the first summer institute. Chavers said, "As it turned out, it was really well worth it." The next semester, Chavers reorganized the way she ran her classroom. "We've gone back to a highly structured way of reading and teaching phonics [using chants]. We'd gotten away from that." She also now teaches the whole class in one group and from one book. She reported that when she first changed, "Some children struggled, but it's surprising when they have their peers reading and reading well, it seems to give them more incentive to read better." Chavers learned how to teach addition and subtraction using chants at the summer institute, but the class at the summer institute had not gotten to multiplication and division. So, Chavers made up her own chants for multiplication and division. She recalled,

And then I told them [her students] one day, I said, "Well, we'll sing this out." Well, they didn't know what that was. I told them, "It's like you're standing on the corner trying to sell something." And even the children who have more difficulty with math, they have been able to pick up on those multiplication tables. They cannot only say them, they can pass their tests! A lot of times after we do them, they'll go out of the room and you'll hear them going down the hall buzzing, singing them. You know, they like to do it. It's really, it's not anything new, it's just the way it's presented.

Chavers talked on about bringing her love of music into the classroom now in ways she never felt authorized to do before. She talked about impressing her friends with her students' written work. She spoke with pride about parents who glow when they see report cards that are better than ever before, who brag that their children are doing work that they themselves did not see until junior high school. Parental interest and participation have clearly increased. According to the district superintendent, "Some parents here were kind of skeptical about going up and bringing 'this Black thing from Chicago'" into this White, mostly rural section of Oklahoma. The same parents became supporters, however, when they saw the difference it made for their children.

Chavers said that her children are convinced that they can do anything. When she plays choral music on the tape recorder, they beg to learn the songs:

> This week they said, "Oh, won't you play the music?" And, "Oh, can't we learn the song?" . . . And they assured me, "Oh, we can learn it." So in 2 afternoons, they pretty well learned it. I was once a music teacher. With this new program, I've been able to incorporate it again.

When asked where she got the permission, she said, "I just did it. I don't have to feel like this isn't part of my work anymore." Other teachers at other schools expressed similar feelings about new freedom to bring their personal interests and talents into their classrooms.

At the time of this interview, Chavers had been teaching for 17 years, but she said,

> With the introduction of this program, it's just been different. The whole atmosphere has been different around here. The discipline problems for me have all but just totally disappeared with this program. And it's not the fact that you're after the kids all the time. It's "This is what I expect of you." You know, "You are here for a job.
>
> "This is your job, and my job here is to teach you. Your job is to be the best student you can be. And that is what I expect of you."

Robarts and Chavers are examples of what is possible, though probably not for all teachers.

According to the head mentor teacher, an effective principal who understands GE appears to be the most important distinction between schools that are doing very well with GE and those that are not. One characteristic of the most effective principals is that they find ways of removing ineffective or uncooperative teachers from their schools.

Outcomes for GE have not been rigorously evaluated. However, several teachers bragged during interviews that their own class-average test scores had risen by 30 or more percentiles—for example, from the 13th to the 45th, and so forth—in the space of 1 year. The key was GE's apparently effective program of professional development. Just how effective the program has been over the long term is something that future evaluations may try to measure.

CONCLUSION

Any conception of bias requires a corresponding conception of neutrality. A major reason that no consensus has emerged from scholarship concerning the importance of racial bias in the classroom is that there is no single benchmark for racial neutrality. Instead, there are at least three: unconditional racial neutrality, race neutrality conditioned on observables (including past performance), and race neutrality conditioned on unobserved potential. Moreover, racial biases can exist in teachers' perceptions, expectations, and behaviors, or in any combination of the three.

Consider teacher perceptions of current student performance. If the benchmark for bias in teacher perceptions of current performance is unconditional racial neutrality, then most teachers are biased; but evidence shows that this is mainly because their perceptions of current performance are correct. When their perceptions early in a school year are inaccurate, the inaccuracies may become true through a process of self-fulfilling prophecy, but there is little evidence that initial inaccuracies or prophecies systematically favor either Blacks or Whites. In fact, where the benchmark is racial neutrality *after taking past performance and other observable predictors into account,* evidence favors the conclusion that teacher perceptions of current performance are generally unbiased. Whether the same applies to expectations and behaviors is less clear. I found no clear evidence of any type on whether teachers' expectations or behaviors are racially biased for students *whom they perceive to be equal on past or present measures of performance or proficiency.* Conversely, taking unconditional racial neutrality as the benchmark, it is clear that teachers' perceptions and expectations are biased in favor of Whites and that teacher behaviors appear less supportive of Blacks. Clearly, the benchmark for neutrality affects the conclusions.

Robert Schuller says, "Any fool can count the seeds in an apple, but only God can count the apples in a seed."[65] Similarly, tests can measure what children know, but only God can measure their latent future potential. Neutrality conditioned on latent future potential relates to a third type of bias and a third way that teachers' beliefs can matter. Because potential is unobserved, racial bias of this type is virtually impossible to gauge with any reliability. Still, it seems especially likely that teachers underestimate the potential of students whose current performance is poor, including disproportionate numbers of Blacks. Similarly, Blacks are underrepresented among students with the very highest scores, and potential for greater Black representation at the top of the distribution is unproven. Thus, at both the top and the bottom of the test score distribution, stereotypes of Black intellectual inferiority are reinforced by past and present disparities in performance and probably cause teachers to underestimate Blacks' potential more than Whites.' If they expect that Black children have less potential, teachers probably search with less conviction than they should for ways of helping Black children to improve and miss opportunities to reduce the Black-White test score gap.

Simply cajoling teachers to raise their expectations for Black children, using phrases such as "all children can learn," is probably a waste of time. However, good professional development programs can make a difference. Recall that some teachers in Oklahoma responded to the GE program with the assertion, "My kids couldn't do that." If they had gone on teaching the way they had always taught, that judgment would have been correct. But when they changed their teaching, they learned that they were wrong. Similarly, outside of GE, Guskey (1982) showed that teachers could learn responsive teaching methods that weaken the link between past and future performance. Teachers who are helped by professional development to improve their classroom practices can have "seeing is believing" experiences that challenge their prior biases. We need more research on how professional development programs affect both test score levels and the Black-White test score gap.

Even without the biases discussed above, teachers' beliefs probably affect Black students more than Whites. Evidence is quite thin, but the few studies that bear on this hypothesis appear to support it. Jussim et al. (1996) found that teachers' perceptions of sixth graders' math performance in October did not contain a racial bias once they controlled past performance and attitudes. Nevertheless, the impact of teachers' October perceptions on May math scores was almost 3 times larger for Blacks than for Whites. Furthermore, the effect was also larger for females than for males and larger for both Black and White students from low-income households. Findings from other studies are consistent. For example, Casteel (1997) found that Black eighth and ninth graders were more eager to please teachers, but Whites were more concerned about pleasing parents. These differences may be due to parenting. For example, White parents might exert more consistent pressure for good grades; Black parents might be less assertive about grades and perhaps more deferential themselves to teachers. We do not know the answers. Future research should actively pursue these questions, including the implications for policy, teaching, and parenting.

My bottom-line conclusion requires speculation because the research is so incomplete. It is that teachers' perceptions, expectations, and behaviors probably do help to sustain, and perhaps even to expand, the Black-White test score gap. The magnitude of the effect is uncertain, but it may be quite substantial if effects accumulate from kindergarten through high school. Unfortunately, the full story is quite complicated and parts of it currently hang by thin threads of evidence. Much remains on this research agenda.

Fortunately, successful interventions can establish that children of all racial and ethnic groups have more potential than most people have assumed. As the evidence accumulates, we should be able to focus with greater determination on cultivating and harvesting all that youthful minds embody.[66] It would then be no surprise if the Black-White test score gap began to shrink again, as it did in the 1980s, and ultimately disappeared.

NOTES

1. See Phillips, Crouse, and Ralph (1998). The Black-White gap in skills at the beginning of primary school is smaller for later cohorts. Hedges and Nowell (1998) found evidence that reductions in Black-White test score disparity across cohorts during the 1970s and 1980s were due primarily to a narrowing of the Black-White gap in years of schooling among parents.

2. Existing evidence on group-level disparity at the mean across grade levels within a cohort is not entirely clear because of measurement issues and data problems. See Phillips et al. (1998) for a discussion of methodological decisions that determine whether the gap appears to be constant or widening with time within a cohort.

3. When possible, this chapter will present effect sizes measured in standard deviation units. For example, if one group of students experiences a particular treatment and an otherwise equivalent control or comparison group does not, the effect size of the treatment on test scores is the difference between average scores for the two groups after the treatment, divided by the pooled standard deviation of scores. For example, for an outcome that is normally distributed, an effect size of .20 moves a student from the 50th to the 58th percentile; an effect size of .50 moves him or her to the 69th percentile; and an effect size of .80 moves the student to the 79th percentile.

4. Her comment is about racial disparity in ability group assignments.

5. This immediate discussion concerns experiments. However, Type I benchmarks are also used sometimes in naturalistic settings. Specifically, unconditional racial neutrality may seem the only morally defensible alternative in the absence of reliable information *about individuals* on which to base a benchmark that is not unconditionally race neutral.

6. Baron, Tom, and Cooper (1985) reported that effect sizes could be retrieved for only 6 of the 16 studies. In these 6 studies, the Black-White differences in teacher expectations averaged half a standard deviation. If 9 of the other studies are assumed to have effect sizes of 0, and the 1 study with a significant result but no effect size is assumed to have an effect size of .36, then the average effect size across all 16 studies is .22.

7. Baron et al. (1985) conducted online computer searches of *Psychological Abstracts,* the Educational Research Information Center, and *Dissertation Abstracts International* as the basis for their initial bibliography. The descriptors that they used were crossings of the following terms: "teacher expect . . . " "teacher attitudes," or "teacher bias" with "racial," "ethnicity," "class," "socioeconomic," "social background," or "social characteristics."

8. To compute effect sizes for each outcome, the standard deviation among Blacks is used as the denominator because the pooled standard deviation was not given. The standard deviation among Whites is virtually the same as among Blacks. All effect sizes reported in this paragraph are calculated from numbers in DeMeis and Turner (1978), Table 2, p. 83. Effect sizes for the Black-White difference among students speaking standard English were 0.57, 0.52, 0.55, and 0.44 standard deviations respectively for "personality," "quality of response," "current academic abilities," and "future academic abilities." For Black English, the analogous numbers were 0.34, 0.44, 0.23, and 0.14. The fact that effect sizes were smaller for tapes on which students spoke Black English is not surprising, because speaking Black English would be an especially negative signal for a White student. Across the four outcomes, within-race effect sizes for Black English versus Standard English ranged from 0.23 to 0.45 for Blacks and from 0.55 to 0.74 for Whites, always favoring standard English.

9. Whatever the reasons, average scores on standardized examinations tend to be lower for Blacks than for Whites. Hence, the most accurate prediction under most circumstances is that Whites will have higher scores. Moreover, given a group of Black and White students starting from equal baseline scores, the average future score among Whites in the group will tend to be closer to the overall future mean for Whites. The average among Blacks will tend to be closer to the overall mean for Blacks, which for most exams in most samples is lower than for Whites (Philips et. al., 1998).

10. See, for example, Eccles and Wigfield (1985) for a line of reasoning that might cause this to be true. Essentially, to deviate from a previously established trajectory, the student may need support from the teacher when

the student begins the process of change. If the teacher continues treating the student as he or she did before the change, the student may decide that the environment is not sufficiently responsive to make the new goal attainable. The student feels a lack of control and returns to the old ways.

11. Experimental studies that expose teachers to different sequences of facts show that teachers' expectations are flexible to remain accurate as new information becomes available (e.g., see Shavelson, Cadwell, & Izu, 1977). The pattern of flexibility among teachers in real classrooms is not known.

12. For example, see the discussion herein of work by Guskey (1982), where improvements in teacher responsiveness *reduced* the accuracy of teachers' early predictions for end-of-semester performance.

13. This study covers 49 teachers and 934 fourth, fifth, and sixth graders in five cities across four census regions (see Haller, 1985, Footnote 4).

14. Discusses findings from Irvine (1985), which was a conference paper (see Irvine, 1990, p. 77).

15. The correlations between 2nd-week rankings and end-of-year test scores were .63 for White males and .62 for Black males. The correlation for Black males dipped by the 10th week but returned to the same range as for Whites by the end of the school year. Irvine (1990) emphasized the *difference* in the pattern for Black and White boys because the correlation dipped for Black boys in the 10th week. It seems to me, however, that the similarity is the more salient finding: Of three comparisons for boys and three for girls, in only one (boys at the 10th week) was the racial difference notable. Some teachers in Irvine's study were consistently more accurate than others. The teacher with the lowest correlations moved from .11 for the 2nd week to .56 for the end of the year. At the high end, one teacher had correlations of .91, .92, and .89 for the 2nd week through the end of the year.

16. Recall, for example, that two lines with different slopes each represent correlations of 1 between the variables on the x and y axes. Similarly, teachers' early perceptions or expectations could have a much larger impact on performance for one race than for the other (as in a steeper line) even though the correlation between teachers' perceptions or expectations and end-of-year performance was the same for both groups. This possibility of different slopes is explored in Jussim, Eccles, and Madon (1996) and discussed herein, after discussing the other two types of racial bias.

17. Members of the task force that produced the report included a number of noted Black scholars: Sara Lawrence Lightfoot of Harvard, who was the principal author; James P. Comer of Yale; John Hope Franklin of Duke; and William Julius Wilson, then of the University of Chicago.

18. Of course, goal setting is affected by more than teachers' expectations of student potential. The curricular materials that are handed down to teachers from the administration and students' actual behaviors matter as well.

19. See Ford (1996) for useful discussions of this issue referring to theories of multiple intelligences. Also consider, using the terminology of the present chapter, that people who think that potential is very distinct from performance and that ability is equally distributed among the races will favor a Type I proxy for Type III. Others might favor a Type II proxy, augmented perhaps by a positive shift factor for all students, if they think that racial differences in performance are good approximations of racial differences in potential. Of course, it is difficult to find anyone willing to suggest this in print.

20. Miller (1995) presents a useful review of trends in surveys regarding beliefs about Black intellectual inferiority. He pointed out that numbers in the Harris poll tend to produce smaller percentages because they ask more directly about whether any Black-White difference in intelligence is genetic.

21. Across different surveys, it is clear that fewer people answer yes to questions about intellectual inferiority of Blacks when the question asks explicitly about "in-born" or genetic differences (see the discussion in Miller, 1995, chapter 8).

22. The phrase "rumors of inferiority" comes from the title to Howard and Hammond (1985).

23. Leading researchers on teacher expectations claim that sustaining expectations are probably more prevalent than self-fulfilling expectations (e.g., see Good, 1987).

24. The most frequent explanation for failure is that teachers do not believe the information about the students. Sometimes teachers figure out the purpose of the experiment. Other times, teachers have their own sources of credible information or they have known the students long enough to form opinions before the experiment begins. In a meta-analysis of 18 experiments in which IQ or a similar measure of ability was the outcome, Raudenbush (1984) showed very clearly that studies finding evidence of the effect were primarily those where teachers had no opportunity to form an independent impression of students before the experiment began.

25. Smith (1980) did not say what percentage of the effect sizes she reported use the standard deviation of test score levels as opposed to test score gains in reporting effect sizes.

26. Actually, Brophy (1985) said that teachers' expectations probably make about a 5% difference, but he did not say whether he was talking about the difference in gain during a school year or the difference in total achievement (as in the level on a test). Brophy's statement was based on his own review of the literature where the period of individual studies is seldom more than a single school year.

27. This multivariate equation includes controls for predictors of performance such as past performance and socioeconomic background. Typically, there may be a tendency for the estimate of self-fulfilling prophecy to be statistically biased upward because of omitted variables that are

positively associated with both teachers' expectations and student performance. Hence, any findings of this sort must be taken as suggestive, not definitive.

28. It is not unusual, for example, for a teacher to say, "Betty is doing well now because she is repeating the grade and has seen some of this material before. I don't expect that she will do as well for the rest of the year." This teacher might be accurate in his or her current evaluation of the student, but still biased in his or her expectation. Other examples could reverse the expectation and make it more positive than current performance. There, too, the expectations might or might not be biased when judged from the perspective of what past performance and attitudes would predict.

29. Also see Jussim (1989) and Jussim and Eccles (1992) for previous studies using the same data to study the accuracy of teachers' expectations, but not emphasizing racial differences. They speculated that the void in the literature stems from the political risk of studying groups who actually do differ. Researchers have avoided the risk by focusing on experimental studies that assume away differences.

30. Of the 1,664 sixth graders, 76 were African Americans. Ideally, one would want a larger number of African Americans in such a study. It is not clear why this data set contained so few. The data came from the Michigan Study of Adolescent Life Transitions, which was not initially designed to study racial differences. For more details about the Michigan Study of Adolescent Life Transitions, see Wigfield, Eccles, MacIver, Reuman, and Midgley (1991).

31. The study does not report raw means by race, but it does report that the correlations of race with grades and standard test scores were −.12 and −.14, respectively (both with $p < .001$), with Blacks having the lower scores and grades. These are probably smaller than in the typical national sample of Black and White sixth graders.

32. Jussim et al. (1996) did separate calculations to measure whether the residual variance in teachers' perceptions left unexplained by the background factors was similar for Blacks and Whites. It was slightly higher for Blacks, but only by a margin so small as to be inconsequential: "The correlations of ethnicity with the absolute values of the residuals from the models predicting teacher perceptions were .06 ($p < .05$), .07 ($p < .05$), and −.02 (not significant) for performance, talent, and effort, respectively" (p. 355). Although 2 of the 3 are statistically significant, these suggest only a very small difference in accuracy, with less accuracy for Blacks than for Whites.

Regarding social class, there was a small positive relationship found between parents' education and the teacher's perception of the student's talent. There were also some small gender effects. Teachers' perceptions of performance and effort were higher for girls after controlling for the factors listed in the text. Hence, it appears that teachers were relying to a small extent on a gender stereotype, though not necessarily a false one.

33. As background variables, the equation to predict scores and grades includes race, math grades from the end of fifth grade, math scores from the end of fifth or beginning of sixth grade, self-concept of ability, self-reported effort at math, self-reported time spent on homework, and indices for the intrinsic and extrinsic value of math to the student. Interactions of student's race with teacher perceptions of effort and talent were tried, but these produced strange results because of collinearity with the interaction for race and performance. The result for performance might best be understood to represent the interaction of race with all aspects of the teacher's perceptions.

34. For Michigan Educational Assessment Program scores, the effect size was only .14 for Whites, but it was .37 for African Americans ($p < .001$). This effect size for Whites is quite close to the effect size of .17 for math achievement scores that Smith (1980) reported in her meta-analysis. For grades, the effect size for African Americans was .56 compared with .20 for Whites ($p < .01$). Calculations conducted by Jussim et al. (1996) after the chapter was published use a specification that includes additional interaction terms. That specification adds interactions of race with the student's past grades and scores. The effect size for Michigan Educational Assessment Program scores rose from the original .37 to become .58 for African Americans and dropped from .14 to .13 for Whites. With the additional interaction terms, the coefficients on past grades and scores were estimated to be somewhat smaller for African Americans than for Whites. Hence, it appears that Blacks' performance was more dependent than Whites' on current teachers' opinions and less anchored in measures of past performance. One might speculate that this is because past grades and scores for Black students were less accurate than for Whites as measures of their knowledge or potential, but we cannot know from the information available.

35. It is not clear what to make of the lack of relationship between self-reports of effort and teachers' perceptions of effort. If teachers are really grossly inaccurate in their assessments of effort, this could contribute to the disengagement of children who are believed not to be trying when they really are. It could also contribute to a lack of challenge for students who are slacking off when they appear to be working hard and actually would be well served by being asked to do more.

36. The fact that teacher perceptions were also stronger predictors for females and for Whites from low-income households makes it more likely that this is a real effect for Blacks. Furthermore, because Jussim et al. (1996) found no unexplained racial differences in October performance ratings for Blacks and Whites after controlling for background factors, and only a trivial difference in unexplained variation, it seems unlikely that the ratings mean very different things or have different implicit scalings for Blacks and Whites. Still, these results need to be replicated several times in future research to be firmly established.

37. Jussim et al. (1996) assumed that current perceptions were good estimates of expectations for the future, and they used the words *perceptions* and *expectations* interchangeably. Jussim (personal communication, 1998) has argued that this is a reasonable assumption based on other research regarding the processes by which people form expectations. This, however, might be inappropriate for the reasons explained in the text. I have not found any research with data on teachers' perceptions of current performance along with expectations for future performance for both Blacks and Whites.

38. The sample included 928 Whites and 761 African Americans from nine schools and 12 classes in two public school districts.

39. See the discussion in pages 46–49. Irvine cites two dissertation studies from the 1970s and one journal article from the late 1960s when she writes, "Researchers have found that black and other minority pupils are more negatively affected by teacher expectations than white students are" (p. 49). The studies she cites to make this point are Baker (1973), Krupczak (1972), and Yee (1968). I have not found any studies that contradict these few.

40. Jussim et al. (1996) cited an earlier paper by Steele (1992).

41. As informal but reliable evidence, I offer my personal experience. As a fifth grader, I moved from a segregated school to one that was integrated. In my new classroom, the top reading group was White with one or two exceptions, the middle group was mixed but mostly Black, and the slow group was Black. Although I did not believe that the pattern was unfair, I wanted the teacher to know and I wanted to know for myself that I was an exception to it. The teacher placed me in the middle group. I could not understand why she could not see from my records that I belonged in the top group, despite the fact that I was Black. I recall being driven to establish myself as an exception to the racial pattern in the classroom and fearing for a while that my performance in the middle group might not be good enough to establish me as an exception. I might be trapped in the middle group! After a few weeks, the teacher moved me up, and my anxiety abated. However, my constant awareness of the racial pattern in group memberships remained.

42. These fourth- and sixth-grade results are from a single year for two different cohorts; hence, although the differences appear consistent with a trend, they do not clearly establish it. Also, Gross (1993) did not give sample sizes broken down by the number who were above, at, or below grade levels. Hence, we are not sure how many children each of these numbers represents.

43. Gross (personal communication, February 1998) reported that she conducted regression analyses using students' classroom performance as predictors, and the CATM test performances of the Black

high achievers were below what was predicted. However, these calculations were unpublished and, because they are a decade old, are no longer available.

44. Mickelson (1990) reported (but did not show) that results with standardized test scores as the dependent variables produced the same story as for grades. In predicting grade point average, standardized coefficients on concrete attitudes in the full specification were .111 ($p < .05$) for Blacks and .190 ($p < .01$) for Whites. These are not large effects. Still, the fact that such a rough index of beliefs is statistically significant at all and that the distinction between abstract and concrete attitudes is demonstrated so clearly in Table 4.2 provide important insight. The coefficient for abstract attitudes was about a fifth as large as for concrete attitudes. The t statistic on the coefficient for abstract attitudes was about 1 for Whites and less than .5 for Blacks. The regressions control for: mother's and father's occupations and educations, a locus of control index, the student's weekly hours worked, the percentage of close friends planning to attend a 4-year college, and an indicator variable for each of the eight schools in the sample.

45. Mickelson (1990) studied 1,193 seniors from eight high schools in the Los Angeles area during the 1983 school year. She analyzed only the responses from Blacks and Whites, who comprised 41% and 59%, respectively, of her working sample. Mickelson's indices measured levels of agreement with the following statements. For each index (abstract and concrete), higher levels of agreement correspond to higher values.

Abstract Attitudes

1. Education is the key to success in the future.

2. If everyone in America gets a good education, we can end poverty.

3. Achievement and effort in school lead to job success later on.

4. The way for poor people to become middle class is for them to get a good education.

5. School success is not necessarily a clear path to a better life.

6. Getting a good education is a practical road to success for a young Black [White] man [woman] like me.

7. Young White [Black] women [men] like me have a chance of making it if we do well in school.

8. Education really pays off in the future for young Black [White] men [women] like me.

Concrete Attitudes

1. Based on their experiences, my parents say people like us are not always paid or promoted according to our education.

2. All I need to learn for my future is to read, write, and make change.

3. Although my parents tell me to get a good education to get a good job, they face barriers to job success.

4. When our teachers give us homework, my friends never think of doing it.

5. People in my family have not been treated fairly at work, no matter how much education they have.

6. Studying in school rarely pays off later with good jobs.

I think that to call these attitudes "concrete" is a gross misnomer and that it has confused the interpretation of Mickelson's (1990) work. They are just as "abstract" as the others. What they measure is ambivalence or doubt about the first list, but "fairness" is not "concrete."

46. The "middle class" or "working class" designation is based on a combination of standard blue/white collar distinctions and the parents' level of education.

47. Also see Babad (1980, 1985) for related research from Israel.

48. The possibility that confederate students' behaviors confounded findings of racial bias in Rubovits and Maehr's (1973) study led Taylor (1979) to try a different experimental design. She placed "phantom" 6-year-old students behind a one-way glass where they could allegedly see the teacher and respond to the teacher's questions and instructions. This removed any effects of targets' actual behaviors. The teachers were told that the students could see and hear them and would respond to their instructions by pushing buttons that lighted up on a panel that the teachers could see.

Teachers in Taylor's (1979) study were 105 White female undergraduates at the University of Massachusetts, Amherst. They were studying education, just as in Rubovits and Maehr (1973). They were told that the purpose of the experiment was "to examine certain aspects of teaching behavior in a situation where feedback from pupil to teacher was limited." Discussions after the experiment showed that the teachers had believed this premise. Each was told in written instructions that the student was Black or White, male or female, and of high or low ability. In fact, unknown to the participants, all of the "student feedback" during the experiment was provided by a single adult who was hidden from view and gave answers by manipulating 10 lights on a panel. The person giving the answers was blind to what any given teacher had been told about the "student." Sessions were videotaped, and teachers' behaviors were coded.

49. There are many sources from which to draw this standard finding. For example, Irvine (1990), in Table 3.3, tabulated studies conducted in naturalistic classroom settings. Of 17 findings from 16 studies, Whites were favored in 9 cases, there was no difference in 4 cases, the opposite race of the teacher was favored in 2 cases, the same race as the teacher was favored in 1 case, and Blacks were favored in 1 case. All but 1 of the studies on the list are from the 1970s and early 1980s; 1 is from 1969. For a discussion of earlier studies, see Brophy and Good (1974).

50. Blacks rate lower by a statistically significant margin for each of the three variables in the index.

51. See Brophy and Good (1974) and other literature that they discuss regarding the types of students that teachers like to teach. Also see below in the present chapter.

52. Teachers' expectations might be less flexible for Black students than for Whites (though we do not know for sure that they are). Inflexible teacher perceptions for Blacks might lead to teacher behaviors that reinforce problem behaviors for low-performing students and promote good behaviors for high-performing students. This is a ripe topic for future research.

53. See the Ferguson (1998) for a discussion of how teacher's race and social class background might affect student performance. Simply matching the race of the student and the child is too simple a prescription because social class and professional competence also appear to be important.

54. One important thing to communicate about academic ability is that it is not immutable—that sustained effort mobilizes and develops ability. Dweck (1991) and Dweck and Leggett (1988) found statistically significant evidence among White children that those believing ability is fixed tend to adopt performance goals, whereas those believing otherwise tend to adopt mastery goals. Among those who believe ability is fixed and that their own endowment is low, the performance goal is to hide their ignorance. Among those who believe ability can be mobilized and developed by sustained effort, both high and low achievers tend toward mastery goals. The same is probably true for Blacks, but the research that would show it has not, to my knowledge, been done.

55. See the literature review section of Cook and Ludwig (1998).

56. In a summary of the literature on wait time, Rowe (1986) reported, [Teachers'] expectations change gradually, often signaled by remarks such as "He never contributed like that before. Maybe he has a special 'thing' for this topic. . . . " *This effect was particularly pronounced where minority students were concerned*

[italics added]. They did more task relevant talking and took a more active part in discussions than they had before. (p. 45)

There are other references in Rowe's (1986) paper to the studies that develop these findings. Wait time is shorter for low-performing students.

57. Studies show mixed results regarding techniques for improving corrective feedback. Some are more successful than others. See, for example, Slavin's (1987) review of the literature of mastery learning.

58. Early in the semester, teachers classified each student into one of five groups of equal size based on "probable achievement" in the course. At the end of the semester, they repeated this exercise, placing students in five groups of equal size based on "achievement potential."

59. Brattesani, Weinstein, and Marshall (1984) found strong evidence that standardized test scores were predicted less well by past performance in classrooms where there was more differential treatment. The point they made in the paper is that teacher expectations become self-fulfilling prophecies only when communicated through differential treatment. They found that teacher expectations are stronger predictors in classrooms with more differential treatment. However, because the teachers' expectations were collected in April of the school year, I regard them as reports from the end of the school year, not self-fulfilling predictions.

60. See Table 4 in Brattesani et al. (1984). The sample sizes are small, so the difference in percentages of low achievers making large gains does not reach statistical significance. Nevertheless, the magnitudes of the gains are large among the small number of students involved. For interesting related work, see Weinstein, Marshall, Sharp, and Botkin (1987), who showed that even first graders can accurately report differential treatment by teachers of their peers, but it is not until third and fifth grade that their reports regarding their own differential treatment become more accurate.

61. This summary draws from Ferguson (1993), which tells the story of the birth of the initiative and its early development.

62. Most of the time, she maintained, the resistance could be reduced by a combination of two responses. First, she would assure the teacher that she could slip into GE gradually, implementing some of it first and other things later. Second, she would model the GE practices to which the teacher was resistant. She would do so at that teacher's school, preferably in that teacher's classroom, and always with the greatest respect and tact. When a teacher witnessed a mentor teacher demonstrating a method with the teacher's own students, and succeeding, he or she usually became (or claimed to become) more open to giving it a try.

63. In one worst case example, a teacher had failed with a new method during the year before the introduction of GE. Several other teachers at her school were using the GE method and doing well. She, however, was sure

that GE could not work for her. So she continued teaching one letter per week to her first-grade class of "slow learners," with no pressure from her passive principal to change.

64. The names of the teachers and schools have been changed, but the facts and quotations are real.

65. Robert Schuller is a popular television minister and proponent of positive thinking.

66. Of course, in addition to strong leadership and professional development, stronger performance incentives for teachers, no matter what their expectations, should be part of the expression of society's determination. The search for ways of designing and implementing such incentives is currently quite active. Three books with chapters that emphasize incentives and accountability are Hanushek and Jorgenson (1996), Hanushek (1994), and Ladd (1996).

REFERENCES

Babad, E. Y. (1980). Expectancy bias in scoring as a function of ability and ethnic labels. *Psychological Reports, 46,* 625–626.

Babad, E. Y. (1985). Some correlates of teachers' expectancy bias. *American Educational Research Journal, 22*(Summer), 175–183.

Baron, R., Tom, D. Y. H., & Cooper, H. M. (1985). Social class, race and teacher expectations. In J. B. Dusek (Ed.), *Teacher expectancies* (pp. 251–269). Hillsdale, NJ: Lawrence Erlbaum.

Brattesani, K. A., Weinstein, R. S., & Marshall, H. (1984). Student perceptions of differential teacher treatment as moderators of teacher expectation effects. *Journal of Educational Psychology, 76,* 236–247.

Brophy, J. (1985). Teacher-student interaction. In J. B. Dusek (Ed.), *Teacher expectancies* (pp. 303–328). Hillsdale, NJ: Lawrence Erlbaum.

Brophy, J., & Good, T. (1974). *Teacher-student relationships: Causes and consequences.* New York: Holt, Rinehart & Winston.

Cabello, B., & Burstein, N. D. (1995). Examining teachers' beliefs about teaching in culturally diverse classrooms. *Journal of Teacher Education, 46*(September/October), 285–294.

Casteel, C. (1997, April). Attitudes of African American and Caucasian eighth grade students about praises, rewards, and punishments. *Elementary School Guidance and Counseling, 31,* 262–272.

Coates, B. (1972). White adult behavior toward Black and White children. *Child Development, 43,* 143–154.

Cook, P. J., & Ludwig, J. (1998). The burden of "acting White": Do Black adolescents disparage academic achievement? In C. Jencks & M. Phillips (Eds.), *The Black-White test score gap* (pp. 375–400). Washington, DC: Brookings Institution Press.

DeMeis, D. K., & Turner, R. R. (1978). Effects of students' race, physical attractiveness, and dialect on teachers' evaluations. *Contemporary Educational Psychology, 3,* 77–86.

Dweck, C. (1991). Self-theories and goals: Their role in motivation, personality and development. In R. A. Dienstbier (Ed.), *Nebraska symposium on motivation, 1990* (pp. 199–235). Lincoln: University of Nebraska Press.

Dweck, C., & Leggett, E. L. (1988). A social cognitive approach to motivation and personality. *Psychological Review, 95,* 256–273.

Eccles, J., & Wigfield, A. (1985). Teacher expectations and student motivation. In J. B. Dusek (Ed.), *Teacher expectancies* (pp. 185–226). Hillsdale, NJ: Lawrence Erlbaum.

Egan, O., & Archer, P. (1985). The accuracy of teachers' ratings of ability: A regression model. *American Educational Research Journal, 22,* 25–34.

Entwisle, D. R., & Alexander, K. L. (1988). Factors affecting achievement test scores and marks of Black and White first graders. *The Elementary School Journal, 88*(5), 449–471.

Evertson, C., Brophy, J., & Good, T. (1972). *Communication of teacher expectations: First grade* (Report No. 91). Austin: University of Texas at Austin, Research and Development Center for Teacher Education.

Feldman, R. S., & Orchowsky, S. (1979). Race and performance of student as determinants of teacher nonverbal behavior. *Contemporary Educational Psychology, 4,* 324–333.

Ferguson, R. F. (1993). *Spreading the paradigm of a master teacher: The Great Expectations initiative in Oklahoma* (Working Paper of the Taubman Center for State and Local Government). Cambridge, MA: Harvard University, John F. Kennedy School of Government.

Ford, D. Y. (1996). *Reversing the underachievement among gifted Black students.* New York: Teachers College Press.

Fordham, S., & Ogbu, J. (1986). Black students' school success: Coping with the "burden of 'acting White.'" *The Urban Review, 18*(3), 176–206.

Gaines, M. L. (1990). *Accuracy of teacher prediction of elementary student achievement.* Paper presented at the annual meeting of the American Educational Research Association. (ERIC Document Reproduction Service No. ED320942).

Good, T. L. (1987). Two decades of research on teacher expectations: Findings and future directions. *Journal of Teacher Education, 38*(4), 32–47.

Gross, S. (1993). Early mathematics performance and achievement: Results of a study within a large suburban school system. *Journal of Negro Education, 62,* 269–287.

Guskey, T. R. (1982). The effects of change in instructional effectiveness on the relationship of teacher expectations and student achievement. *Journal of Educational Research, 75,* 345–348.

Haller, E. J. (1985). Pupil race and elementary school ability grouping: Are teachers biased against Black children? *American Educational Research Journal, 22*(4), 465–483.

Hanushek, E. A. (1994). *Making schools work: Improving performance and controlling costs.* Washington, DC: Brookings Institution Press.

Hanushek, E. A., & Jorgenson, D. W. (Eds.). (1996). *Improving America's schools: The role of incentives.* Washington, DC: National Academy Press.

Hedges, L.V., & Nowell, A. (1998). Are the Black-White differences in test scores narrowing? In C. Jencks & M. Phillips (Eds.), *The Black-White test score gap* (pp. 254–281). Washington, DC: Brookings Institution.

Herrnstein, R. J., & Murray, C. (1994). *The bell curve: Intelligence and class structure in American life.* New York: Free Press.

Hoge, R., & Butcher, R. (1984). Analysis of teacher judgments of pupil achievement level. *Journal of Educational Psychology, 76,* 777–781.

Howard, J., & Hammond, R. (1985, September). Rumors of inferiority. *New Republic, 72,* 9.

Irvine, J. J. (1985, April). *The accuracy and stability of teachers' achievement expectations as related to students' race and sex.* Paper presented at the meeting of the American Educational Research Association, Chicago.

Irvine, J. J. (1990). *Black students and school failure: Policies, practices, and prescriptions.* Westport, CT: Greenwood.

Jencks, C., & Phillips, M. (Eds.). 1998. *The Black-White test score gap.* Washington, DC: Brookings Institution Press.

Jussim, L. (1989). Teacher expectations: Self-fulfilling prophecies, perceptual biases, and accuracy. *Journal of Personality and Social Psychology, 57,* 469–480.

Jussim, L., & Eccles, J. (1992). Teacher expectations II: Construction and reflection of student achievement. *Journal of Personality and Social Psychology, 63,* 947–961.

Jussim, L., Eccles, J., & Madon, S. (1996). Social perception, social stereotypes, and teacher expectations: Accuracy and the quest for the powerful self-fulfilling prophecy. *Advances in Experimental Social Psychology, 28,* 281–387.

Kleinfeld, J. (1972). The relative importance of teachers and parents in the formation of Negro and White students' academic self-concepts. *Journal of Educational Research, 65,* 211–212.

Kluegel, J. R. (1990). Trends in Whites' explanations of the Black-White gap in socioeconomic status, 1977–1989. *American Sociological Review, 55*(August), 512–525.

Ladd, H. F. (Ed.). (1996). *Holding schools accountable: Performance-based reform in education.* Washington, DC: Brookings Institution Press.

Lightfoot, S. L. (1978). *Worlds apart: Relationships between families and schools.* New York: Basic Books.

Merton, R. (1948). The self-fulfilling prophecy. *Antioch Review, 8,* 193–210.

Mickelson, R. A. (1990). The attitude-achievement paradox among Black adolescents. *Sociology of Education, 63,* 44–61.

Miller, L. S. (1995). *An American imperative: Accelerating minority educational advancement.* New Haven, CT: Yale University Press.

Mitman, A. (1985). Teachers' differential behavior toward higher and lower achieving students and its relation to selected teacher characteristics. *Journal of Educational Psychology, 77,* 149–161.

Monk, M. (1983). Teacher expectations? Pupil responses to teacher mediated classroom climate. *British Educational Research Journal, 9,* 153–166.

Ogbu, J. (1978). *Minority education and caste: The American system in cross-cultural comparison.* New York: Academic Press.

Ogbu, J. (1983). Minority status and schooling in plural societies. *Comparative Education Review, 27,* 168–203.

Ogbu, J. (1987). Opportunity structure, cultural boundaries, and literacy. In J. Langer (Ed.), *Language, literacy, and culture: Issues of society and schooling* (pp. 149–177). Norwood, NJ: Ablex.

Pedulla, J., Airasian, P., & Madaus, G. (1980). Do teacher ratings and standardized test results of students yield the same information? *American Educational Research Journal, 17,* 303–307.

Phillips, M., Crouse, J., & Ralph, J. (1998). Does the Black-White test score gap widen after children enter school? In C. Jencks (Ed.), *The Black-White test score gap* (pp. 229–272). Washington, DC: Brookings Institution Press.

Puma, M., Jones, C., Rock, D., & Fernandez, R. (1993). *Prospects: The congressionally mandated study of educational growth and opportunity* (Interim Report prepared for the U.S. Department of Education, Planning and Evaluation Service).

Raudenbush, S. W. (1984). Magnitude of teacher expectancy effects on pupil IQ as a function of the credibility of expectancy induction: A synthesis of findings from 18 experiments. *Journal of Educational Psychology, 76*(1), 85–97.

Rosenthal, R. (1994). Interpersonal expectancy effects: A 30-year perspective. *Current Directions in Psychological Science, 3*(6), 176–179.

Rosenthal, R., & Jacobson, L. (1968). *Pygmalion in the classroom.* New York: Holt, Rinehart & Winston.

Rowe, M. B. (1986). Wait time: Slowing down may be a way of speeding up! *Journal of Teacher Education, 37*(1), 43–50.

Rubovits, P. C., & Maehr, M. L. (1973). Pygmalion Black and White. *Journal of Personality and Social Psychology, 25,* 210–218.

Shavelson, R. J., Cadwell, J., & Izu, T. (1977, Spring). Teachers' sensitivity to the reliability of information in making pedagogical decisions. *American Educational Research Journal, 14,* 83–97.

Slavin, R. E. (1987). Mastery learning reconsidered. *Review of Educational Research, 57*(2), 175–213.

Smith, M. L. (1980). Teachers' expectations. *Evaluation in Education, 4,* 53–56.

Solorzano, D. (1992). An exploratory analysis of the effects of race, class, and gender on student and parent mobility aspirations. *Journal of Negro Education, 61,* 30–44.

Steele, C. M. (1992, April). Race and the schooling of Black Americans. *Atlantic Monthly,* 68–72.

Steele, C. M., & Aronson, J. (1998). Stereotype threat and the test performance of academically successful African Americans. In C. Jencks & M. Phillips (Eds.), *The Black-White test score gap* (pp. 401–428). Washington, DC: Brookings Institution Press.

Taylor, M. C. (1979). Race, sex, and the expression of self-fulfilling prophecies in a laboratory teaching situation. *Personality and Social Psychology, 6,* 897–912.

Weinstein, R. S. (1985). Student mediation of classroom expectancy effects. In J. B. Dusek (Ed.), *Teacher expectancies* (pp. 329–350). Hillsdale, NJ: Lawrence Erlbaum.

Weinstein, R. S., Marshall, H. H., Sharp, L., & Botkin, M. (1987). Pygmalion and the student: Age and classroom differences in children's awareness of teacher expectations. *Child Development, 58,* 1079–1092.

Wigfield, A., Eccles, J. S., MacIver, D., Reuman, D., & Midgley, C. (1991). Transitions at early adolescence: Changes in children's domain-specific self-perceptions and general self-esteem across the transition to junior high school. *Developmental Psychology, 27,* 552–565.

Willis, S. (1972). *Formation of teachers' expectations of students' academic performance.* Unpublished doctoral dissertation, University of Texas, Austin.

Willis, S., & Brophy, J. (1974). The origins of teacher attitudes toward young children. *Journal of Educational Psychology, 66*(4), 520–529.

CHAPTER FIVE

Early Schooling and Academic Achievement of African American Males

James Earl Davis

Temple University

One factor that has been consistently associated with the achievement gap is school disengagement by African American males (Carter, 2003; Polite, 2000). Despite the prevalent view that achievement matters, research studies provide only modest evidence about the effects of disengagement among Black boys[1] in the early grades. Little evidence is available on the antecedents of underachievement for young males—the exception being the negative effects of some family and schooling background variables (Ferguson, 2000; Polite & Davis, 1999). This is due, in part, to the sparse data available on the experiences and outcomes of African American males in the early grades. However, the negative consequences of the achievement gap are more widely known and accepted. In general, we know that for these students, lower levels of achievement appear to have the most significant consequences for future development of social identity, cognitive ability, emotional capacity, and social competence—each negatively influenced by poor schooling experiences (Heath & MacKinnon, 1988). Similarly, the inherent social and economic limitations associated with underachievement are also supported by research across the disciplines (Anderson, 2000; Jencks & Phillips, 1998; Mincy, 1994; Murnane, Willett, & Levy, 1995). Thus, rather than ask questions about known negative effects of the achievement gap for African American males, one might pose the following question: What are the mechanisms at work that are responsible for African American males' achievement lags and apparent disengagement in early years of schooling?

This chapter centers on African American males in the early years of their formal schooling (kindergarten through third grade), specifically their experience and achievement outcomes. Research on African American boys' achievement, performance, and school behavior will serve as the core of this chapter. Initially, I provide an overview of the achievement status of African American males coupled with attention to the gender and racial context, particularly at school, in which these boys develop academically and socially. Published research from a variety of sources grounds the chapter in the most useful and reliable data that substantiate the achievement gap between African American males and their school peers, as well as provide direction to addressing lags in educational achievement. In doing so, I identify variables and factors that are needed to fully understand the achievement gap for African American males in early education. I try to situate achievement status and disengagement experience as well as anchor the discussion about explanations within a larger argument about the role of schools and teachers as gender socializing agents for African American males.

Some assumptions are apparent in this chapter. I assume that African American males need to be cared for and nurtured in responsive schools; that these schools and teachers need to be supported in meeting the needs of Black males; and that a critical component of support includes increasing the ability of schools to contribute to Black males' social, cognitive, gender, and academic development. Based on these assumptions, I focus on findings from the research literature on Black male achievement and factors, such as school organization, that are associated with achievement outcomes. Second, I explore the degree to which schooling and gender identity help to explain possible disengagement and opposition to schooling experienced by Black boys in the early years. Throughout the chapter, I critique current research efforts and recommend a research agenda for understanding disparities in achievement and attitudes toward schooling among African American boys.

GENDER AND RACIAL CONTEXT OF ACHIEVEMENT

Considerable attention has been directed toward understanding gender differences in education. Central to this effort has been the investigation of the effects of gender on schooling experiences and achievement. In most of this work, gender is viewed from a social constructivist perspective, where qualities of masculinity are culturally attributed and defined (Connell, 1995; Ferguson, 2000; Thomas, 1990). Schooling contexts are often cited as important sources for gender construction and development (Thorne, 1986). Likewise, school experiences and opportunities are also circumscribed by race and ethnicity. Yet the intersection between gender and race in these contexts is often overlooked in educational research. In particular, the current plight of young African American males in schools demands much more focus, both theoretically and methodologically. Namely, issues of race and gender are central to any discussion about African American males and achievement (Delpit, 1988; Fine, 1991; Fordham, 1996; Williams, 1996). Whether related to background and family resources (Corcoran & Adams, 1997) or opportunities to learn and develop that are influenced by gender relations (Adler, Kless, & Adler, 1992; Best, 1983), Black males are too often disadvantaged by this perplexing and misunderstood intersection of race and gender.

Although research on the schooling experiences of African Americans has a long history, recent discussions, particularly those presented by popular media about the unique plight of Black males and the racial achievement gap, have captured the interest of many. These discussions surrounding the educational status of Black males and the nature of their precarious educational position are infused with compelling descriptors such as worlds apart, epidemic of failure, and left behind. From this discourse has emerged an urgency to address the education achievement problems of Black males. Given this urgency, it seems ironic that scant attention has been given to the educational experiences and perspectives of Black boys in early schooling. In particular, little is known about the processes and experiences of early schooling, particularly issues of masculinity and how it influences schooling. To be fair, the idea of Black masculine identity and underachievement has gained currency in some literature and popular press (Boyd-Franklin & Franklin, 2000), yet the main of education research remains silent.

To be Black and male in American schools places one at risk for a variety of negative consequences: school failure, special education assignment, suspensions, expulsions, and violence (Ferguson, 2000; Polite & Davis, 1999). Rates of Black male school attrition, relatively poor academic performance, and college enrollment and persistence are seen, in part, as a function of Black males' inability or disinterest in fulfilling their roles as conventional learners in school settings. These negative school experiences and outcomes are viewed, to varying degrees, as products of structural factors, results of cultural adaptations to systemic pressures and maladaptive definitions of masculinity (Boykin & Bailey, 2000; Hare & Hare, 1985; Majors & Mancini Billson, 1992). What has emerged from this focus on the educational problems of Black males is an archetype of masculine behavior that is either deficient or distorted under the weight of racism, economic marginality, and cultural pathology (Hunter & Davis, 1992). Although masculinity is generally seen as being important (Akbar, 1991; Connell, 1995), it is regarded, however, as unidimensional and implicitly universal. Thus, this framework obscures the diversity and complexity of the constructions of so-called masculinities and how they are played out for African American males in schools.

Contrary to the generally accepted objectives of schooling, the current thinking of many researchers and educators is that schools are not meeting the particular social and developmental needs of African American males (Brown & Davis, 2000). In response, gender-exclusive school environments are being suggested as a measure to reverse disproportionate rates of school failure experienced by Black males (Span, 2000). It is argued that consistent and positive males in educational settings provide models for young Black males to emulate. These positive role models are believed to counter inappropriate sex role socialization and maladaptive masculine identity (Cunningham, 1993). In turn, conceptions of masculinity are developed that are not antithetical to expected behaviors, roles, and expectations in school settings.

Broader sociological and economic forces are seen as undermining both the development and the appropriate expressions of masculinity among African American boys, particularly among the inner-city poor. In contrast, alternative models of masculinity (Akbar, 1991; Winbush, 2001) are being prescribed. However, its image of masculinity as either evasive or arrested still dominates the discourse. The ties between the meaning of masculinity and schooling objectives are believed to be incongruent and often diametrically opposed. One reason commonly mentioned for the disengagement, alienation, and poor academic performance of Black males is that they perceive most educational activities as feminine and irrelevant to their masculine identity and development. Furthermore, it is also believed that schools, specifically teachers, impose a feminine culture on males that induce oppositional behaviors. Given the reactions to these school contexts and gender expectations, many Black boys are seen as both victims and participants in their own educational demise.

RESEARCHING BLACK BOYS AT SCHOOL

During the past decade, a corpus of journal articles, reports, and scholarly and popular books have detailed the precarious nature of Black males in school and society (Boyd-Franklin & Franklin, 2000; Brown & Davis, 2000; Garibaldi, 1992; Majors & Gordon, 1994; McCall, 1994; Mincy, 1994; Polite & Davis, 1999; Williams, 1996). Although the current plight of young Black males in school is the focus of some of this work, very little is known about how early schooling contexts and experiences affect achievement outcomes. This interaction of school context, identity, and socialization is important to consider.

In the midst of trying to get a handle on the education crisis of Black boys, we have unfortunately learned too little about how boys construct personal meaning for their social and academic lives. We do know that Black boys are both loved and loathed at school. They set the standards for hip-hop culture and athleticism while experiencing disproportionate levels of punishment and academic failure. This juxtaposition leads to a range of behaviors and strategies within school that set the tone for the overall problematic educational experience of Black boys (Sewell, 1997). The response of these boys to a context that defines them as both sexy and as sexually threatening is often problematic. The spaces they create in response offer a sanctuary for the development of a set of relational and performance patterns that are unique to this group. These masculine spaces are erected, consciously or subconsciously, in schools that construct them as alien and undesirable. Clearly, schools are critical sites for young Black males as they make meaning of who they are, what they are supposed to do, and how others perceive them.

Although Black boys as well as Black girls are negatively affected by schooling, some research suggests that the problems facing Black boys are more chronic and extreme, thus deserving of special policy and programmatic attention (Garibaldi, 1991, 1992; Polite, 1993; Watson & Smitherman, 1991). Others cite cultural messages about Black males and how they are negatively constructed in the media and perceived in everyday life (Belton, 1995; Blount & Cunningham, 1996; Harper, 1996). These images portray the Black male as violent, disrespectful, unintelligent, hypersexualized, and threatening. These cultural messages, without a doubt, carry over into schools and negatively influence the ways young Black male students are treated, positioned, and distributed opportunities to learn. For instance, Black boys' demeanors are misunderstood by White middle-class teachers and seen as defiant, aggressive, and intimidating (Majors, Tyler, Peden, & Hall, 1994; Slaughter-Defoe & Richards, 1994). Furthermore, in almost every category of academic failure, Black boys are disproportionately represented (Entwisle, Alexander, & Olson, 1997). One study documents that only 2% of African American males enrolled in the public school system of a large midwestern U.S. city achieved a cumulative grade point average of at least a 3 on a 4 point scale. At the same time, three fourths of Black males in that system were performing below average (Leake & Leake, 1992). In addition, a report on academic performance comparing Black males in a large urban and suburban school district found that fewer than 3% of Black males were enrolled in advanced classes (Wright, 1996). Clearly, by all measures of school attainment and achievement, Black males are consistently placed at risk for academic failure. In addition to lags in test score performance and grades, African American males are referred for special education placement at a much higher rate than all other students and they are much more likely to be suspended or expelled from school (Harry & Anderson, 1999). There is growing evidence that Black males disengagement with schooling develops in the early grades and continues to intensify as they progress through school (Carter, 2003). By all indicators, Black males consistently fall behind other students in early school performance and lead their peers in school infractions and other negative outcomes. The direction of the relationship between these negative educational experiences and school disengagement are surprisingly unclear. From the current literature, it is difficult to establish whether disengagement or achievement is the antecedent.

Although the body of research on Black boys in the early grades is limited, it provides some useful insights. Much of this work, comparative in nature, examines the academic experiences and outcomes of Black boys relative to other students. Slaughter-Defoe and Richards (1994) suggested that as early as kindergarten, Black males are treated differently than other male and female students. Throughout elementary and middle school, Black boys consistently receive lower ratings by teachers for social behavior and academic expectations (Rong, 1996). In their study of factors related to school outcomes for Black males, Davis and Jordan (1994) found that boys' school engagement reflected in study habits and attendance were positively related to achievement and grades. Black boys who spend more time on homework and attend school regularly also perform better academically and are more engaged in their schooling. They also found that remediation, grade retention, and suspensions induce academic failure among Black boys. A longitudinal qualitative study of young African American males from their preschool years into late adolescence is informative concerning parental involvement. Rashid (1989) found that the extent of parental involvement in the early years of schooling was critical, including the preschool program in which the boys were initially enrolled. Likewise, parental mediation of peer contacts and the availability of positive adult male role models were important in the lives of these boys.

Although recent attention has been paid to the relatively poor academic performance of African American boys in school, its scope and focus are clearly not enough. Much of this work, I contend, is not really about understanding the achievement gap among Black boys and their peers. Rather, the field has been concerned about documenting poor performance and achievement deficits of Black males throughout their schooling years. Therefore, despite research attention directed toward Black males in school, insights about effective ways of countering the achievement gap and reversing high levels of disengagement go wanting. One research area that has been neglected deals with issues of Black boys' early childhood schooling and home experiences, such as school readiness. This area of investigation would provide potentially useful information on Black males' trajectory of achievement and differences in school engagement over time.

Indeed, the early educational experiences of African American boys are by far the most important in the developmental trajectory of achievement throughout school (Best, 1983; Entwisle et al., 1997). Data on early schooling are spare and are usually limited to test scores and other measures of achievement. The large national data sets that are available, such as Children of the National Longitudinal Survey of

Youth (prekindergarten–fifth grade), Prospects (first and third grades), and the National Assessment of Educational Progress (fourth grade), although potentially useful, have been underused. Specifically, achievement and personal background information about African American boys from these data sources may be helpful in establishing achievement patterns and explanatory factors during the early years of schooling. On the other hand, qualitative and ethnographic studies of early childhood and schooling of Black boys are rarer. When these studies are published, they are usually focused on issues of socialization, attitudes, and peer relations without much linkage to achievement outcomes (Tyson, 2002). Using a developmental perspective to study changes in African American boys' achievement and performance from kindergarten to third grade and beyond should frame both quantitative and qualitative research on achievement. Research questions that pay attention to specific changes in achievement with respect to grade level, subject area, school culture, and student characteristics (e.g., socioeconomic background, attitudes, and identity) would benefit from longitudinal studies in this area.

For preschool Black boys, three common criteria often used as indicators of school readiness include student academic skill development, attitude, and behaviors (U.S. Department of Education, National Center for Education Statistics, 1993). Using data from the National Longitudinal Survey of Youth, some interesting patterns of Black boys' academic readiness skills appear (Nettles & Perna, 1997). Boys have lower test scores relative to girls on motor and social development tests. Similarly, boys score lower on verbal memory test. However, there are no differences in scores on the Peabody Picture Vocabulary Test, a language-independent measure, between the two groups. Furthermore, Black boys fidget more, begin speaking much later than girls, and are more likely to have a verbal stuttering or stammering problem. These indicators of early literacy for Black boys should prompt a research and intervention agenda that seeks to uncover meaningful explanations for achievement outcomes.

EXPLAINING BLACK MALE SCHOOL ACHIEVEMENT AND DISENGAGEMENT

Reasons cited for African American boys' academic achievement and disengagement in the early years of schooling are numerous.

Although many of the theories and explanations are attractive and popular, particularly among some policy makers and social activists, they tend to lack substantial research support. In general, macro- and micro-explanations about the declining performance of African American boys relative to their White and female peers need more empirical study.

The most influential theories currently proposed to account for the relatively low academic performance of African American boys center on three areas: (a) student attitudes, (b) social organization of schools, and (c) masculine identity. Much research about student attitudes focuses on student resistance and cultural opposition to schooling and achievement (Cook & Ludwig, 1998; Fordham, 1996; MacLeod, 1995). The notion that attitudes of Black students are the results of negative cultural orientation toward schooling is most closely associated with Fordham (1996). The idea of a cultural ori- entation implies that negative school attitudes can be found among Black students because it is learned behavior that is community enforced. The assumption that young children in school, especially Black boys, are participants and victims in this anti-achievement milieu guides this work. Data from the Early Childhood Education Component of the National Household Education Survey (U.S. Department of Education, National Center for Education Statistics, 1993) revealed some early patterns concerning school engagement for Black boys. For instance, 5-year-old Black boys are more likely to lack confidence about their abilities in school compared with Black girls (23.5% vs. 9.7%), and boys are less likely to speak out in class compared with girls. However, parents report no differences in their reading levels. But parents indicate they played more with Black girls (e.g., arts, crafts, toys, and games). In general, African American boys have very positive experiences in early schooling. Almost all of them (98%) report looking forward to going to kinder- garten each day, and the vast majority of them like their teacher and say good things about their school. These findings are supported by an ethnographic study that found Black boys to be achievement oriented and very engaged in the process of learning in elementary school. Interestingly, only boys who were struggling academically expressed negative attitudes toward school (Tyson, 2002).

From the evidence reported here, although limited, the picture about disengagement of Black boys in the early school years becomes less clear. I posit that the inconsistency of findings of disengagement of Black boys in school is due to differences in the developmental experiences and attitudes of young boys relative to older students in middle and high school. Most of the research on schooling opposition and attitudes focus on adolescents and not during the early years of school (Ainsworth-Darnell & Downey, 1998; Fordham, 1996; Solomon, 1991; Welch & Hodges, 1997). The research that exists on Black males' attitudes in the early grades is relatively recent and typically focuses on peer relations. Little attention is given to how young Black males construct personal meaning of education and achievement inside and outside school. Particularly, discussions about how young Black males make sense of their own gender/race identity connected with achievement and engagement attitudes have been noticeably absent from research studies.

Explanations of the achievement gap relating to how schools are organized have concentrated on curriculum issues, teaching strategies, school achievement climate, and expectations. How schools structure students' opportunities to learn has been shown to influence academic achievement (Epstein & MacIver, 1992; Lee & Bryk, 1988). Access to academic experiences and achievement through the curriculum, teachers, and other school activities are of particular importance for African American males who may be already marginalized at school (Finn & Cox, 1992; Sanders & Reed, 1995). Elementary schools, particularly those in low-income inner-city and rural areas, traditionally have been neglected, underfunded, and burdened with limited parental and community support. Because of complex social and economic reasons, young Black males in these schools setting are acutely at risk for limited achievement and school disengagement. For instance, classrooms that require a tremendous amount of disciplinary attention may produce limited learning environments that shortchange Black boys in terms of academic instruction and learning activities. If school and classroom climate are negatively affected by discipline problems, academic engagement and instructional focus will surely suffer. This link between school climate and student achievement is documented (Irvine, 1990; Polite, 2000) but requires much more research specifically focused on African American boys.

Ability grouping of Black boys in elementary schools also appears to have negative consequences on their achievement levels. Although much evidence on Black boys is not readily available, a few studies point in this direction. Simmons and Grady (1992) reported that Black boys in the early grades were overenrolled in lower-level courses. For instance, throughout the third grade, Black boys perform equally well as their peers on districtwide assessment in reading and math. Beginning in the fourth grade, however, Black boys experience a sharp decline in their test scores. The percentage of Black males in the top reading group dropped from 23% in Grades 1 and 4 to 12% in Grade 6. These declines correspond to the ability grouping of Black boys in which they only have access to lower-level courses. When elementary Black boys have unequal access to the curriculum, achievement inequalities in the later grades are not surprising. Other school organization efforts such as magnet schools, charter schools, after-school programming, block scheduling, looping, extended, and year-round schooling are important areas for study to determine if specific achievement effects of these strategies occur for Black boys in the lower grades.

The need for early school-based intervention for African American boys who are placed at risk for school disengagement is supported by findings from research on schooling success. Interventions such as Success for All (Madden, Slavin, Karweit, Dolan, & Wasik, 1993), where implementation generally begins in kindergarten through the third grade or preschool through the third grade and then continue up to Grades 4 and 5, appear appropriate and effective. Although evidence suggests that substantial reading effects typically occur in the first year of implementing the program at kindergarten and first grade, some large effects are found in the second and third grades after the initial year of implementation. To ensure academic success for African American boys, curriculum improvement, instruction, and support for teachers should begin in preschool and earlier before boys begin to underachieve. It is clear that program interventions are less effective if they are implemented after boys have fallen too far behind. Although early intervention strategies for Black boys are necessary, they are not always sufficient. The effects of early interventions alone generally fade over time, particularly for cognitive outcomes (Wasik & Slavin, 1993). Thus, more research on early and sustained interventions, particularly whole-school reform initiatives such as Success for All, Comer School Development Program, Title I, and Reading Recovery, is needed to accurately map achievement during the early schooling years of African American males.

Another explanation for Black male underachievement centers on gender identity. One reason commonly mentioned for the alienation and poor academic performance of Black males is that they perceive schooling activities as feminine and irrelevant to their masculine sense of self (Noguera, 2003). Others contend that the increased presence of committed and successful Black male adults in educational environments is essential for enhancing Black boys' academic and social identity development. An array of program initiatives has captured the attention of school administrators, local communities, and parents as possible solutions to school-related problems associated with Black males. Some of these programs are school affiliated, with local groups and organization teaming with school districts to offer support services and mentoring for Black boys. Others are community-based program that operate independently from schools in their efforts to mobilize proactive community resources to improve the academic chances of Black boys (Hopson, 1997). All these programs seek to support school activities by providing a positive presence of adult Black men. Mentoring programs that assign professional Black men as role models for young boys, typically in elementary and middle schools, have been established in many school districts. Professional Black men serve as teachers' aides, tutors, and reading partners for Black boys needing academic support and guidance. The justification for these initiatives points to the need for consistent and positive Black men in educational settings who provide models for young Black males to emulate. It is no surprise that Black male organizations such as Concerned Black Men, Inc., Black men's church groups, Black fraternities, and Million Man March chapters are at the forefront of these school-based programs.

Others contend that the increased presence of committed and successful Black male adults in educational environments is essential for enhancing Black boys' academic and social development (Jeff, 1994; Span, 2000). This positive male presence is meant to diffuse traditional masculine behaviors and counters negative gender role socialization of Black boys. The development of conceptions and expressions of masculinity that match positive behaviors and deportment in school settings is the primary objective of these interventions.

Approaches such as organizing all-male schools and classrooms take a more radical approach to schooling conditions. Given the severity of problems associated with Black boys in schools, advocates for race- and gender-exclusive schooling defend these strategies that attempt to reorganize the gendered nature of schools and classrooms as the best approach (Watson & Smitherman, 1991).

Many advocates for Black boys see teachers as responsible for imposing feminine standards of behavioral expectations that induce school disengagement attitudes and behaviors (Holland, 1992). These all-male academies serve as compensatory devices aimed at restoring a normative masculinity to the center of Black boys' schooling experiences.

Alternative Afrocentric models of masculinity are also being proposed (Akbar, 1991; Jeff, 1994; Kunjufu, 2001) and used in manhood development programs and curricula for younger males. These models call for an overthrow of Western models of male socialization and a regrounding of Black boys and men in a new cultural awareness. African American immersion schools and curricula that stress African and African American history and culture are viewed as positive strategies in building self-esteem and self-confidence and promoting dispositions for learning (Brown, 1995; Murrell, 1994, 2002; Pollard & Ajirotutu, 2000). These schools embrace a new conception of masculinity that shifts from dominate ideas of male socialization to a cultural awareness grounded in the positive experiences and history of African people, particularly Black men. The intent of these models are transformative; however, images of a normative masculinity being either unfulfilled or misdirected still dominate and limit policy and practice solutions.

There has been much controversy on the development of all-male public schools (Span, 2000). A few of these schools, located primarily in large urban areas, exist only in theory as all male because their enrollment also includes African American girls (Watson & Smitherman, 1991). Another area of so-called gender tracking that experiences less political and legal resistance is the single-sex classroom. A number of school districts have experimented with within-school single-sex instruction. The Baltimore City public schools and Washington, D.C., public schools are two large urban systems that successfully implemented single-sex classes (Ascher, 1992). These classes, particularly aimed at Black boys, were designed to help boys catch up to the achievement and performance levels of girls. Unfortunately, very little is known about the effectiveness of these gender-tracked classrooms as well as all-male academies and school-based and community interventions. Recent studies on the effectiveness of culturally themed and African-centered schooling experiences for Black boys have been mixed. Fifth-grade Black boys enrolled in a cultural immersion school were found to take more personal responsibility for their intellectual and academic achievement than their peers in a traditional school. The immersion school, however, appears to account for no other achievement or identity differences (Sanders & Reed, 1995). In addition, Hudley (1995, 1997) identified potential effects on academic self-concept for Black males enrolled in separate Afrocentric classrooms but little effects on achievement.

PROMOTING RESEARCH ON ACHIEVEMENT IN EARLY SCHOOLING

Much of the attention paid to highlighting and understanding Black male underachievement has ironically hindered our understanding of why some African American boys actually achieve and perform well in school. Too often, our research efforts have focused on failure instead of profiling Black boys who are high achievers in elementary school (Ford & Harris, 1996). Studying high achievers also acknowledges teaching strategies, school structures, and student attitudes that are effective in producing achievement results. There is a need to rethink how African American boys with similar demographic backgrounds and shared schooling environments produce differential achievement outcomes. Lessons to be learned from this research approach would be incredibly insightful.

Not all Black boys are the same. This simple point is not an obvious one given most of the discussions about the so-called Black boy problem in American schools. But where are the high-achieving African American boys? It is apparent from the national conversation on troubled boyhood that the inclusion of high-achieving Black boys' experiences muddles the discussion. In essence, we have created a separate conversation and agenda that removes Black boys with competitive test scores and positive school experiences from an important national debate. Racism, stereotypes, lower expectations, and pervasive peer and popular culture define the "other" boyhood crisis that many Black boys face daily. African American boys create major problems and challenges for schools: These challenges are cultural and gender based. The difficulty for schools, in part, rests in their inability to deal with where these Black boys are coming from and their authentic experiences of being young, Black, and male in U.S. public schools. Although educational institutions acknowledge that these students often bring diverse backgrounds and perspectives, little is understood about the complex lives African American boys lead inside and outside school.

The dismal statistics of the achievement gap and behavioral problems are compelling, but understanding the so-called Black male achievement problem calls for a solutions-oriented research agenda. This includes a research focus on the active role African American boys themselves play in creating their own school experience and opportunities for achievement. This is not to say that how schools structure students' opportunities to learn is not important. For sure, inequalities in schooling have potentially lifelong consequences for Black male educational attainment, employment, and family relations. Access to quality academic programs, curricula, and teacher quality are extremely important (Ferguson, 1991, 2003) for these Black boys who bring to school many skills, dispositions, and behaviors that marginalize. But to always cast these young males as victims strips them of any agency in how they make meaning of who they are at school. New gender-centric research projects in the schooling of Black boys are also required—ones that seek to capture the complexity and variations in the voices and experiences of Black boys at school. Understanding the role of peers, in addition to teachers and families, in the social construction of masculinity for Black boys in early education would constitute a major research effort in addressing issue of disengagement and achievement. Studying Black boys' constructions of masculinity and framing how they link these constructions to achievement motivation and performance will be extremely important in unpacking the achievement gap problem.

Also, a new research agenda on the role of teachers in increasing the achievement levels of Black boys is being called for. Teacher accountability is a dominant theme in school reform efforts across the United States. Much of this concern for accountability centers on student learning and achievement outcomes (Boykin, 1994). But should teachers be held responsible for the social outcomes and experiences of Black boys? It goes without saying that teachers play a very significant role in the school lives of students. Because most of the school day is spent in classrooms under the supervision and guidance of teachers, their influence on Black boys should never be taken for granted. Although teachers are blamed for many problems Black boys face, ironically, most of the proposed solutions aimed at remedying the educational plight of African American boys have excluded teachers. The rationale for this position is that teachers are blamed for students' poor levels of academic performance and engagement

(Holland, 1992). Teachers' influence on Black boys is too important, however, to silence them and reduce their contribution to this national conversation. Black males in general share this desire for a more personal connection with teachers (Davis, 1999). They feel they are often misunderstood and wrongly judged because of how they look and act. Teachers bear a disproportionate role in monitoring social relationships not only in their classrooms but also in other social settings at the school. Traditionally, teachers have felt that their student social networks and relationships were off-limits to them. As teachers are being held accountable for structuring student's learning opportunities, so must teachers take a more active role in understanding Black boys and intervening when necessary with social lessons that cultivate an appreciation for the importance of school and achievement.

CONCLUSIONS

As I have tried to illustrate in this chapter, research on early schooling for African American boys is crucial in mapping achievement trajectories as well as in understanding the reasons for underachievement and school engagement. Unfortunately, studies in the field have been limited in their ability to reasonably account for the achievement gap problem. Given the strengths and weaknesses of these studies, both theoretically and methodologically, the range and focus of research in the field of Black male educational studies can be strengthened. Research findings about effective program and policy intervention outcomes that appear to be robust and consistent over time should be the goal of a progressive research agenda in the study of Black boys in early education. With the zeal to improve the educational and life chances for Black males should also come a renewed interest and urgency in doing outcome-based research that informs policy and practice.

I have suggested three explanatory areas (student attitudes, social organization of schools and curriculum, and masculine identity) that have the greatest potential for structuring a broad research agenda on Black boys' achievement outcomes in the early years of schooling. Related to these research areas is the pressing need to effectively use national databases in which data on Black boys are analyzed both comparatively and independently. Furthermore, research and program evaluation efforts need to be more deliberately focused on Black boys' experiences and achievement outcome in national early interventions such as Head Start, Early Head Start, and Healthy Start.

Early schooling is a place in which Black boys begin to make sense about their various identities at school. In the process, counteridentities are created inside and outside school that feed on a traditional masculine hegemony of behaviors and attitudes. I am well aware that the development of Black boys' social identity is complicated by the heavy dosages they get from immediate and distance sources, such as family, community, church, and the media. Indeed, these social messages provide young males with information about their place and purpose. Schools, for sure, are contested sites in which Black boys learn to negotiate the endorsement and participation in a variety of gendered identities that could enhance or restrict their achievement possibilities. Sadly, too many schooling experiences of Black boys represent yet another disappointing aspect of their young lives. For many of them, schools ignore their aspirations, disrespect their ability to learn, fail to access and cultivate their many talents, and impose a restrictive range of their options. Within this overwhelming oppressive schooling context, too many Black boys simple give up—beaten by school systems that place little value on who they are and what they offer.

Certainly, a concerted research program and research-based interventions aimed at disentangling the achievement quagmire hold the possibility for ensuring that African American males reach their highest achievement potential. The nation's social and economic stability are dependent on these efforts.

NOTE

1. The terms *boys* and *males* are used interchangeably throughout the chapter. However, *boys* denotes a more developmentally appropriate description of early childhood students.

REFERENCES

Adler, P. A., Kless, S. J., & Adler, P. (1992). Socialization to gender roles: Popularity among elementary school boys and girls. *Sociology of Education, 65,* 169–187.

Ainsworth-Darnell, J. W., & Downey, D. B. (1998). Assessing the appositional culture explanation for racial/ethnic differences in school performance. *American Sociological Review, 63,* 536–553.

Akbar, N. (1991). *Visions of Black men.* Nashville, TN: Winston-Derek.

Anderson, E. (2000). *The code of the streets.* Chicago: University of Chicago Press.

Ascher, C. (1992, June). School programs for African-American males . . . and females. *Phi Delta Kappan,* pp. 777–782.

Belton, D. (1995). *Speak my name: Black men on masculinity and the American dream.* Boston: Beacon Press.

Best, R. (1983). *We've all got scars: What boys and girls learn in elementary school.* Bloomington: Indiana University Press.

Blount, M., & Cunningham, G. P. (Eds.). (1996). *Representing Black men.* New York: Routledge.

Boyd-Franklin, N. B., & Franklin, A. J. (2000). *Boys into men: Raising our African American teenage sons.* New York: E. P. Dutton.

Boykin, A. W. (1994). Reformulating educational reform: Toward the proactive schooling of African American children. In R. J. Rossi (Ed.), *Educational reforms and students at risk.* New York: Teachers College Press.

Boykin, A. W., & Bailey, C. T. (2000). *The role of cultural factors in school relevant cognitive functioning: Synthesis of finding on cultural context, cultural orientation, and individual differences* (Report No. 42). Washington, DC: Johns Hopkins and Howard Universities, Center for Research on the Education of Students Placed at Risk.

Brown, K. (1995). African American immersion schools: Paradoxes of race and public education. In R. Delgado (Ed.), *Critical race theory: The cutting edge* (pp. 373–386). Philadelphia: Temple University Press.

Brown, M. C., & Davis, J. E. (Eds.). (2000). *Black sons to mothers: Compliments, critiques, and challenges for cultural workers in education.* New York: Peter Lang.

Carter, P. L. (2003). Black cultural capital, status positioning, and the conflict of schooling for low-income African American youth. *Social Problems, 50,* 136–155.

Connell, R. W. (1995). *Masculinities.* Berkeley: University of California Press.

Cook, P. J., & Ludwig, J. (1998). The burden of "acting White": Do Black adolescents disparage academic achievement? In C. Jencks & M. Phillips (Eds.), *The Black-White test score gap* (pp. 375–400). Washington, DC: Brookings Institution Press.

Corcoran, M., & Adams, T. (1997). Race, sex and intergenerational poverty. In G. Duncan & J. Brooks-Gunn (Eds.), *Consequences of growing up poor.* New York: Russell Sage.

Cunningham, M. (1993). Sex role influence on African American males. *Journal of African American Males Studies, 1,* 30–37.

Davis, J. E. (1999). Forbidden fruit: Black males' constructions of transgressive sexualities in middle school. In W. J. Letts & J. T. Sears (Eds.),

Queering elementary education: Advancing the dialogue about sexualities and schooling (pp. 49–60). Lanham, MD: Rowman & Littlefield.

Davis, J. E., & Jordan, W. J. (1994). The effects of school context, structure, and experience on African American males in middle and high school. *Journal of Negro Education, 63,* 570–587.

Delpit, L. (1988). The silenced dialogue: Power and pedagogy in educating other people's children. *Harvard Educational Review, 58,* 280–298.

Entwisle, D. R., Alexander, K. L., & Olson, L. S. (1997). *Children, schools, and inequality.* Boulder, CO: Westview.

Epstein, J., & MacIver, D. (1992). *Opportunities to learn: Effects of eighth graders' curriculum offerings and instructional approaches* (Report no. 34). Baltimore, MD: Johns Hopkins University, Center for Research on Effective Schooling for Disadvantaged Students.

Ferguson, A. A. (2000). *Bad boys: Public schools in the making of Black masculinity (law, meaning and violence).* Ann Arbor: University of Michigan Press.

Ferguson, R. F. (1991). Racial patterns in how school and teacher quality affect achievement and earnings. *Challenge: A Journal of Research on Black Men, 2*(1), 1–35.

Ferguson, R. F. (2003). Teachers' perception and expectations and the Black-White test score gap. *Urban Education, 38,* 460–507.

Fine, M. (1991). *Framing dropouts: Notes on the politics of an urban high school.* Albany: State University of New York Press.

Finn, J. D., & Cox, D. (1992). Participation and withdrawal among fourth-grade pupils. *American Educational Research Journal, 29,* 141–162.

Ford, D., & Harris, J. (1996). Perceptions and attitudes of Black students toward school, achievement, and other educational variables. *Child Development, 67,* 1141–1152.

Fordham, S. (1996). *Blacked out.* Chicago: University of Chicago Press.

Garibaldi, A. M. (1991). The educational experiences of Black males: The early years. *Challenge: A Journal of Research on Black Men, 2,* 36–49.

Garibaldi, A. M. (1992). Educating and motivating African American males to succeed. *Journal of Negro Education, 61*(1), 12–18.

Hare, N., & Hare, J. (1985). *Bringing the Black boy to manhood: The passage.* San Francisco: Black Think Tank.

Harper, P. M. (1996). *Are we not men? Masculine anxiety and the problem of African-American identity.* New York: Oxford University Press.

Harry, B., & Anderson, M. G. (1999). The social construction of high-incidence disabilities: The effects on African American males. In V. C. Polite & J. E. Davis (Eds.), *African American males in school and society: Policy and practice for effective education* (pp. 58–92). New York: Teachers College Press.

Heath, P. A., & MacKinnon, C. (1988). Factors related to the social competence of children in single-parent families. *Journal of Divorce, 11,* 49–65.

Holland, S. (1992). Same-gender classes in Baltimore: How to avoid the problems faced in Detroit/Milwaukee. *Equity and Excellence, 25,* 2–4.

Hopson, R. (1997). *Educating Black males: Critical lessons in schooling, community, and power.* Albany: State University of New York Press.

Hudley, C. A. (1995). Assessing the impact of separate schooling for African American male adolescents. *Journal of Early Adolescence, 15*(1), 38–57.

Hudley, C. A. (1997). Teacher practices and student motivation in middle school program for African American males. *Urban Education, 32,* 304–319.

Hunter, A., & Davis, J. (1992). Constructing gender: Afro-American men's conceptualization of manhood. *Gender & Society, 6,* 464–479.

Irvine, J. J. (1990). *Black students and school failure: Policies, practices, and prescriptions.* Westport, CT: Greenwood.

Jeff, M. F. X. (1994). Afrocentrism and African-American male youth. In R. Mincy (Ed.), *Nurturing young Black males: Challenges to agencies, programs and social policy.* Washington, DC: Urban Institute.

Jencks, C., & Phillips, M. (Eds.). (1998). *The Black-White test score gap.* Washington, DC: Brookings Institution Press.

Kunjufu, J. (2001). *State of emergency: We must save African American males.* Chicago: African American Images.

Leake, D. O., & Leake, B. L. (1992). Islands of hope: Milwaukee's African American immersion schools. *Journal of Negro Education, 61*(1), 4–11.

Lee, V., & Bryk, A. (1988). Curriculum tracking as mediating the social distribution of high school achievement. *Sociology of Education, 61*(2), 78–94.

MacLeod, J. (1995). *Ain't no making it: Leveled aspirations in a low income neighborhood.* Boulder, CO: Westview.

Madden, N. A., Slavin, R. E., Karweit, N. L., Dolan, L. J., & Wasik, B. A. (1993). Success for all: Longitudinal effects of a restructuring program for inner-city elementary school. *American Educational Research Journal, 30,* 123–148.

Majors, R. (2001). *Educating our Black children: New directions and radical approaches.* London: Routledge Falmer.

Majors, R. G., & Gordon, J. U. (1994). *The American Black male: His present status and his future.* Chicago: Nelson-Hall.

Majors, R. G., & Mancini Billson, J. (1992). *Cool pose: The dilemmas of Black manhood in America.* New York: Lexington.

Majors, R. G., Tyler, R., Peden, B., & Hall, R. E. (1994). Cool pose: A symbolic mechanism for masculine role enactment and copying by Black males. In R. G. Majors & J. U. Gordan (Eds.), *The American Black male: His present status and his future* (pp. 245–259). Chicago: Nelson-Hall.

McCall, N. (1994). *Makes me want to holler: A young Black man in America.* New York: Vintage Books.

Mincy, R. B. (Ed.). (1994). *Nurturing young Black males: Challenges to agencies, programs, and social policy.* Washington, DC: Urban Institute.

Murnane, R., Willett, J., & Levy, F. (1995). The growing importance of cognitive skills in wage determination. *Review of Economics and Statistics, 77*(2), 251–266.

Murrell, P. C. (1994). In search of responsive teaching for African American males: An investigation of students' experiences of middle school mathematics curriculum. *Journal of Negro Education, 63*(4), 556–569.

Murrell, P. C. (2002). *African-centered pedagogy: Developing schools of achievement for African American children.* Albany: State University of New York Press.

Nettles, M., & Perna, L. (1997). *The African American data book: Higher and adult education* (Vol. 2). Fairfax, VA: Frederick D. Patterson Research Institute.

Noguera, P. (2003). The trouble with Black boys: The role and influence of environmental and cultural factors on the academic performance of African American males. *Urban Education, 38,* 431–459.

Polite, V. (1993). Educating African-American males in suburbia: Quality education? Caring environment? *Journal of African American Male Studies, 1,* 92–105.

Polite, V. C. (2000). When "at promise" Black males meet the "at risk" school system: Chaos! In M. C. Brown & J. E. Davis (Eds.), *Black sons to mothers: Compliments, critiques, and challenges for cultural workers in education.* New York: Peter Lang.

Polite, V. C., & Davis, J. E. (Eds.). (1999). *African American males in school and society: Policy and practice for effective education.* New York: Teachers College Press.

Pollard, D., & Ajirotutu, C. (2000). *African-centered schooling in theory and practice.* Westport, CT: Bergin & Garvey.

Rashid, H. (1989). Divergent paths in the development of African-American males: A qualitative perspective. *Urban Research Review, 12,* 12–13.

Rong, X. L. (1996). Effects of race and gender on teachers' perception of the social behavior of elementary students. *Urban Education, 31,* 261–290.

Sanders, E. T., & Reed, P. L. (1995). An investigation of the possible effects of an immersion as compared to a traditional program for African-American males. *Urban Education, 30,* 93–112.

Sewell, T. (1997). *Black masculinities and schooling: How Black boys survive modern schooling.* London: Trentham.

Simmons, W., & Grady, M. (1992). *Black male achievement: From peril to promise* (Report of the Superintendent's Advisory Committee on Black

Male Achievement). Upper Marlboro, MD: Prince George's County Public Schools.

Slaughter-Defoe, D. T., & Richards, H. (1994). Literacy as empowerment: The case for African American males. In V. L. Gadsden & D. A. Wagner (Eds.), *Literacy among African American youth: Issues in learning, teaching, and schooling* (pp. 125–147). Cresskill, NJ: Hampton.

Solomon, R. P. (1991). *Black resistance in high school.* Albany: State University of New York Press.

Span, C. (2000). "Black schools for Black children": Black males, Milwaukee, and immersion schools. In M. C. Brown & J. E. Davis (Eds.), *Black sons to mothers: Compliments, critiques, and challenges for cultural workers in education.* New York: Peter Lang.

Thomas, K. (1990). *Gender and the subject of higher education.* London: Open University Press.

Thorne, B. (1986). Girls and boys together, but mostly apart: Gender arrangements in elementary schools. In W. Hartup & Z. Rubin (Eds.), *Relationships and development* (pp. 167–184). Hillsdale, NJ: Lawrence Erlbaum.

Tyson, K. (2002). Weighing in: Elementary-aged students and the debate on attitude toward school. *Social Forces, 80,* 1156–1190.

U.S. Department of Education, National Center for Education Statistics. (1993). *National household education survey.* Washington, DC: Office of Educational Research and Improvement.

Wasik, B. A., & Slavin, R. E. (1993). Preventing early reading failure with one-to-one tutoring: A review of five programs. *Reading Research Quarterly, 28,* 179–200.

Watson, C., & Smitherman, G. (1991). Educational equity and Detroit's male academies. *Equity and Excellence, 25,* 90–105.

Welch, O., & Hodges, C. (1997). *Standing outside on the inside: Black adolescents and the construction of academic identity.* Albany: State University of New York Press.

Williams, B. (Ed.). (1996). *Closing the achievement gap: A vision for changing beliefs and practices.* Washington, DC: Association for Supervision and Curriculum Development.

Winbush, R. A. (2001). *The warrior method: A program for raising healthy black boys.* New York: Amistad Press.

Wright, D. L. (1996). *Concrete and abstract attitudes, mainstream orientation, and academic achievement of adolescent African-American males.* Unpublished doctoral dissertation, Howard University, Washington, DC.

CHAPTER SIX

What's Happening to the Boys?

Early High School Experiences and School Outcomes Among African American Male Adolescents in Chicago

Melissa Roderick

University of Chicago

Rising payoffs to skills and dramatic declines in the economic prospects of the noncollege bound have now made completion of high school, and even participation in postsecondary education, a

AUTHOR'S NOTE: This research was supported by grants from the Spencer Foundation, the Annie E. Casey Foundation, and the Office of Educational Research and Improvement under the Center for Research on the Education of Students Placed at Risk. The content does not necessarily represent the policy of the Department of Education, and the reader should not assume endorsement by the federal government. I am indebted to the comments and contributions of Kneia DaCosta and Susan Stone. This chapter could not have been done without all the students and parents who participated in the Student Life in High Schools Project and who gave so much to us over the course of 2 years. Thanks also to the interviewers and research team who worked to collect this data, including Michael Arney, Michael Axelman, Kneia DaCosta, Leticia Villareal Sosa, Richard Contreras, Ron Strong, Milan Sevak, and James Chiong.

requirement for future success. At the same time, many school systems have raised the bar of what is expected of students to attain that goal. We now expect all students to take more rigorous academic courses in high school. And, increasingly, schools are requiring that students demonstrate achievement on standardized tests to graduate. All of this means that during adolescence, schools are asking all students, not just the highest performers, to work harder, invest in schooling, and demonstrate increased academic achievement.

Too often, however, the high school years are a time of decline in student motivation and engagement. There is a common perception that African American adolescents, particularly males, are the most likely to turn away from school and form peer groups that discourage them from working hard and succeeding. Scholars debate about the degree of evidence that supports the contention that African American adolescents are less likely to see doing well in school as something they value (Cook & Ludwig, 1997; Ferguson, 1998; Fordham, 1996; Fordham & Ogbu, 1986; Jencks & Phillips, 1998; Smerdon, 1999). We do know, however, that African American urban students, particularly males, have the poorest rates of high school completion. In Chicago, for example, among the entering 1992 Chicago Public School ninth-grade class, only 37% of African American males graduated 4 years later compared to 55% of their female counterparts and 58% of White students.[1]

What happens as adolescents move through their early high school years that could explain declines in motivation and school engagement and increasing divergence between gender and racial groups? There is an emerging body of evidence that school transitions are critical points in students' school careers. Research on motivation, for example, finds that adolescents' engagement and performance in school decline markedly as they move from elementary school to junior high and high school and that urban students are the most at risk. These declines are linked to school dropout (Blyth, Simmons, & Carlton-Ford, 1983; Crockett, Petersen, Graber, Schulenberg, & Ebata, 1989; Eccles, Lord, & Midgley, 1991; Felner & Adan, 1989; Felner, Primavera, & Cauce, 1981; Reyes, Gillock, & Kobus, 1994; Roderick, 1993; Seidman, Allen, Aber, Mitchell, & Feinman, 1994; Simmons, Black, & Zhou, 1991; Simmons & Blyth, 1987). In urban areas, students often experience marked declines in their grades, involvement, and perception of the quality of their school environments as they move into secondary schools (Reyes et al., 1994; Roderick, 1993; Seidman et al., 1994; Simmons et al., 1991; Simmons & Blyth,

1987). For example, in Chicago, although the average eighth grader reports attending school regularly, the average tenth grader reports 30 days of absence (Sebring, Bryk, Roderick, & Camburn, 1996). Many urban freshmen experience academic difficulty. More than 40% of entering ninth graders in Chicago fail a major subject in the first semester of high school and 20% fail two or more (Roderick & Camburn, 1999).

Evidence also suggests that minority males have the greatest academic difficulty following the move to middle-level schools and high school (Felner et al., 1981; Roderick & Camburn, 1999; Simmons et al., 1991).[2] Roderick and Camburn (1999) found that African American males in Chicago were approximately 50% more likely to fail major subjects in the first semester of ninth grade than African American females. These dramatic changes in school performance as students move to high school suggest that declines in engagement in school may not simply be a process of adolescence but may be strongly shaped by the academic and social environments that students encounter in urban high schools.

This chapter takes a close look at the transition to high school among a group of African American males who were part of a longitudinal study in Chicago. It focuses on two questions. First, what does the school performance of African American males and females in this study look like both prior to and after the transition to high school? Second, what are the school, familial, and developmental processes that shape the school performance of African American male adolescents during this period? The article first provides a quantitative look at gender differences in school performance of 32 African American students over the period from eighth to twelfth grade and as students transitioned to a large urban high school in Chicago. It then presents an in-depth qualitative look at the experiences of the 15 males in the longitudinal study. By looking carefully at individual students' experiences, this article seeks to gain insight into how school and families may better assist African American males in negotiating the tasks of adolescence and in promoting positive school engagement.

THE PERIOD OF ADOLESCENCE: IDENTITY FORMATION AND SCHOOL ATTACHMENT

Jacquellyne Eccles and her colleagues (1991) have argued that declines in performance and motivation following school transitions occur because of a mismatch between the developmental needs of adolescents and the educational environments of junior high and high schools. Many of the issues that arise in studying African American adolescents' achievement motivation also center on the interaction of children within their environment, in particular how emerging peer groups combined with adolescents' increasing awareness of racial barriers and stereotypes shape students' behaviors and goals. Thus, a starting place in thinking about school performance during the transition to high school is to examine the developmental changes of adolescence and how school environments shape developmental demands and supports.

Adolescence is often recognized as a time of biological change, but it is also a time of rapid cognitive and social change. It is during adolescence that children develop an increased capacity for formal operations and logical abstract thinking, one of the implications of which is that children develop a new awareness of the self (Galatzer-Levy & Cohler, 1993; Harter, 1990). They become more aware of their own capacity to make decisions and choices. And they begin to focus in new ways on questions of identity development: Who am I? What am I good at? What affiliations and activities make me feel valued and competent?

The answers to these questions of identity are shaped by perceptions and experiences of both the present and the future. During adolescence, children develop an increased capacity to think about the future as connected to the present (Galazter-Levy & Cohler, 1993). An expanding sense of self and of the future means that children begin to evaluate the present in new ways, in search of competence and belonging (Newmann, Wehlage, & Lamborn, 1992). And, adolescents begin to look around them, to their relative status among their peers and to clues they receive from adults and even from the larger society and media for messages about who they are and what they could become.

At the same time that adolescents become more sensitive to their social environments, they also become very real players in shaping relationships with others as well as their performance through differing their own levels of attachment and effort (Spencer, Dupree, & Swanson, 1996). This is why adolescence is often called "a time of choice" (Csikszentmihalyi & Larson, 1984). But adolescence is also a time of choice because social changes in families, in communities, and in schools during this period support these cognitive changes and heighten the importance of identity and decision making. Families often give adolescents increased independence, heightening their ability to make choices and increasing both time spent with peers and nonfamilial adults. In addition, school transitions present an array of new developmental and academic tasks, all of which force the appraisal of personal competence and heighten the need for students to make critical choices.

As students make the transition to high school, they must cope with dramatic increases in school size, the structure of an academic schedule, and the complexity of school environments (Felner & Adan, 1989). These changes are particularly marked in urban areas in which most students attend large high schools. Increase in school size means that students are faced with dramatic changes in the composition of their peer group while receiving greater autonomy in making decisions. The move to high school also involves increases in academic demands. Students begin to take algebra and laboratory sciences and begin work in content areas such as social studies that require different levels of reading comprehension and skills. Adolescents are suddenly faced with less time with teachers, and they are required to learn more in more concentrated periods of time, often in more traditional classrooms with less opportunities for teacher-student interaction, hands-on activities, and group work (Eccles et al., 1991).

The transition to high school becomes important because students' ability to manage these new academic demands and adjust to new learning environments will determine whether they successfully progress through high school. But this period is also important because these rapid changes in tasks and relationships accelerate identity formation. More time with peer groups and more complex social environments heighten the need for adolescents to make decisions about peer affiliations. Increases in the number of adult relationships mean that students must find ways to establish connections with adults and communicate who they are to teachers, administrators, and peers—a process that heightens developmental demands and the need for self-definition. Greater skill demands and differentiation in coursework combined with policies such as tracking that further emphasize relative comparisons, force student assessment of their academic competence, identity as learners, and goals. In essence, as urban students move into high school, they begin to focus on these questions: Am I going to be successful here? Do I have a place here? Have I been realistic in my goals and aspirations? Coming at a development point in which adolescents are forming a sense of their identity and goals, the early years of high school are a time when students are, in new ways, making decisions about their involvement in school, their investment in the work of school, and their goals.

AFRICAN AMERICAN MALES AND THE TRANSITION TO HIGH SCHOOL: ALTERNATIVE HYPOTHESES

Why would African American males in urban environments have greater difficulty during the transition to high school? This article focuses on three not mutually exclusive explanations—differences in external supports and skills, disproportionate effects of school environments, and coping resources and strategies. The first explanation posits that African American males are particularly at risk because they, on average, have the fewest resources to meet new academic and social challenges. First, African American males versus other groups are least likely to have the academic skills that provide a basis for meeting new academic challenges. In 1999, for example, the average reading and mathematics achievement test scores of eighth-grade African American males in Chicago were a year below grade level, the lowest scores of any racial, ethnic, or gender group (Easton et al., 2000). In comparison, the average White male eighth grader in Chicago had test scores over a year higher than those of African American males (Easton et al., 2000). In addition, adolescents with poor academic skills have the greatest difficulty in meeting new academic demands, including moving on to more advanced material (e.g., algebra), coping with increased study demands, and adjusting to changes in teaching style and pedagogy (Eccles et al., 1991).

African American males have also been shown to have fewer familial resources and may receive less guidance and support from families as they make these school moves (Simmons & Blyth, 1987). Adolescents whose parents maintain high involvement and support during high school do significantly better and are more likely to adopt positive coping strategies in response to academic difficulty and stress (Baker & Stevenson, 1986; Newman, Myers, Newman, Lohman, & Smith, 1998; Rumberger, Ghatak, Poulos, Ritter, & Dornbusch, 1990; Simmons & Blyth, 1987; Spencer et al., 1996). In general, parental involvement in school and in monitoring children's education declines during adolescence (Eccles & Harold, 1993; Roderick & Stone, 1998). These declines may be more acute for African American males. Ronald Taylor (1989) argued that the lack of male role models in the lives of African American males deprives them of critical levels of support, particularly during adolescence. In addition, although there is inconsistent evidence to support this, a common argument is that African American parents respond differently to the behavior of boys and hold them to lower expectations (Fordham, 1996; Hare & Castenell, 1985; Hill, 1999; Lewis, 1975; Taylor, 1991).

A second explanation is that African American males, more than any group, experience the most dramatic declines in support and the quality of relationships and school experiences as they make the move to high school. Analyses of surveys and attitudinal scales find that urban adolescents' perception of the quality of their school environment, degree of challenge from their course work, the academic expectations of their teachers, and the quality of their relationships with peers and teachers decline markedly as students move into secondary schools (Reyes et al., 1994; Seidman et al., 1994; Simmons et al., 1991; Simmons & Blyth, 1987). But we might expect these changes to be more marked for males. Any move to more anonymous settings makes it more likely that teachers will rely on stereotypes and prior expectations in forming their relationships with students (Irvine, 1990). Teachers may also be less proactive in reaching out to African American males and less likely to provide them with academic support and high expectations. Furthermore, increased use of tracking in high schools makes it more likely that African American males will be placed in classrooms and tracks that further heighten relative comparisons between students and present even greater declines in academic opportunity and expectations.

African American males may also be disproportionately affected by the increased emphasis on discipline that occurs in large schools. Simmons et al. (1991), for example, found that African American males showed the greatest increase in the incidence of suspensions and probations after the transition to junior high school. The trend throughout the 1990s toward get-tough approaches to violence has disproportionately affected African American males. The conflict in Decatur, Illinois, in which a group of African American males engaged in a brawl and then received tough expulsions that essentially ended their high school careers exemplified the trend in school policies that give no room for mistakes made by African American males. Thus, the second hypothesis is that high schools are too often environments in which African American males are marginalized and unsupported, thus decreasing motivation and sending messages that undermine a positive sense of competence and efficacy in school settings (Davidson, 1996).

The third explanation is that even if African American males have similar skills and supports, minority males would remain at risk because they have fewer positive coping resources and are more likely to adopt negative coping mechanisms, such as avoidance or withdrawal. Managing the stresses and demands of transitions requires that students have coping resources that provide both motivation and strategies for working through problems. Researchers studying motivation and achievement have demonstrated the importance of a sense of efficacy, of competence, and of a clear sense of goals and the future in shaping response to new stresses (Ferguson, 1994; Markus, Cross, & Wurf, 1990; Markus & Nurius, 1986). More negative previous school experiences and students' awareness of teachers perceptions of their group may lead African American males to feel less competent and less efficacious in shaping their school performance through effort, leading to negative coping reactions (Steele & Aronson, 1998). The lack of clear payoffs to education also deprives African American males of a critical coping mechanism (Markus et al., 1990; Markus & Nurius, 1986). Although many youths are clear about the negative payoffs to dropping out, the lack of clear payoffs to persistence and well-defined pathways to success makes it difficult to invest in the future (Oyserman, Gant, & Ager, 1997).

An important extension of this coping hypothesis is offered in the work of Signithia Fordham and John Ogbu (Fordham, 1996; Fordham & Ogbu, 1986; Ogbu, 1985). Coming at a developmental point in which students are forming a sense of their identity and goals, the transition to high school accelerates the need to make decisions about school attachment and identity. As discussed above, African American males may be more likely to receive negative messages from teachers in these new environments about assessment of their academic competence and promise as students. Faced with uncertain payoffs, new academic demands, and negative messages from schools, African American males may begin, as Ogbu and Fordham suggested, to form peer groups and identities that reject performance and the kinds of behaviors that academic success requires.

Understanding whether and why African American males face greater difficulty in the transition to high school can be addressed by asking either how males and females differ in their experiences or by asking the question why some males do better than others. In exploring the evidence for each of these hypotheses, this article focuses on the second question. This chapter begins, however, by examining gender differences in performance during the transition to high school.

THE DATA SET

This study draws on research conducted in an elementary school and high school on the south side of Chicago that served a 100% African American student body population. These schools were one of three elementary-high school pairs in the Student Life in High Schools Project (SLP), a longitudinal study of 98 students in the transition to high school in Chicago.[3] The SLP followed these students from the spring of eighth grade (April 1995) through the end of tenth grade (June 1997).[4] Every three months, students participated in semistructured interviews for a total of nine interviews. Interviewers asked students about their aspirations and plans, discussed their activities in classes and school, and charted their progress as they made the transition. Students discussed their experiences with class work, relationships with teachers, peers, and parents, and involvement both within and outside of schools. The study collected school transcript records, assessments from two of each student's eighth-grade teachers, and three from each student's ninth- and tenth-grade teachers, and data from parents. A formal parent interview was conducted during ninth grade. The study conducted a one-year follow-up at the end of eleventh grade and followed students through official school records and informal contacts through spring of 2000. This article uses data from student interviews, teacher assessments, parent interviews, and official school records collected over the course of the study.[5]

South Side High[6]

The goal of the SLP was to study the transition to high school in an average achieving urban high school.[7] South Side High School is a vocational magnet school. It presented a good choice for those who could not get into the more selective magnet schools but wanted to avoid the closest neighborhood high school. South Side High is one of the largest schools in Chicago, with an entering ninth-grade class of more than 700 students. The high school is somewhat selective, excluding students with very low (three stanines or below) scores in reading and mathematics. Despite its selective status, the percentage of tenth graders reading at or above national norms in the early 1990s was about average for the city. The dropout rate was also slightly lower (35%) than the city average (50%). Ninth-grade transition outcomes were not, however, significantly better. At the time of the study, almost two thirds of all South Side freshmen failed one or more courses at the end of ninth grade.

The Student Sample

Students in the SLP South Side sample were slightly higher achieving than the average Chicago high school student because the minimum achievement criterion at South Side excluded students with very weak skills.[8] The South Side sample was largely a working parent and single-parent sample.[9] Of South Side parents, 78% were employed, with 21% of the households reporting dual incomes. Almost half of the South Side students lived in single-parent homes: 30% lived in dual parent homes, 14% in homes with a parent and other guardian or parental partner, and 11% lived with other relatives. Three quarters of South Side parents or guardians had graduated from high school, and most had either attended trade school (39%) or completed some college (21%).

Elementary School Performance of Males and Females in South Side Elementary

This article reports results for 32 of the 35 students in the SLP South Side sample.[10] Of these students, 17 were female and 15 were male. Table 6.1 compares males and females in the sample on the basis of eighth-grade performance and teacher assessments. As seen in Table 6.1, African American males and females in the South Side sample were quite similar at the eighth-grade level in their school performance, grade point average (GPA), attendance, and achievement test scores. The achievement test scores of both groups were, on average, about a year below grade level based on national norms for entry into high school.

Table 6.1   Description of African American Male and Female Students in South Side High School Sample in Eighth Grade: Eighth-Grade Performance, Teacher Assessments, and Prior School Background

Item	Male	Female
n	15	17
Eighth-grade school performance[a]		
Median GPA 8th grade	2.48	2.45
Median GPA major subjects	2.00	2.00
Median percentage attendance	96	98
Average Illinois Test of Basic Skills (in 8.8 = grade level)		
Reading grade equivalent	7.65	7.72
Mathematics grade equivalent	7.98	7.90
Teacher assessments (average)[b]		
Does this student work hard for good grades? (0 = never, 2 = most of the time)	1.36	1.38
How often does/is student (0 = never, 2 = most of the time):		
Complete homework assignments	1.54	1.65
Receive detention	.32	.04
Disruptive in class	.32	.23
Absent	.13	.34
Engaged in the class work	1.59	1.58
How often spoke to parents (0 = never, 2 = often):		
About a discipline problem	.77	.19
More generally	1.04	.85
How involved are parents (0 = little, 2 = very)	1.18	1.19
Compared to other students in the class, how would you rate this student's (1 = bottom 10%, 3 = average, 5 = top 10%):		
Academic skills	3.23	2.96
Motivation	3.18	2.92
Social skills	3.54	3.31
Home support for learning	3.18	3.11
How likely is it that this student will go to college? (0 = not likely, 2 = likely)	.82	.96

(Continued)

Table 6.1 (Continued)

Item	Male	Female
Prior background		
Percentage ever retained	33	23
Prior school changes		
Percentage none	40	29
Percentage one	27	18
Percentage two to four	20	30
Percentage four or more	13	23

a. Grade point average and attendance were obtained from students' elementary school records kept at the elementary school. These records were missing for 1 female and 1 male.

b. Teacher assessments were collected from two of each student's elementary school teachers: a homeroom teacher and a second teacher, either English or mathematics, depending on what the primary teacher taught. The data in this table represent the average of both teacher assessments when two were available. Unfortunately, one homeroom teacher in South Side Elementary School did not complete teacher assessments.

Eighth-grade teachers in their assessments of students' behavior and skills did not rate the South Side male and female students differently. However, they did report that boys were more likely to receive detentions and be disruptive in class and, not surprisingly, reported much more contact with the parents of male students about discipline problems. This finding is consistent with national data on gender differences in parent/teacher contacts (Bae, Choy, Geddes, Sable, & Snyder, 2000). Gender differences in behavior, however, were not reflected in teachers' assessments of the students' levels of engagement and potential as learners. Moreover, eighth-grade teachers rated the boys slightly higher, on average, in terms of academic skills and motivation. This suggests that in the more personal environments of Chicago's elementary schools teachers may become more tolerant of gender differences in classroom behavior and can find ways to engage boys in the academic process.

Student Transition to High School: Gender Differences in Performance

This study provides a unique opportunity to examine the set of factors that shapes the academic performance of males in the transition to high school. Here we have a sample of eighth-grade boys and girls who live in the same community, attended the same elementary school, and for the most part moved on to the same high school. On most measures, these students showed little differences in elementary school performance.[11] What happened to these students in the transition to high school?

Changes in Grade Point Average and Attendance

Table 6.2 presents changes in GPA, GPA in major subjects (core GPA), and attendance between fifth grade and the end of ninth grade. The median is presented to account for the fact that students who withdrew during ninth grade had a GPA of zero attendance. Both males and females experienced dramatic declines in their school performance during the first semester of high school. Boys experienced significantly larger declines in their grades. Differences in school attendance were not as severe.

Changes in Teacher
Assessments of Students' Behavior

Teacher assessments provide both a look at gender differences in student performance over the transition as well as the extent to which high school teachers viewed males more negatively. Table 6.3 presents eighth- and ninth-grade teacher reports of the average behavior of students in the South Side sample. Ninth-grade teachers reported much more negative behavior than eighth-grade teachers for both males and females. Changes in teachers' reports, however, were more marked for males than for females. For example, although eighth-grade teachers assessed males and females similarly on their engagement in class and completion of homework, ninth-grade teachers reported that males, on average, displayed significantly less effort and engagement than females. Ninth-grade teachers rated the average African American male as being disruptive and a discipline problem.

Ninth-grade teachers also viewed the skills and motivation of their male students more negatively than those of their female students. In eighth grade, teachers reported that the boys had, on average, above-average academic skills. Conversely, ninth-grade teachers rated these same students as having closer to below average academic skills. We saw similar patterns in ratings of home support for learning and motivation.

Table 6.2 Trends in Student Performance Over the Middle Grade and First Four Quarters of High School

African American Males and Females in the South Side High School Sample

	Elementary School		9th-Grade Quarters				Change 8th to end of 9th Grade
	Average Grades, 5th to 7th	8th Grade	First	Second	Third	Fourth	
Median GPA							
Males	2.31	2.48	1.14	1.57	.86	1.00	−1.48
Females	2.51	2.45	2.14	2.00	1.64	1.69	−.76
Median core GPA[a]							
Males	1.83	2.00	.75	1.25	.67	.67	−1.33
Females	1.83	2.00	1.67	1.50	1.00	1.46	−.54
Percentage attendance, median							
Males	.97	.96	.98	.93	.91	.89	−.07
Females	.97	.98	.93	.89	.82	.88	−.10

a. Core GPA and core class refers to performance in a major subject (English, mathematics, science, and social studies).

Table 6.3 Eighth- and Ninth-Grade Teacher Reports of Student Behavior, Skills, Motivation, and Supports: African American Males and Females in the South Side High School Sample

	Males			Females		
	8th Grade	9th Grade	Change	8th Grade	9th Grade	Change
How often is this student (0 = never, 2 = most of the time):						
Sent out of class because of discipline?	.05	.32	.27	.15	.04	-.11
Engaged in class work?	1.59	.93	-.66	1.58	1.26	-.32
Absent?	.13	.92	.79	.34	.93	.59
Disruptive in class?	.32	.73	.41	.23	.27	.04
How often does this student (0 = never, 2 = most of the time):						
Receive detention?	.32	.70	.38	.04	.31	.27
Have unexcused absences?	.23	.99	.76	.31	.71	.40
Complete homework?	1.54	.86	-.68	1.65	1.10	-.55
Compared with other students in the class, how would you rate this student's (0 = bottom 10%, 4 = top 10%):						
Home support?	3.18	2.57	-.61	3.11	2.83	-.26
Social skills?	3.54	3.03	-.51	3.31	2.96	-.12
Motivation?	3.18	2.40	-.78	2.92	2.80	-.35
Academic skills?	3.23	2.40	-.83	2.96	2.70	-.28
How likely is it that this student will go to college? (0 = not likely, 2 = very likely)	.82	.65	-.17	.96	.88	-.08
Does this student work hard for good grades? (0 = never, 2 = most of the time)	1.36	.74	-.62	1.38	1.24	-.14

Differences in gender outcomes over the transition are most pronounced when we look at course failure. In eighth grade, only two students, one male and one female, failed a course. In the first quarter of ninth grade, as seen in Table 6.4, 60% of South Side males failed one or more courses versus 41% of females. By the end of ninth grade, 80% of the males were failing one or more subjects, and more than 25% were failing virtually all their courses or had dropped out. In comparison, at the end of ninth grade, 41% of females were failing a course and only 12% were having serious academic difficulty. Thus, for most males in this study, the transition to high school was devastating. It was marked by significant declines in their performance in school and by extremely high rates of failure. After 90 days in high school, males were already in the position of being at risk of not moving forward. Table 6.4 charts the continued progress of these students through the end of eleventh grade. It shows that the differential pattern in male and female performance persisted and initial course failures developed into continued deterioration of school performance.

Dropout and Graduation Outcomes

The result, as seen in Table 6.5, is that by twelfth grade, 60% of the males in the South Side sample had dropped out of school compared to only 20% of the females. Just as disconcerting, of the six African American males who graduated, only one graduated in the top third of the class whereas four graduated in the bottom third. Graduating in the bottom third of the class means that students have enough credits to graduate but do not have the requisite courses or GPAs that allow them to move on to a competitive college. In comparison, of the 12 South Side African American females who graduated, 4 graduated at the top of their class and 4 graduated in the middle of their class, and 2 in the bottom third of their class. The graduating ranks of 2 students are unknown because they completed high school outside of Chicago.

These dropout and graduation outcomes refer to the percentage of the initial sample that completed a high school credential at a 4-year public or private high school. National data suggest that African American males are equalizing high school outcomes through later completion of degrees.[12] Patterns in dropout behavior among males at

Table 6.4 Trends in Average Course Failure and Dropout Rates by Semester, 9th Through 11th Grade: African American Males and Females in the South Side High School Sample

	9th Grade		10th Grade		11th Grade	
	Percentage Semester 1	Percentage Semester 2	Percentage Semester 3	Percentage Semester 4	Percentage Semester 5	Percentage Semester 6
Males						
Passed all classes	40.0	20.0	20.0	33.3	26.7	33.3
Failed one or more courses or dropped out	60.0	80.0	80.0	66.7	73.3	66.7
Fs in < 33% of courses	40.0	46.7	33.3	20.0	13.3	13.3
Fs in 33% to 75% of courses	6.7		20.0	.0	6.7	6.7
Fs in 75% or more of courses	20.0	13.3	0.13	.3	6.7	.0
Dropped out		13.3	26.7	33.3	46.7	46.7
Females						
Passed all classes	59.8	58.8	52.9	47.1	58.8	64.7
Failed one or more courses or dropped out	41.1	41.2	47.1	52.9	41.2	35.3
Fs in < 33% of courses	17.6	17.6	11.8	23.5	23.5	11.8
Fs in 33% to 75% of courses	17.6	11.8	23.5	11.8	.0	.0
Fs in 75% or more of courses	5.9	5.9	5.9	.0	.0	5.9
Dropped out		5.9	5.9	17.6	17.6	17.6

Table 6.5   Final Graduation and Dropout Outcomes and Class Rank
for Graduates: African American Males and Females in the
South Side High School Sample

Description	Males	Females
Percentage dropped out	60	20
Percentage graduated	40	80
Graduating class rank		
Top one third of graduates	1	4
Middle one third of graduates	1	4
Bottom one third of graduates	4	2
Rank unknown	0	2

NOTE: Dropout and graduation rates refer to the percentage of students who did not graduate from a regular 4-year high school. Several males completed a GED or high school credential in an alternative high school or GED program.

South Side reflect this trend. Of the nine male dropouts in the sample, seven ultimately attended alternative schools or GED programs. Completion rates in these programs, however, could not be determined.

The SLP South Side African American male and female sample is small. These patterns in course failure and school dropout are quite similar, however, to that observed in the larger Chicago Public School system (Roderick & Camburn, 1999). As noted above, the South Side sample is also a more advantaged inner-city sample. These students did not come from the worst Chicago neighborhoods. They did not come from low-performing elementary schools, and they had higher skills than the average Chicago ninth grader on entry into high school. The gender differences in this sample in elementary school also do not reflect the national and Chicago-wide data that would suggest that African American males have substantially lower skills and poorer school performance than females during the middle school years. The unique nature of the sample, however, is a strength. How could such similar students have such dramatically different outcomes over the course of essentially one year and often only one semester? The conventional explanation that African American males are disadvantaged early (and thus the roots of failure are planted long before middle school) cannot explain the differences we observe in this sample.

The Withdrawers, the Disengaged, and the Resilient: A Qualitative Look at Patterns in the Experiences of Males in the Transition to High School

This section presents a qualitative analysis of patterns in the school development of the 15 African American males in the South Side sample during the transition to high school. The qualitative analysis was based on a three-stage methodology. In the first stage, case studies of each student were developed to examine trends in behavior, performance, and enrollment over the transition. In the second stage, case studies were analyzed to identify common patterns in student experiences and students were placed in three identifiable groups. For each group, detailed case studies (see Appendix, pp. 195–220) were developed to illustrate common themes while also revealing the individuality of each particular student. The third stage looked within groups to identify trends and commonalities (themes) in the following four areas: (a) prior school performance and skills, (b) levels and changes in parent/guardian involvement and community supports, (c) experience with class work and relationships with teachers and administrators, and (d) changes in attitudes, goals, and identity.

Withdrawers: Tim, Robert, Marvin, and Eli[13]

The cases of Tim and Robert (all names are pseudonyms) illustrate the main themes observed in the first group. Withdrawers made a very early exit from high school, and that exit was precipitated either by expulsion from school or by withdrawal after a violent incident. This section also draws on data from two other students in this group—Eli, the only student expelled from school for fighting, and Marvin (see Table 6.6). There were five common themes in these students' experiences.

First, all these students had extremely low skills prior to entering high school. Low skills indicated that doing high school work was going to be difficult for these students even with high levels of support. As early as first semester, Marvin was struggling:

> I don't like algebra that much. That be messin' me up. That be confusin' me, and the numbers be messin' me up, and then I get

Table 6.6   The Withdrawers: Eighth-Grade Performance, Family Status, and Summary of Transition Outcomes

Participant	8th-Grade Performance	8th-Grade Teacher's Assessment	Family Status	Outcomes in Transition
Tim (see case)	Prior retention, core GPA = 1.75, reading achievement = 6.5, math achievement = 6.9.	Below-average academic skills and motivation.	Lived with his mother and grandmother. Both died during study.	First semester ninth grade, core GPA fell to .67. He was skipping regularly. In winter, Tim left school after a conflict with gangs. He enrolled in an alternative school.
Robert (see case)	Prior retention, two prior school changes, core GPA = 1.0, reading achievement = 4.9, math achievement = 6.4.	Below-average academic skills and lowest levels of motivation, very likely to drop out.	Lived with his mother and older sister.	Robert attended high school for one quarter. He failed all of his classes. After a conflict with gangs, he withdrew. Attended a GED program but did not complete.
Marvin	Prior retention, prior special education, three prior school moves, core GPA = 2, reading achievement = 8.4, math = 6.3.	Below-average home support for learning and motivation, likely to drop out. Almost never works for grades.	Lived with both parents.	First semester, core GPA fell to .67. He completed the year but did not have enough credits to be a 10th grader. After a conflict with gangs in 10th grade, he withdrew and his parents sent him to Arkansas.

Participant	8th-Grade Performance	8th-Grade Teacher's Assessment	Family Status	Outcomes in Transition
Eli	No prior retention, reading achievement = 6.8, math achievement = 6.4.	Below-average home support and motivation and academic skills, very likely to drop out and likely to have difficulty in high school.	Lived with mother and sometimes father. Older siblings, all of whom graduated from high school.	Attended ninth grade for one semester. First quarter, Eli flunked all his courses, and he skipped and missed school regularly. After a fight, school expelled him and referred him to an alternative school.

NOTE: Core GPA = GPA in major subjects. Achievement scores on the Iowa Test of Basic Skills. 8.8 = grade-level national norms. Data from teacher assessment are based on the responses of teachers on scale items (e.g., *not likely* to *likely*) to specific questions (see Tables 6.1 and 6.2).

bad grades. I don't know—like, I do all my math homework, but I just get bad grades in it. You know, I be tryin.' . . . Biology just get me mixed up. Like, those hard definitions and those long words. Stuff like that.

The changes that students encountered in adjusting to new teaching styles were particularly difficult for this group. As Eli explained, suddenly he was expected to learn the material the first time around with little help.

Different classes, the work, you know, got more advanced . . . it seemed like in elementary school, they . . . care about you a little bit more. . . . Like, in high school, you another one of the 10,000 students or something. Like here, this work [they] explain ya all only one time. . . . And after that, that's it. Eighth-grade teachers, they'll take the time to see you understand it.

Second, students adopted avoidance as a coping mechanism, which allowed them to maintain an abstract involvement in school without participating in the work of school itself. Attendance rates for this group plummeted between eighth and ninth grades. Going to school but not to class was common. Third, parents in this group lost these children to negative peer groups who provided an alternative to school. Researchers have suggested that as boys experience failure in school, they begin to look to peer groups for self-esteem and a sense of belonging (Hare & Castenell, 1985; Spencer, 1995; Taylor, 1989). Peers became an increasingly negative and central force in these youths' lives, providing recognition for students such as Tim (see Appendix, pp. 195–199).

Researchers on African American males have suggested that protective responses from parents and lower expectations for sons contribute to disengagement from school (Hare & Castenell, 1985; Hill, 1999; Staples, 1984). For the most part, parents in this group were not concretely involved in their male children's education and did little monitoring of out-of-school activities. Moreover, these parents often reacted to their son's experiences by trying to protect them. As Tim and Robert's cases illustrate (see Appendix), there was good reason why these parents were worried about the safety of their sons, having had previous experience with loss and violence. In addition, decreasing involvement over the transition may reflect confusion as to how to support adolescent males who have low skills and learning barriers.

Marvin (see Table 6.6) provides an excellent example. Marvin had extremely low skills and, early in his school career, he spent 2 years in a special education classroom. After he failed several courses in the first semester, his parents increased their involvement. His mother tutored him in math and his father worked closely with him on biology. Marvin appreciated his parents' support and attributed their intervention to his being able to pass biology. When asked who or what was the person or thing that influenced him most this year, Marvin answered,

> My father . . . like, when I get in trouble, he will, you know, watch me do my work. . . . He's the one who . . . made me sit in his room and do my work. . . . so I wouldn't of got that grade in biology if it wasn't for my father. . . . I wouldn't have done it, you know . . . you get lazy and stuff.

Marvin's parents enrolled him in a summer program after ninth grade. He had a positive experience in the program, where he found good teachers and supportive peers. This intervention, however, did not sustain him back in his old school. His continued academic problems and involvement with gangs seemed to wear his parents down. After a conflict with gangs early in the year, his parents sent him to live with his brother in Arkansas. To Marvin, this was a rejection. To his parents, it might have been the best that they thought that they could do. Marvin attended school in Arkansas for a while and then moved back to Chicago to live with his sister. He eventually returned to Arkansas where, in 11th grade, he was living with a friend and enrolled in a GED program. Marvin felt that his parents had given up on him and admitted that he "did not call much."

This pattern of decreasing parental involvement as African American males become more involved in peer groups is a familiar one. In his study of African American males in a midwestern high school, Vernon Polite (1995) concluded that the parents of African American male students self-effaced and abandoned their role in the education of their sons (p. 599). Although the parents of this group struggled with how to deal with their children, school personnel did not. They escorted them out the door. It seemed that a goal of South Side administrators was to find students who were either peripheral or core gang members and get them out of school. For Robert and Tim, this process seemed passive: simply let them leave and do not help them solve their problems, so that they feel they are not safe and are unwelcome. In some ways, this response might seem understandable. Administrators in urban high schools are under pressure from parents to make schools safe by getting rid of gangs. The main tactic taken by this school was not to try to reduce gang membership. Instead, the school used any evidence of bad behavior or victimization as a way of labeling students and ultimately rejecting them.

Finally, despite significant difficulties in school, these students continued to maintain high academic aspirations and a strong commitment to finishing school. Mickleson (1990) suggested that African American adolescents maintain abstract commitments to the goals of education but see no probable returns to education based on their day-to-day experiences. The maintenance of this abstract commitment may be an important coping mechanism. As Tim's life (see Appendix) got more difficult, he seemed to reiterate the importance of education as a way of keeping his hopes high. For others, maintenance of goals may reflect a struggle with how to work out the disjunction between the goals that these students thought they should have and the reality of their experiences. Eli often sounded as though he was mimicking lectures from adults. In ninth grade, Eli, who was on the verge of getting expelled, argued that even if he was failing classes, he was going to stay in school. "If I drop out of school, how I get a job, you know. Go to college . . . I'm gonna just stay in there no matter if I get some F's or not—hey, I'll just keep putting more effort into it."

And even after he was placed in an alternative school, which he eventually left because of gang conflicts, he reiterated the importance of these goals. When asked if he thought that gang membership was hurting his future, Eli responded,

> I wouldn't let nothing like that distract me . . . you know, 'cause . . . it all up to you. I want an education, I want a diploma, you know, I wanna get a good job, have a family, and stuff. . . . My main goal in here is trying to get out of here and go back to regular public school . . . do what I gotta do.

Rather than adopting an alternative identity, students in this group seemed to struggle with how to form a new identity in the context of their reality and their aspirations. These students seemed confused about how to resolve the mismatch between what expectations are applauded by adults and their own need for a feeling of competence. Psychologists term this as identity diffusion—lack of identity formation as a reaction to failure (Spencer & Markstrom-Adams, 1990; Taylor, 1989). Thus, although these students expressed high aspirations and the need to do better, their behavior reflected avoidance and flight. For the students in this first group, low skills, lack of support and expectations in their home and school contexts, and the lack of opportunity to find relationships and activities in which they could feel successful, led increasingly to feelings of isolation.

The Disengaged: Malik, Eddie the Mover, Levon, and Reggie the Skipper

Malik's case (see Appendix, pp. 204–209) illustrates patterns in the school behavior of a second group of youth whom I refer to as the disengaged. This section also refers to the experiences of two other students in this group, Eddie and Reggie. Charles (see Appendix), although a graduate, also exhibited many of the themes in this group. The pattern in this second group's behaviors was very different from that of the first group. All these students attended high school regularly and had no involvement in gangs. These students participated in school through the 11th and 12th grades, and their inability to graduate stemmed primarily from a lack of accumulated credits.

Although students in the withdrawal group were distinguished by their very weak skills, students in this second group had significantly better skills and elementary school performance. Their eighth grade teachers would probably be shocked at their school outcomes. Like Malik, these students were recognized by eighth-grade teachers as being very bright. Reggie's teachers called him "highly motivated." Eddie was so bright that he skipped fourth grade and was placed in an honors classroom. Eighth-grade teachers rated these students as hard workers with good skills and with high home support for learning.[14] These students also strongly identified themselves as smart, students who were successful in school.

A common theme in this second group is that of family stress and disruption. Most students lived with one parent and often changed residences during ninth and tenth grade. Malik (see Appendix) changed residences twice during the study. Reggie lived with his mother and sister but during the study moved multiple times and, at one point, lived with an aunt because his mother was having financial problems. Eddie's case was the most extreme and illustrates the stresses faced by students who have multiple residences. In the beginning of the study, he lived with his grandmother, his father, who was a fireman, and his sister and brother. During the study, Eddie moved in and out of residences occupied by his mother, who moved multiple times during the period of the study. In addition, he moved in and out of his father's home and sometimes lived with his grandmother. At some points, he talked about living in all three places: "Like, I stay over my mother's one week, and go over my dad's one week, and then over my grandma's the next week." However, it seemed as though Eddie moved temporarily between residences until people got tired of him or other problems developed. For example, in ninth grade, he temporarily moved in with his mother,

'cause my mother, first she wanted me to come stay over there, so I moved over, and when I was over there, I got into it with some boys around there, she told me to move back with my dad. . . . She didn't want me around there.

Despite obvious home stress, initially the disengaged each had an adult who was involved in his education. That adult involvement, however, was often abstract and disconnected from day-to-day monitoring of the student's work. Parents and guardians stressed education and saw their roles, like Malik's father, as pushing high aspirations, but did not engage in concrete behaviors.

These students, like those in the first group, experienced difficulty handling the new academic and developmental demands of high school. Malik's case (see Appendix) represents the predominant theme in the school behavior of this second group. In the first quarter, these students seemed to enjoy high school but reported having difficulty understanding the work and adjusting to teachers whose attitudes were less than supportive. These students expressed shock at the change in their relationships with teachers. Suddenly, school was not easy and teachers were not nice people who cared about them and their progress. Their coping mechanism was to begin picking and choosing among teachers and differentiating work effort across classes. Reggie, for example, initially had difficulty in both English and Spanish (see Table 6.7). But, although his Spanish teacher was a favorite among the boys for her engaging and

Table 6.7 The Disengaged: Eighth-Grade Performance, Family Status, and Summary of Transition Outcomes

Participant	8th-Grade Performance	8th-Grade Teacher's Assessment	Family Status	Outcomes in Transition
Malik (see case)	One prior school change, core GPA = 1.75, reading achievement = 8.6, math achievement = 8.4.	Likely to very likely to go to college. Not likely to have trouble in high school. Average academic skills. Above-average motivation.	Lived with his father, during study moved back with his mother.	First semester of high school did well, failing only algebra. Second semester and remainder of high school were marked by high rates of course failure and skipping. In eleventh grade, he withdrew.
Reggie (see case)	No prior retention, seven school changes, core GPA = 3.0, reading achievement = 8.3, math achievement = 8.6.	Above-average academic skills, motivation and home support. Always works hard for good grades. Likely to go to college.	Lived with mother and sister. Multiple residence changes.	First semester, his core GPA fell to 1.0. End of year, he had multiple course failures and a pattern of course skipping. Continued in tenth grade. Reggie failed all his courses end of second semester tenth grade. Left for alternative school.
Eddie	One prior retention and one grade skip, one prior school move,	Above-average academic skills, motivation and home	Lived originally with father and	First semester, Eddie failed English. By end of year, he was skipping regularly. GPA fell to 1.0 at the end of ninth grade. In tenth grade,

(Continued)

Table 6.7 (Continued)

Participant	8th-Grade Performance	8th-Grade Teacher's Assessment	Family Status	Outcomes in Transition
	core GPA = 3, reading achievement = 11.0, math = missing (prior year, 9.0).	support. Always works hard for good grades. Likely to go to college.	grandmother. Multiple residence changes.	skipping and course failure escalated so that he did not have enough credits to be an eleventh grader. Eddie stayed in school through twelfth grade before dropping out.
Levon	One prior school change, no prior retention, core GPA 8th = .75, reading achievement = 6.4, math achievement = 5.6.	Below-average academic skills and motivation. Not likely to go to college. Likely to have difficulty in high school. Seldom works hard for good grades.	Lived with his mother.	First semester, Levon failed two courses. By second semester, he was skipping regularly. He continued this pattern of course skipping and failure throughout high school. At end of tenth grade and again in eleventh grade, he failed all major subjects. Middle of twelfth grade, he dropped out.

NOTE: Core GPA = GPA in major subjects. Achievement scores on the Iowa Test of Basic Skills. 8.8 = grade-level national norms. Data from teacher assessment are based on the responses of teachers on scale items (e.g., *not likely* to *likely*) to specific questions (see Tables 6.1 and 6.2).

supportive personality, his English teacher had a reputation for being boring and uncaring. At the end of the year, Reggie passed Spanish because he did extra work and went for help after school. He failed English largely because he stopped going to class.

Differentiation among this group was not limited to work effort in classes. It was also about differentiating effort across the school year. Because quarter grades did not count, many boys thought that they could ignore work in the first quarter and make it up the second quarter. Many of these students did manage, through bursts of attention, to bring up their grades and pass most of their classes. This pattern of differentiation and realizing that they could get by with little effort became a major problem. For all of these students, class cutting was the major factor that undermined their grades. Like Malik, not attending class just became too attractive.

Vernon Polite (1995) argued that a major cause of academic underachievement among African American males is benign neglect from teachers and an administrative structure that does little to intervene and make sure that students are on track and getting proper guidance. Polite (1995) concluded that "it is possible to consider the education of African American males as a complex avoidance process involving parents, teachers, administrators, and the schools themselves" (p. 597). The behavior of students in this second group, their course skipping and course failure, went unchecked. The fact that Malik played cards in the lunchroom for periods on end, and that Reggie came to school but was absent from most of his classes, suggests a disorganized environment that allowed these students to fail miserably. Teachers were only somewhat engaged in the process of trying to get kids to class, but their efforts were disorganized and uncoordinated by the central administration. Although Reggie's teachers in eighth grade called him "highly motivated," one of his ninth-grade teachers commented, "This student does not have the maturity to perform well in high school or the motivation." Another teacher complained,

I called Reggie's mother and told her that he was not attending class. I even got an attendance sheet so she could monitor his attendance daily. I have too many students to continue to run him down.

These comments reflect an expectation that students should be able to handle the demands of high school with little guidance and support. High school teachers' comments also reflected little knowledge of the student's home environment. By the end of ninth grade, Eddie, the student who was constantly moving, was fatigued and showed the stress of living in different places by withdrawing from other students. Eddie's teachers' comments showed little knowledge of this situation. One teacher commented, "Eddie is certainly capable of becoming an exceptional student. Unfortunately, he is very lazy." A second teacher noted, "The student is pleasant when he can have his way. He likes to work alone and he wants to have his own way." Rather than acting as a warning sign of a bright student in trouble, Eddie's behavior was interpreted as oppositional.

Benign neglect allowed these students to discover that they could push limits, pick and choose the classes where they exerted minimal effort, and meet very weak social and academic norms and get by. Benign neglect allowed them to engage in behavior that they themselves knew was wrong without adult intervention designed to correct it. These were all "good kids" who were not in gangs and thus were doing nothing to upset the administration other than undermining their own future. Although these students were disengaged from the work of school, it does not mean that they could not at any point become engaged. Malik's and Charles's geometry teacher (see Appendix) demonstrated that these students could engage in substantive work and demonstrate enjoyment and commitment to learning when in classroom environments that they found set high expectations, provided them a sense of competence and self-esteem. Each of these students had experiences with individual teachers that were positive and to which they responded with equal levels of engagement. But these moments of quality education were islands in a sea of disorder and experiences that consistently undermined their engagement with school.

These students were not, however, getting by. They were failing courses and not accumulating credits needed for high school graduation. The second way that the school engaged in avoidance was in allowing students to progress through high school without making up courses or credits. Students in this group were allowed to stay in high school for three years or more with little prospect of graduating. Eddie, the multiple mover, entered twelfth grade needing to pass four semesters of English, one semester of mathematics, and make up several additional credits to graduate. His twelfth-grade transcript looked just like a twelfth-grade course schedule of a student who wanted a light year: one world literature course, a history elective, his shop major, and physical education. Obviously, Eddie had been allowed to sign up for this schedule with no one explaining that he would not graduate in June. In the winter of twelfth grade, Eddie dropped out.

Although adults in the school can be blamed for a lack of intervention and for not providing guidance to these students, the students also knew that their behaviors were inappropriate. How can we understand the strong disjuncture between these students' school behaviors and their potential? Claude Steele has suggested that racial stigma is an unrecognized component of underachievement among African Americans. As Steele (1992) argued,

> Doing well in school requires a belief that school achievement can be a promising basis of self-esteem and that belief needs constant reaffirmation even for advantaged students. Tragically, I believe the lives of Black Americans are still haunted by a specter that threatens this belief and the identification that derives from it at every level of schooling. (p. 72)

The specter Steele referred to is the fact that even if students are smart, they believe that they are constantly being judged as inadequate and vulnerable. Although Steele focused on college students, for many students in this group, the change in school setting occasioned a similar reassessment of their academic competence, leading to vulnerability and coping strategies that were self-defeating and would sabotage their future success (Murray & Fairchild, 1989).

Students in this second group seemed particularly vulnerable to their experiences in high school in part because they relied so heavily on their elementary school teachers for support and on their success in elementary school in forming a positive sense of themselves. For Malik and Charles, their concept of themselves as good kids who were smart and did well in school was critically important to them. For Charles, whose father was in jail and whose mother was an addict, this identity was a shield to confirm for himself that he was not like his parents and would not follow in their footsteps. But what these students encountered in their high school environment was quite the opposite. They were no longer viewed as good kids who were trying to do the best despite overwhelming odds. They were no longer viewed as smart and as being at the top of their class. Instead, they were viewed by their teachers as unmotivated students with only limited attachment to schooling. They were also, for the first time, experiencing academic difficulty without adults to help them make sense of their problems and cope positively. This academic difficulty further undermined their confidence and made them even more vulnerable to negative interactions with teachers and other school personnel. Research on motivation finds that when students who have academic difficulty react by decreasing their assessment of their underlying ability, they tend to reduce rather than increase effort (MacIver, Stipek, & Daniels, 1991). Students in this group displayed such behavior by running from their classes rather than seeking help.

The negative views of these students that teachers expressed in written assessments must surely have been experienced by the students themselves. These changes sent students such as Malik into a tailspin. The result, as characterized by Claude Steele (1992), is disidentification:

> In reaction, usually to some modest setback, she withdraws, hiding her troubles from instructors, counselors, and even other students. . . . She disidentifies with achievement, she changes her self-conception, her outlook, and values so that achievement is no longer so important to her self-esteem. She may continue to feel pressure to stay in school from her parents even from the potential advantages of a college degree. But now she is psychologically insulated from her academic life, like a disinterested visitor. Cool, unperturbed . . . disidentification undoes her future as it relieves her vulnerability.

Disidentification was central to the process by which students in this second group continued to go to school while failing miserably and avoiding classes. This coping process was painfully illustrated in an interaction that an interviewer had with a teacher and Reggie, who the interviewer usually found wandering the halls. In the spring of tenth grade, the interviewer found Reggie in his drafting class. In front of Reggie, the drafting teacher proceeded to talk about what a poor worker Reggie was, how he never did his work, and implied that I (the interviewer) should have no interest in him anyway. A quick glance at Reggie made it apparent that he was either oblivious to the comments or at least acting like it. The interviewer later brought the incident up with Reggie. Her interviewer's notes read:

Throughout the interview, Reggie was very polite, cooperative, and relaxed as usual. He was attentive and serious as well. At some point, I casually asked Reggie what he thought of his drafting teacher and the class. Reggie denied having any conflicts and in fact suggested that he enjoyed the class, was doing his work, and was doing rather well.

Reggie's "cool pose" in the face of this interaction has been identified as a common coping mechanism among Black males (Majors & Billson, 1992). In response to academic problems, students react with denial, avoidance, and then retreat, a cycle of withdrawal that reinforces the problem. Students retreat because they are not doing well and are confronted with teachers who they perceive as unsupportive and blind to who they really are as individuals. This retreat then undermines the potential for addressing the problem and reinforces the teacher's beliefs that they are unmotivated.

What does this mean for their identity formation? Consistent with Steele's observation, these students did not withdraw from school largely because they were stuck between their parents' and their own expectations of what they knew they should and could do and the reality of their day-to-day experiences in school. Billson (1996) called this coping technique ritualism; the goals no longer seem attainable or relevant but the means to achieve them persist. Jason Osborne (1997) has tested Steele's hypothesis and found that as African American males move through high school, the correlation between their academic performance and measures of their self-esteem declined consistently and dramatically, a pattern not observed in other groups. Unlike the first group, in which failure was met with an increase in abstract attachment to the goal of schooling, among this group, disidentification became a more general confusion over who they were and where they were going. At the end of his 10th-grade interview, for example, Malik exclaimed, "I never wanted to be a lawyer, that was my parents' dream." But he was clearly struggling with who he should be instead. Malik's comments in his last interview demonstrates this struggle for identity:

It just feels awkward. . . . Not knowing which way I wanna go. . . . They want me to do right. It's like I wanna do what they want me to do, but I wanna do what I wanna do.

The Resilient: William, Charles, Donald, Cedric, John, and Scottie

William's and Charles's cases (see Appendix, pp. 209–220) represent themes in the third group of students, those that graduated. This section also refers to Charles's close friends Cedric, Donald, and Scottie. There was very little in this group's elementary school performance that distinguished them from the previous group. All had average to above-average grades in eighth grade. They were recognized by their teachers as bright and committed students who would do well in high school. Almost all the boys in this group, like William and Charles, also struggled with the transition to high school. Because these students look so much like the second group, we have to ask the question, Why did these students make it whereas the others did not? There were four themes that distinguished these students from the previous group.

The first theme was strong family support. Two students in this group lived with both parents, two lived with a mother and had no contact with their father, and two lived with grandparents. Parents and grandparents in this group maintained or increased their support throughout the transition from elementary to high school. All these students had families that were very involved in their son's education, in day-to-day monitoring of behavior and providing support and encouragement. In addition, parents and grandparents in this group placed a high priority on getting their sons involved in structured activities such as sports, academics, and social programs that kept them active and pushed their talents. As adult role models, they also set high expectations, had strong reactions, and actively intervened when their children did not do well, letting their children know that failure was not an option. William's family's reactions to his difficulties in ninth grade and Charles's grandmother's advocacy for him at school (see Appendix) were examples of how parents in this group handled problems in ways that let the boys know that they had high expectations and believed in them. Cedric provided the most poignant example. Cedric fell in love in ninth grade, a relationship that kept him away from his schoolwork. At the end of the year, his girlfriend became pregnant. Cedric's parents had a meeting at their house with the girl's mother and both children, and it was decided that she should have an abortion. This was devastating to Cedric, but his parents were firm and supportive. They spent a great deal of time talking to him, his mom shared her own stories, and his aunt explained that she had made this decision once in her life, too. This experience changed Cedric:

> I'm understanding my whole family more . . . everything started happening, you know. . . . I wanted to grow old so fast. . . . I didn't realize what I was doing. . . . And my father. I got real close to my father like never before . . . one night, I was sitting on the porch . . . I looked at the sky and was talking to God . . . then my father, he came out here, he sat with me, he said, "It's not your fault, you know." . . . And my mom, I learned so much . . . to see my mom sit there and cry about what she went through in the past.

Cedric's story, like William's, is one of parents and families who set high expectations but who spend time talking to their children, helping them make sense of their lives, and guiding their decisions. This pattern of parental involvement is consistent with research that finds that a major difference between dropout and graduates is the extent to which families intervene after academic difficulty and are involved on a day-to-day basis in talking about work in school (Rumberger et al., 1990). Although these families were often positive in dealing with their children, rules and strong discipline were important components. Spencer et al. (1996) have argued that although parental encouragement is significant in determining children's academic expectations and behavior, the degree of family "hassles" reported by youth, such as rules and monitoring, is strongly related to measures of learning responsibility. As Spencer and her colleagues argued, hassles are not always negative. With the exception of Charles, all these students talked about their relationships with their parents and families as getting closer and better between eighth and tenth grade because of high levels of intervention and because problems were worked out.

Families in this group were distinguished by having high levels of nonfamilial supports around them. All but one family were very involved in church, which meant that many other adults were part of these children's lives. Many of these young men found male mentors in pastors and uncles. Families also communicated with one other. Charles and Donald remained best friends throughout high school and Charles's grandmother and Donald's mother talked often.

A second theme was that students in this group took responsibility for their academic difficulty and were proactive in seeking support. Charles's volunteering for the after-school program, which he also got Donald to attend, was critical for both boys in allowing them to make up credits and graduate. These students were honest about when they were having problems and sought help. In the first semester, for example, Donald was disappointed in his grades and was struggling in English and biology. At the end of the year, when asked what teachers he thought he really knew well, he named his English and biology teachers. Incredulous, his interviewer asked, "How come the people in the classes that you're doing the worst in know you the best?" Donald responded that these were the teachers who had tried to help and were the most encouraging, telling him he had to get himself together and "boosting me up." Donald's teachers concurred. His English teacher related,

> Donald is doing well. . . . One day he told me he was tired of failing. Since that day, he has made many accomplishments. Donald has the potential of being a model student at South Side. I hope he keeps up the good work.

This teacher's comment illustrates a third theme. Through their own reaching out for support, the resilient were able to push through stereotypes to get teachers to recognize them as individuals, even though, as William's teachers noted, their day-to-day behavior was often not in line with their ability. As a result, many students in this group were recognized for particular talents, whether it be sports, writing, or music, or simply for their personality. John, like many students, made a strong connection to Ms. R., the Spanish teacher whom he visited after school, and to another teacher for whom he volunteered in the after-school program. Both teachers commented on how much they enjoyed his personality.

The boys' capacity to reach out to their teachers allowed teachers to understand their behavior in a different light. Scottie (see Table 6.8) provides a poignant example. Scottie gave his teacher's name to his social worker to contact for an evaluation of his placement with his grandmother. At the time, his mother had reentered his life, had a baby, and wanted custody of him. His teacher's comments at the end of the year reflected how this knowledge gave her insight into behavior that too often was interpreted as lack of motivation.

Table 6.8 The Resilient: Eighth-Grade Performance, Family Status, and Summary of Transition Outcomes

Participant	8th-Grade Performance	8th-Grade Teacher's Assessment	Family Status	Outcomes in Transition
William (see case)	No prior retentions or school moves, core GPA = 3.25, reading achievement = 9.4, math achievement = 9.8.	Above-average motivation, home support, and skills. Likely to go to college. Always works hard.	Lived with both parents and siblings.	First quarter, William flunked two courses, by the end of the year had raised his core GPA to 2.5. Maintained mainly A's and B's throughout his high school career. He graduated in the top third of his class.
Charles (see case)	One prior school change, core GPA = 1.85, reading achievement = 8.7, math achievement = 8.3.	Motivation rated as above average to top 10%, average to above-average academic skills, likely to go to college.	Lived with grandmother. Later with mother and uncle.	Struggled academically throughout high school with high rates of course failure and skipping. He graduated in bottom third of class.
Cedric	No prior school moves, core GPA = 2.5, reading achievement = 8.4, math = 8.5.	Teacher assessments unavailable.	Lived with both parents.	Initially, good transition. First semester core GPA = 2.0. End of ninth grade, failed two courses. Many course absences. Struggled academically throughout high school. He graduated bottom third of class.
Donald	No prior school changes, core GPA = 2.25, reading achievement = 8.1, math achievement = 9.8.	Works hard all the time, very likely to go to college. Motivation and academic skills rated between above average to top 10%.	Lived with mother and aunt.	Initially good transition, but performance worsened. Consistently Cs and Ds in major subjects. Regular attender. He graduated bottom third of class.

(Continued)

Table 6.8 (Continued)

Participant	8th-Grade Performance	8th-Grade Teacher's Assessment	Family Status	Outcomes in Transition
Scottie	No prior school moves, core math = 8.8, reading achievement = 6.8.	Teacher assessment unavailable.	Lived with grandparents.	Consistent performance in high school. High levels of attendance. Mostly Ds and Cs in major subjects. He graduated bottom third of class.
John	Three prior school changes, core GPA = 3.0, reading achievement = 7.3, math achievement = 8.5.	Average academic skills and motivation. Always does work and is engaged in class. Likely to go to college.	Lived with mother and sister, strongly involved uncle.	Consistent academic performance throughout high school. First semester 9th grade, core GPA 2.75. He graduated middle of class.

NOTE: Dropout and graduation rates refer to the percentage of students who did not graduate from a regular 4-year high school. Several males completed a GED or high school credential in an alternative high school or GED program. Core GPA = GPA in major subjects. Achievement scores on the Iowa Test of Basic Skills. 8.8 = grade-level national norms. Data from teacher assessment are based on the responses of teachers on scale items (e.g., *not likely* to *likely*) to specific questions (see Tables 6.1 and 6.2).

Scottie is a soft-spoken young man whom I like a lot. But there are so many times he seems lost. At times, he seems depressed, and a couple of times he had asked to go to the back of the room because of a headache. When he does his work, it is done well. But there are many times he seems just too tired to do his work. . . . I feel he has untapped potential . . . . I received an evaluation from a social services agency. . . . This indicates there are some family situations that need intervention. . . . I don't know if this is a fair evaluation, but I have a feeling that Scottie needs a secure home . . . this is a feeling I have and the reason I refer to him as lost.

In summation, these students adopted coping mechanisms that allowed teachers to get to know them. These strong relationships that went beyond the classroom allowed them to put up with the daily hassles that were a constant threat to their school performance. Where did these students get such strong coping mechanisms? Research on resilience highlights the role of disposition of having a pleasant outlook and personality in shaping people's capacity to cope positively with stress (Masten, 1994). Differences in personality may come into play. But it is also likely that students in this group were modeling the strategies that their parents used with them in handling problems by communicating and taking responsibility. Such familial patterns may not only have allowed the boys to develop these capacities—being verbal and communicating with adults—but also provided them with successful strategies to deal with problems. Students in this third group also evoked their parents' strategies of involvement in extracurriculars as an important protective mechanism. This involvement, moreover, ended up providing these students with critical identities.

The last theme is that these students developed alternative identities that allowed them to distinguish themselves from peers and resist peer pressure. William (see Appendix) found in religion an identity that allowed him to have a positive sense of self and a strong achievement ideology while saying no to peers. For others, involvement in sports provided a healthy athletic identity that promoted positive school performance because of required GPAs, and gave them a reason to work hard. Cedric, who was also a marginal student, found a nonacademic identity that worked similarly. In ninth grade, Cedric participated in a church music camp and found that he was quite talented. Over the next three years, music became Cedric's life, ultimately providing an avenue to college and high levels of involvement outside of school. Cedric describes how music changed his relationship with the security guards after he found a practice piano at school:

It's like, security guards and all them, they come so they can hear me. . . . remember one of the security guards, you know, they just didn't like me for some reason. . . . I don't know why, I ain't never do nothin to them. . . . But now everywhere I go, they just love it. They wanta hear me play and everything, you know?

These students did not develop an alternative identity that chose White culture over African American culture. At no point did these students express that they felt that they were rejecting an identity as an African American male. Instead, these students often used racial ideology to justify the need to reject the behavior of their peers, a finding consistent with findings from Bowman and Howard's (1985) and from Sander's (1997) work that indicates high levels of racial identity and parental discussion of racial barriers promote achievement. It did, however, mean that, like William, they were aware that they were rejecting their peers, if not their racial identity. Cedric, for example, explains why he did not hang out with people in his neighborhood, even in elementary school.

Because, you know, it's kind of hard for a Black man, so, basically, I have to say no because we gotta have school. . . . So we can learn. Learn everything we need to know so it won't be so hard for us . . . so we won't end up like people out there. You know, the people you be seeing on the corners. So we won't have to go through . . . peer pressure, gangs, stuff like that.

I termed this final group the resilient because they replicate the major findings of studies of resilience. Strong families, high levels of connectedness to adults, involvement in structured activities, coping mechanisms that allow them to reach out for help and form relationships, strong problem-solving and communications skills, and the development of positive racial and achievement identities are all characteristics that have been linked to resilience in high-risk settings (Masten, 1994; Wang, Haertel, & Walbert, 1994). With all of this in their lives, these young men's outcomes still look like underperformance. Most of these students left high school with low GPAs and barely enough credits to graduate. In the end, the high school did not rise to what these students brought to it. Resilience in school communities with weak academic and social norms, particularly for African American males, means that success was graduating from high school and surviving, not excelling in it and pursuing additional schooling.

CONCLUSION

A researcher encountering the African American male students in the SLP at tenth grade would most likely conclude that there is strong evidence for disengagement from school and underperformance. The withdrawers were out of school, pursuing alternative degrees with varying levels of participation, were unemployed, and not engaged in any meaningful activity. The disengaged were attending school regularly, doing nothing, seldom going to classes, and failing courses. Many of the graduates were just barely getting by academically. But this cross-sectional look misses the process by which these students' day-to-day experiences in school undermined academic engagement and performance, by which adults' reaction to difficulties ranged from neglect to rejection, and by which students' own coping mechanisms, in the absence of any adult guidance and within environments of weak academic structure and norms, undermined their performance. This section discusses some of the policy implications of this analysis.

Students in the first group, the withdrawers, faced significant barriers to doing the work of high school. They had extremely low skills, little parental support for their education, and high rates of family disruption and loss that made them vulnerable to gang pressure and provided them with few coping resources to manage developmental demands. An important policy debate is whether the national trend to end social promotion and reliance on high-stakes testing will place these vulnerable students at even greater risk. The students in this study were one of the last groups of Chicago eighth graders to enter high school before Chicago ended social promotion by adopting minimum test score requirements for promotion. None of the students in this first group would have met the eighth-grade promotional test cutoff. They would most likely have been retained. But the experiences of this group demonstrate that the alternative of allowing them to progress without intervention sets them up for failure. For this group, the first policy response is to increase the basic skills of African American males through much earlier intervention.

Many of the students in this first group found alternative schools that met their need for personalized small environments that provided alternative avenues to work and training. At present, however, such opportunities are rare and often come after students have had substantial difficulty and are facing an uphill battle in trying to turn themselves around. For these students, the options of alternative schools and GED programs came after failure and withdrawal and were presented as punishment for their behavior rather than as alternative options. Developing programs, both within and outside high school, that could successfully serve students such as Robert and Tim is not, however, the way that most school systems are moving. In the time since Robert and Tim entered high school, Chicago, like many school systems, has adopted core academic requirements for all freshmen and is moving toward mandatory subject area exams for promotion. Even if Robert and Tim had managed to stay in school in their freshman year, such requirements would place them in a position of fighting an uphill battle where they would consistently be sent the message that they are at the bottom of the queue. Although such approaches may benefit many, these approaches may not serve the need for students such as Robert and Tim who might most benefit from a focused program in which adults are not trying to pull them over hurdles and avoid failure but working with them to develop alternative avenues that build their skills and develop their self-esteem and goals.

The second group also experienced academic difficulty, stress, and lack of support. These students also experienced significant familial stress that reduced the supports available to them. But this group entered high school with high levels of engagement in learning, high expectations and commitment to schooling, and adequate skills to take on the task. Policies that work to increase students' skills are inadequate if we continue to operate high schools such as South Side High. For this second group and also for the graduates, the most direct policy implication is high school reform. A central theme in this article is that the traditional large anonymous urban high school with its uneven quality, disconnected programming, and lack of attention to guidance and student development is simply not up to the task of promoting high levels of engagement and achievement for minority adolescents in urban communities. For this middle group, a lack of consistent and concrete home support for their education and the stresses that these students experienced outside school made them even more vulnerable to their experiences at school. Rather than being a place of consistency, quality, engagement, and support, high school for these students was an arena of risk and failure, an arena in which their day-to-day interactions undermined their school attachment and sense of competence and self-esteem.

The reality of urban environments and the complexity of families should not be an excuse. Rather, it is even more paramount that high schools develop effective school environments that give African American males the best opportunities possible and are not places in which only the resilient can be successful. Research has demonstrated that urban schools can promote high achievement and engagement of students when they provide students with high expectations, quality teaching, and approaches that are both highly structured and personalized (Lee & Bryk, 1989; Lee & Smith, 1995; Lee, Smith, & Croninger, 1997). Effective personal environments are those that develop a web of support that combines individualized attention and monitoring of student progress, opportunities for students to develop relationships with adults, and safe and orderly learning environments that provide consistent expectations for behavior. The conclusion one draws from the experiences of both the disengaged and the resilient is that these students needed an effective high school if they were to be successful. But although we are continually asking more of students, we are not asking this of high schools. The reform of high school environments should be a top priority in addressing the racial achievement gap and in improving the college prospects of African American students, particularly males. In urban areas, there must be a systematic attempt to reduce the size of high schools and promote extensive reform of educational environments so that they provide personalized assistance and allow teachers to develop cohesive communities that meet the academic and developmental needs of the youth that they serve. A critical policy question is, How can schools and communities provide for urban students the kinds of supportive relationships that were identified as critically important in shaping the school performance of the resilient? At present, the most popular approach to improving educational support and outcomes for minority students has been mentoring and out-of-school support programs such as GEAR UP. The popularity of these programs stems from the demonstrated success of mentoring and enrichment programs (Heckman & Lochner, 2000; Mincy, 1994; Walker & Freedman, 1999). The results of this article would also provide support for such initiatives because they attempt to provide resilience supports for students. As we saw with the resilient group, the presence of non-familial adults who were willing to be coaches and guides was critical in forming their sense of persistence and coping. Their extracurricular engagement allowed them to identify talents and develop positive alternative identities and life themes. The success of these approaches suggests that community and youth organizations can play a pivotal role in developing academic interventions for African American males.

A final policy question is, Is there a role and need for African American male-centered approaches? There are two alternative approaches in developing gender- and race-centered approaches. The first option is to provide student development and specialized support programs within high schools. Evaluation of African American male-centered programs and classrooms has found positive effects on student-teacher relationships and student effort and engagement as having the most recent peer or "posse" support programs (Hopkins, 1997). The use of advisory groups, support groups within the high school, and the beginning of student development programs in which African American males within school environments can find supportive relationships and opportunities for engagement may be a promising approach. Such efforts not only build peer and adult support for African American males and provide in-school opportunities for problem-solving and skill development, they also send a strong symbolic message to males that the school sees their education as a priority.

A second approach is to raise the consciousness of teachers and parents about the developmental and academic needs of African American males. This was the successful approach used by the American Association of University Women in their efforts around girls. This approach calls for national analysis of gender differences in performance within racial and ethnic groups, dissemination of data and public informing, and the development of materials and opportunities that provide professional development opportunities for teachers and schools. A first step in this direction is to gain adequate national data. Although the analysis presented in this article suggests that African American males in inner-city environments are at significant risk for school dropout and failure in their early high school years, there is scant nationally available data and analysis that allow us to assess the extent to which these patterns in school performance vary across community, school, and family contexts. The U.S. Department of Education reports almost all outcomes in publicly available tables by gender and by race/ethnicity, not by gender within racial categories. The lack of regularly reported and widely accessible national data and analysis that investigates whether these differences are reflected in national samples and can be used as indices to track progress in addressing problems creates a substantial gap in our ability to create informed public discourse and policy approaches. There is a role for professional organizations, advocacy organizations, the Department of Education, and the foundation community in working to build research, knowledge, and public informing activities around the educational and developmental progress of African American males.

APPENDIX: FIVE CASES

Case 1: Tim, Waiting on That Big Day

Tim in Eighth Grade. Tim was an adolescent who had always struggled academically. His eighth-grade achievement test scores placed him almost two years below grade level in both mathematics and reading. He was older than his classmates because of repeating second grade. Tim's teachers assessed his academic skills and motivation as below average and reported that he was only somewhat engaged in their class. Despite his low skills and lack of substantive engagement, Tim was very committed to the goals of schooling. He maintained an average GPA throughout elementary school and had better than 95% attendance.

In eighth grade, the future was Tim's main focus. Tim wanted to be a criminal lawyer, a goal he maintained throughout his first two years of high school despite all his difficulties. Tim was excited about high school.

I'm really happy about going. I think it's going to work out. . . . As long as I stay in school, it's going to work out. I'm going to get an education. I'm going to stay in school, I'll cause no problem . . . you got to have an education to get a job. Can't be no dummy. I want to be a lawyer. . . . I want to help these people out that's in jail. They ain't supposed to be in there.

Tim believed that having high self-esteem was the way to reach his goals. He was an only child who lived with his grandmother and mother. In the spring of eighth grade, his grandmother had just been admitted to the hospital and was in critical condition. His mother was also ill. Tim's out-of-school time included taking care of the house, trips to the hospital, and accompanying his mother on visits to the doctor.

Tim felt very supported by his eighth-grade teacher, whom he described as a "good man." He liked the way the teacher talked to them about the importance of staying away from gangs and how he believed in his students. Even a year later, when asked to describe highs and lows in his life, Tim picked his eighth-grade experience as his high. At the end of ninth grade, Tim reflected on how eighth grade was different because teachers believed in students, worried about how students were doing, and cared. Tim explained,

My eighth-grade teacher, he was something else. He said the day I give you the diploma . . . I'm gonna set you free. . . . He mostly gave us this . . . respect. That's mostly—that's what this world is about. Respect. . . . If you respect me, I'll respect you.

Tim in Ninth Grade. Two days before his graduation, Tim's grandmother died. Tim spent the summer hanging out with friends, taking care of his mom, and "hanging with the females." He was becoming very social, a trend that concerned his mom. Tim's mother attended his high school orientation and used the opportunity to talk to him about his need to attend to his schoolwork. "She said I gotta keep focused on what I'm doin' instead of the girls and all that. . . . I gotta keep my mind that I'm graduatin' from South Side High."

During the first semester, Tim passed all his courses except English. He attended school regularly but was also "playing" a lot. He admitted that he was having difficulty in his classes and was disappointed with his work. After report card pickup, his mother urged him to get to work. "She just say I gotta improve more and stop talking on the phone like 2, 3 hours, playing outside, and get down to these books. . . . I just need to slow down . . . that's all, me and my friends, that's all we do is hang out, hang out with females, that's about it. But now I gotta get down to these books."

Despite his good attendance, Tim's activities outside of school time were getting increasingly dangerous. His friends from eighth grade were in a gang that was in conflict with another gang in the school. In the fall, he was worried that hanging out after school might lead to conflicts and fights. By spring, this prediction came true. Tim's associates met with another gang and had a confrontation. Someone pulled a gun on him, and his friend got hurt. When his mother got no positive response from his counselor, she pulled him out of the school.

> Well, I left South Side third marking period 'cause me and a couple of my friends was having a little trouble up there. One of my friends had got, um, jumped on and they was pulling guns on people and all that . . . so my mother just decided to just transfer me out of there 'cause my life was way important than just, you know, going to school. I'm gonna tell you the truth, it was mostly the guys I was hanging with. . . . It was like . . . gang bangers, but the kids I graduated with, we always hung together . . . and my boy had got jumped on real bad. Why stay somewhere you know you're in danger. . . . That's like my mama told me, we ain't going to no other funerals.

Tim's mom enrolled him in an alternative high school downtown. The small school offered him a break from his peers and provided the structure he needed. He liked the way teachers treated students with respect. Tim continued to maintain his goal to become a lawyer. When asked what he learned this year, Tim responded,

> I learned a whole lot. I learned . . . you don't have to hang with a certain group of people to be recognized. You can hang by yourself and you do better off by yourself in a way. If you dress like a gangbanger, you're gonna get acknowledged as a gang-banger. If you dress with nice clothes on, you're gonna be presented as a nice person. . . . But, see, I'm going downtown and I don't have to worry about every few steps . . . watching my back or nothing.

His goal was now

to keep my mind on my schoolwork. Get all good grades and stuff. Keep out of gang activity. Keep on straight ahead. . . . I got a plan and I'm gonna get it done. If it take me a couple of years, I'm gonna get it done. . . . You always can't go straight to the top. You're gonna get stopped somewhere. But it's a matter of staying focused. Knowing what you have to do, right?

Tim in Tenth Grade. During the summer, Tim started getting very serious with one girlfriend. Tim's trouble's, however, were not over. In the fall, his mother became very ill and his best friend was going to die.

But my best friend right now is my mama. And my best friend ain't done too well. . . . One day, you're gonna have to take care of yourself, and right now I'm taking care of mama.

Her death only increased his resolve that he had to keep going to school and

just keep on going. Just like a whole lot of people out here say they're tired of school. How can you get tired of school? You gotta have an education to get a job. Not one of these flipping burger [jobs]. I'm talking about a real job. In a big office one day. Get a secretary or something. Ain't got time to be behind nobody's hot grill. I can't, can't stop going to school. She would have wanted me to finish, so I gotta finish. Gotta make her proud. . . . Gotta keep movin.'

After his mother's death, Tim moved in his with aunt and continued to go to school. Now, however, there was a new responsibility in his life, a son. In the spring of tenth grade, this new responsibility and the need to get a job and work out his relationship with his son's mom was taking precedent. It was clear he was getting tired.

Oh well, you know, Mike [the interviewer], it's the same old, same old. Me trying to get my work done and get out of school. And just, finish, finish high school for right now. . . . Staying on track. Going every day. Keeping good attendance, good grades. Everything is working out for the best . . . gotta start making your own money. Can't be no dependent on nobody the rest of your life. Older you get, gotta get on your own. . . . Man, I really don't know right now. 'Cause I'm just trying, you know, get everything situated. . . . 'Cause I'm young, gotta raise another life. But, hey, you drop your pants and play, you gotta pull out your wallet to pay.

The problem was that his ex-girlfriend was mad at him and living in a very dangerous project with her grandmother. Tim did not feel safe going to visit his son, but he was clearly taking responsibility.

But me and her ain't on real good terms right now. So long as I take care of him, that's what's important. My responsibility. . . . It's gonna be a struggle, but, you know, you gotta love what's yours and that's it. You just can't get down, "Oh man, I'm young, got a baby." Can't be, can't be ignorant. You just gotta do what you gotta do. . . . I'll try to help 'em, help, help out the best way I can, put effort to pitch in, that's all I can do. For now. When I get a job, it's gonna be a little something different.

When reflecting over the year, Tim noted that he felt that between ninth and tenth grade, he grew up "from a little boy to become a man." When asked what was the best thing that had happened that year, however, Tim's answer reflected his discouragement and pain. He could not think a best thing that happened that year, rather he answered, "I'm waiting on that big day. Best is yet to come. Save the best for last." Tim continued attending the alternative school. His 11th-grade transcripts from the school did suggest that he was attending regularly and received an alternative degree.

Case 2: Robert, Trying to Find a Way

Robert in Eighth Grade. Robert was going to face an uphill battle in high school. His eighth-grade achievement scores placed him more than two years below grade level in reading and mathematics. In elementary school, he had difficulty with behavior problems and discipline. Outside school, Robert had a fight in which he was stabbed and, in a separate incident, had been arrested. He was on probation. Robert's goal in eighth grade was to be a police officer and go to the police academy.

Robert lived with his mom, who worked part time, and his older sister. At the time, his brother was in jail, and Robert's parents were separated. Like his brother, his older sister had also had problems. His sister had dropped out of high school after getting involved in a gang dispute and being severely attacked and stabbed.

Robert in Ninth Grade. During the summer before high school, Robert was involved with a tough crowd. He spent the summer "playing" and lost several friends to gang violence. Robert enrolled at South Side High but was not attending regularly. He was absent 15 of 45 days the first quarter and, when in school, was skipping often. He explained that his mother was not waking him up on time. "She ain't been waking up. . . . I ain't got no alarm clock. She gonna get me an alarm clock." Robert's mother had a different explanation. He was leaving the house but not going to school. Robert's mother knew that he was a struggling student and had tried to get his elementary school to test him because "Robert is sort of slow."

By the winter of ninth grade, Robert's mom wanted to transfer him to another high school because of his refusal to go to South Side. She was driving him back and forth from school so he would go. When asked what was the hardest thing about raising a teenager, she replied, "protecting him." Robert's mom complained that she found him increasingly moody and distant. She was struggling with Robert. When asked what she was most proud of about Robert, she paused before replying that she did not know.

Early in the school year, Robert was having gang conflicts. In the winter, his mother witnessed an incident in which he was threatened by other boys. After this episode, she allowed Robert to stay home. Robert explained,

One day, I was leaving out, and they started following me and, um, I guess they thought I was gonna get on the bus, 'cause they be trying to jump a lot of students on the bus, but my momma come and picked me . . . so I walked over to the car, and they were following me, and they asked me if I was a Blackstone, and I said no . . . they asked me what am I, and I just kept walking. Then, they said something, "Yeah, you better get in the car" or something like that, and my momma heard them too, and that's when she got out of the car, 'cause she thought they was gonna jump on me, 'cause it was about 10 boys, and she had gotten the club out of the car. So, they had walked off, said whatever, you know, "You better not come to school tomorrow" . . . so I haven't been there for a couple months.

Robert's mom went to the school to talk to the assistant principal and principal. Because this was the most recent of several incidents, the principal assumed that Robert was in a gang and gave him a list of alternative schools. Robert insisted that he was not a gang member.

But, the principal didn't understand that, she thought I was something in another gang, that's why the boys kept messing with me, that's what she said. [Interviewer: Are you in a gang?] No! And that's what I told the assistant principal, too. [Interviewer: But, they wouldn't believe you, 'cause they keep, these gang kids keep messing with you.] Yeah, the incidents keep happening. The assistant principal asked me, what organization was I in, and I told her I wasn't in no organization. And the principal told me, "Well, you know you're lying." She said it like that. And she gave me this list of alternative schools to give to my mother, she told me to call some of these schools up.

Robert's mother called several area high schools, but they were all full. She called the alternative school that his friend Eli was also attending and signed him up for July when he would turn 16. But when July came, Robert reported that he really did not want to go to an alternative school and would wait for the summer when he could go back to a regular high school. In the meantime, his mother got him a Big Brother through his aunt.

At first, I didn't want to think about it . . . more like I thought it was more like a counselor or something. But, it was like the big brother, you . . . somebody to go out with and everything, and kick it. . . . Like that. Saturday, we'll go get something to eat, go to breakfast or something, just ride around and talk about most things . . . about things that I wanted to do when I get older and stuff like that. He'll tell me things I gotta do to accomplish [being a policeman], and stuff like that.

By the end of ninth grade, most of Robert's friends had left school. He spent the summer "driving with his friends." Robert's aunt offered him a job working at her chicken shack. He did not take her up on her offer. His explanation for not taking this job was a similar refrain for him.

> She told me to come up there. I just didn't go. I was tired that day, and, uh, I haven't talked to her since then. [Interviewer: How about the next day?] I wanted this summer job, . . . I filled out a whole bunch of applications. [Interviewer: But you aunt was kind of handing you a job there?] Yeah, but I didn't really want to work there. I wanted to work like around my house . . . Dominicks [a supermarket] or places they got clothes stores and stuff, got few applications . . . I didn't get no contact, yet.

By the summer, Robert had also lost contact with his Big Brother, admitting he had let that relationship slide. In response to the question of when was the last time he had seen the mentor, Robert responded,

> Not since that last day. I was supposed to see him again in, um, I had something to do that day and I didn't call him back. I got to call him, though. But I had to do something that day we supposed to have met up. I haven't talked to him since that day. Forgetting and stuff.

Robert's response of "forgetting" was somewhat selective. During the entire SLP project, Robert never missed an interview and called after the project was over whenever the study asked students to check in.

Robert in Tenth Grade, Fall. Robert did not go to his neighborhood high school as planned. Instead, he enrolled in a GED program. Robert found his niche. It was small and he felt successful. He liked the individual attention he received and particularly made a connection with his law teacher, a policeman. He felt that all his teachers would "talk to you solo, you know what I'm saying. . . . The way they explain it. If you don't understand it, all you gotta do is ask for help. And they'll teach you how to do it individually. . . . You understand?"

The first time he took his GED exam, he failed. But he persisted in attending the program and planned to take the test again. Unfortunately, Robert was arrested in the middle of the semester because he had broken parole. The police arrested him at school. Robert felt positive about how his teachers at school, particularly his law teacher, handled it.

> Like, the police had came with the warrants to come get me from school. . . . So he's [his teacher] talking to them. . . . He said that, uh, that Robert Smith is turning himself in, so that really helped me out. . . . He was always trying to check because he's the police, so I knew he was checking up on my name and stuff like that. He's real cool. . . . you know how police is, towards Black teens too? . . . when it was time for me to go down and stuff, he'd tell us, say, "Stay out of the streets." Things like that, so, you know, he really be helping us out. . . . I turned myself in. It looked really good to the judge.

Robert was in the juvenile detention center for a month before his case came to trial. He was released but felt he could not go back to the program because he had missed too much time. He continued to talk about becoming a police officer and studying law and was thinking about the Job Corps. At his court appearance, Robert's mom seemed very down. The interviewer's notes read,

> She looked very weary and expressed concerns not only about her son's run-in with the law but also the threat of her having to find a new place to live, as her Section 8 housing status was coming under scrutiny. She perused the apartment listings while we waited. The subtext of her conversation seemed like surrender and defeat. She seemed almost resigned to the fact that Robert would not be released from the center. The actual hearing was very brief. The judge looked at his report card (he was taking classes at the center) and smiled at me. She said, "Excellent student," read his A's and B's out loud, and asked Robert why he couldn't do the same outside the classroom. She let him go.

Follow-Up Contacts With Robert. After the court appearance, Robert's mother moved. Several months later, Robert checked in with his interviewer, leaving a phone message with his new number. The interviewer tried several times, but his mom reported that he was not home much. His mom reported that she was still planning to get him into the Job Corps. At the end of the year, in an official check-in,

Robert reported that he was sort of looking for a job and that his mom was supposed to call the Job Corps. His sister had moved out, his brother was back in jail, and he had not seen his father in some time. He reported that he was spending most of his time playing basketball and hanging around the house. He admitted he was pretty bored. Robert stayed in contact. One year later, Robert was still living in the same apartment and was not working and not in a GED or Job Corps program. He was still talking about doing it.

Case 3: Malik, Goals of Being a Valedictorian Wasted in the Lunchroom

Malik in Eighth Grade. Malik stood out among eighth graders as a bright young man who was challenging himself and others around him. An eighth-grade teacher's description captures his spirit.

> Malik is an acute student. He does his work. He's very outgoing and egotistical. (Confident). He can be overbearing in his opinions. Academically, he does well. He believes he knows it all. He needs to listen more—Learn to listen and listen to learn.

In elementary school, Malik was very involved in extracurricular activities. He played basketball on both his elementary school and church teams. His goal for high school was to get on the basketball team, get straight As, and be "top of the basketball team headed for valedictorian." He described himself as a motivated adolescent who liked learning and liked teachers who set high standards. For example, Malik thought it was good for teachers to be tough— "'coz it makes you wanna push to do better. 'Coz you know that they won't, um, give you a break, so it makes you want to prove them, prove to them you can do better."

In elementary school, Malik had a positive peer group who he described as Black-identified and high performers. His friends called him the little Malcolm X because he liked to "read a lot of Black books." Malik was proud of his identity. When asked how he thought smart students were treated, Malik responded,

> Most of the time, they happy for 'em, but some might try to talk about 'em, and call 'em nerds, and things. . . . Like, when we do Black history stuff and I get good grades, they say, "Aw, he just

Malcolm X, that's the only reason why he get good grades." In a way, it's a compliment 'coz they . . . admittin' that I'm smarter, and in a way, it's kind o' like they're a little jealous. [Interviewer: Um, and what does that, what does that do to you?] It just makes me wanna do even better and make them even MORE jealous.

In eighth grade, Malik and his little sister moved in with his dad because his mom was drinking and "kind of wacko." He liked living with his dad because he was a man and gave him more responsibility, including making him share in chores like cooking and cleaning. Malik's dad was a role model and source of support. In a parent interview, his dad stressed that he emphasized work ethic and church involvement and felt that his biggest strengths as a parent were "role modeling, work, responsibility, promptness, and consistency." He wanted Malik to be a lawyer and worried that he would "give up on education, following in his relatives' footsteps and have low motivation in the face of low opportunity." Malik's dad found that the hardest thing about being a parent is to "keep him in perspective." He admitted that Malik had an attitude that bothered his teachers, but he clearly enjoyed and was proud of his son.

Malik in Ninth Grade. In the first semester, Malik got Bs and Cs. He was playing football and, despite being surprised at how much gang activity there was in the high school, felt positive about the school. He flunked algebra, a course he admitted was hard, and he was going to tutoring. "I used to be a good math student. I mean, I just wonder. How come I can't get that algebra? It just makes me mad that I can't get it."

To Malik, the biggest difference between elementary school and high school was the independence. When asked what he would tell an eighth grader about high school, Malik explained,

To expect a big change. . . . Like, my 8th-grade teachers told me. I didn't really believe them. . . . It's not that they [elementary school teachers] care more about youth, the grammar school teachers are more on you about getting you work in. But in high school, if you don't get it in, that's your fault.

Malik's dad was also initially positive. At report card pickup, he found the teachers wanted to talk and that they knew and liked his son. He was worried about Malik's work effort and increased his monitoring of his homework but found it a bit hard to help.

In the winter of ninth grade, Malik's school performance took a dramatic turn. In his third quarter, he flunked three courses and got Ds in the remainder. He started skipping both his academic support class and algebra. By the spring, his performance deteriorated further. In the second semester, Malik missed only one day of school but had 18 absences in biology and 8 in algebra, both of which he flunked. His ninth-grade teachers reported that he rarely completed homework and was not engaged. As one teacher commented, "Student has excellent potential. Student is lackadaisical and little motivated until the last minute to do his work. Quite playful. He does not get serious until time for grades." Malik explained that he thought he was just slacking off a bit because quarter grades do not count. "The first two marking periods, I was just, like, getting used to the school and I had to do my best, but this one because I figure because this one didn't count, I could slack off a little bit and it wouldn't hurt nobody." His father reacted strongly, punishing Malik.

> I know I am going to get in trouble. He been on me a lot and getting me on the right track, and I'm on punishment until the end of time.
>
> [Interviewer: Until the end of time?] Until I move out of the house!

During the summer when asked to reflect back on his problems, he attributed his failures to "playing."

> Playing . . . and gambling. . . . Playing cards at school. . . . You see, the problem was, I don't know why I started hanging around two guys, and they got to playing cards, and then it's— be like one of them, like, aw, you can miss this class this one day to go in the lunchroom. . . . And I do it, and that's what messed me up, this following them and trying to do what they do.

In addition, Malik admitted that he had continued to struggle with algebra because it was so hard. When asked why he did not get help, he explained that he was too proud to ask. "It wasn't beyond me. . . . I don't never think I need help in nothing."

Malik in Tenth Grade. Malik made up his algebra credit during the summer and entered 10th grade resolved to behave differently. This resolution was not followed. By the fall of tenth grade, Malik's interest in school deteriorated even further. Given his father's persistence, he continued going to school on a regular basis, but he spent most of the time in the cafeteria playing spades. In the first semester, he missed more than 20 days in all of his classes except geometry. His lower grades kept him off the sports teams. Malik was frustrated with himself. When asked what would make him feel better about school, he responded,

> Well . . . if I didn't play so much. If I could just come back and do what I'm supposed to do. . . . I don't know. . . . I'm not focused. . . . I'm still really messing up in grades and that. I'm staying unfocused. . . . I stay focused for a minute and then I, uh, get lazy. [Interviewer: What do you think it's gonna take to help you get off that particular track?] To be honest, I just don't know.

The biggest problem was playing cards and the fact that skipping was so easy.

> All we do is really play cards for money. . . . Me and my partner, we play good. . . . Beat everybody. . . . And you know how it's just the thrill of having the money, you know, so I lied to miss third period today, we ain't gonna do nothing in there.

This behavior did not apply to his geometry class. Malik and Charles both had the same geometry teacher, who had the same affect on them.

> This time, I was surprised. The teacher makes you want to learn. . . . She just comes and say, "You all I'm making sure you're all learning something, you all ain't gonna be sittin' here doing nothin,' gotta learn more" . . . And everybody basically in the class learns something. . . . Even people that don't never do nothin,' they somehow find ways to learn. . . . And it's fun the way she teacher us . . . she makes it a challenge against everybody. . . . She told us at the beginning of the year, two cuts is automatic. You cut a class twice, automatic F, scared everybody. . . . Class is full every day. . . . Nobody misses her class.

His geometry teacher felt equally positive about Malik and his performance. She commented,

> Malik did very little work the first semester. This last marking period, Malik realized he was at risk of failing and has been making more effort, coming for help sometimes during lunch. I have grown to like Malik a great deal and appreciate his enthusiasm and energy. However, he often frustrates me because, like most sophomore boys, Malik is often silly. I have seen some growth from Malik this year, which gives me hope for his future.

Malik was not positive about his other teachers. For example, he described his English teacher as

> he a White teacher. . . . I guess he just come and occupies the class with the amount of time he's supposed to and then leaves! And you know, he's not too much worried about whether we get ahead in life or not. . . . Every day, no more than 10 people come. . . . He doesn't seem to care.

In tenth grade, Malik's father was having health problems. His dad admitted that he was having a hard time giving Malik the attention he needed. By the end of tenth grade, Malik was frustrated, confused, and down on himself. He did not want to talk about the future: "I'm just gonna have to wait till I get out of high school cause right now, I can't see myself in the future now." He talked not knowing how to turn himself around.

> It just feels awkward. . . . Not knowing which way I wanna go. . . . But I wanna do the right thing. . . . I know it just seems hard for me. . . . When I was a little kid, I was so focused in doing good at school. . . . But now in high school, to be honest, I don't even care about the future no mo'. . . . You can get into the habit of not doing it right and then, when you know its time for you to do right, it's just so hard for you to do it. . . . It just like, "I'm trapped, man!" They want me to do right, it like I wanna do what they want me to do, but I wanna do what I wanna do . . . that how it is. . . . I like to do my own thing. . . . I was saying, I'm lazy.

Malik returned for 11th grade but only had credits to be a 10th grader. In the first semester, he missed most of his classes, including more than 20 days in English and physics. In the winter of 11th grade, he transferred to an alternative school, where, to the best of our knowledge, he received a GED. In 11th grade, he moved back with his mom, citing conflicts with his dad.

Case 4: Charles, The Making of an Underachiever

Charles in Eighth Grade. Charles is a bright young man with an engaging personality. His eighth-grade teacher commented, "Charles will do well. He is very personable, a charmer. He tries hard to succeed. Good communication skills." Charles's test scores placed him on grade level. His teachers rated Charles as a hard worker, with high home support for education and above-average academic skills and motivation. They thought it was likely that he would go to college. This assessment reflected Charles's strong commitment to education. Charles's goal for high school was to get the best grades he could get so that he could get into a good college. When asked what he would need to do to achieve that goal, he commented, "Keep my grades in the A department straight and work hard, hard, hard."

Charles had not had an easy life. His father had been in jail since he was born. His mother, a professional, had problems with drugs and in eighth grade had been hit by a car, leaving her with serious health problems. Charles and his little brother lived with his grandparents and his uncle. They were important role models and sources of support. Charles also found support in his church, where he was involved in youth activities and was close to the pastor. Charles worked hard to help his grandmother with his 5-year-old brother.

Charles was extremely positive about his elementary school experience, particularly his teachers who were a source of support. He credited his fifth-grade teacher with turning him around after he moved to the school and in with his grandmother. Charles was focused on the importance of maintaining good behavior. When asked what advice he would give other kids who had behavior problems, he explained,

> I'd try to tell them this gonna be your future. If you act this way now, ain't no way the rest of your life gonna end up good or something, ain't no jobs or be a bum or something. Have to go

to crime, you know, and the next thing you know, you will end up in jail for a long time.

Charles knew he was bright and did not feel that that was a problem. He saw right through our question about whether smart kids get teased. In answer to the question "What do classmates think about the kids who do really well in school?" Charles responded,

They don't call them names and stuff. That's what you're thinking, right? If you're smart, you're smart. A lot of people—they want to be like them. They want to be smart and they . . . try to be like them. Try to learn, act good. . . . I'm almost at the top. I'm one of the smartest people in my classroom.

During the summer, Charles's grandfather enrolled him in a triathlon camp at a local university, "'Cause he don't want me on the streets." His uncle drove him every morning and afternoon. It was a positive experience. He was excited about the rigors of triathlon training and talked at length about its discipline. During the summer, his mom also entered drug treatment, which allowed him to talk to her daily on the phone.

Charles in Ninth Grade. Charles had a rocky transition to high school. He had a hard time with algebra. He thought the teacher gave too much unnecessary homework and required too much detail. He liked his English teacher but was also struggling in that class. He was not involved in any after-school activities and did not want to be. "'Cause I don't like staying in school. I'm tired of staying in school." But he continued to be involved in church, spent a lot of time reading, and was interested in getting a job. His grandmother kept pushing him to get involved; "My grandma wantin' me to do something. Stay off the street, get a job."

Throughout the year, Charles had problems with the main disciplinarian of the school. His carefree style and his playing with identity through fashion and hairstyle got him into conflict with the school administration. His first suspension was for having his hair braided. After this began a series of suspensions for anything from being out of uniform to playing cards. Charles's grandmother was irate and constantly bothering the school. She made visits to the counselor and the principal to no avail. She knew that he was having problems in algebra. She got him into a tutoring program, and he was bringing his grades up. At the end of the year, Charles admitted that he had been "acting the fool" and playing a lot, but his grandmother thought that this picking on Charles was completely inappropriate. At orientation, the principal said that kids would not be suspended for the little stuff but over the course of the year, Charles received multiple suspensions for violations such as being out of uniform. Charles was aware of her advocacy and was articulate about his problems that year. He argued that his low grades were caused by being in the office so much.

> I can't even count it was so much. . . . You need to call my grandma. My grandma know they be sending me there for stupid reasons 'cause she be telling them stop calling here for stupid stuff like this. . . . All crazy reasons. . . . I could see if this was fighting or something. . . . I don't do none of that. . . . I never had no knife or nothing. . . . It's all for silly reasons every time I go there . . . 'Cause Coach C, he does not like me. Every time I go in there, I get suspended. And my grandma will call, and she'll talk to the principal and tell him that it was a stupid reason like that, and they let me back at school. I'm not a bad student. I don't do nothing just to be bad. My grandma know it too. . . . And you can tell by the way he acts that he don't like me and grandma. 'Cause my grandma speaks up. . . . My grandma calls the principal all the time. They just trying to make me fed up. Coach C, he's trying to make me fail.

Despite his grandmother's effort, this experience had an affect on Charles. He felt bad about himself, felt bad about his performance, and by the end of the year, he was very down on himself. When asked what he most looked forward to during the day, he commented,

> Just getting out of these classes. Passing them . . . [Interviewer: Hmm.] Getting home. When I get home just watch TV for a little while. I don't ever get homework. . . . I could do it if I want to. [Interviewer: Right.] I just be lazy.

Charles's grandmother also noticed this decline in his attitude, noting that "he was a bit excited starting off high school and now he has just settled." Charles's teachers did not have a good view of him. His English, algebra, and biology teachers commented that Charles rarely completed homework assignment and was often absent. They felt that he never worked hard and was not likely to go to college. According to his English teacher,

> Charles is bright but lazy. He spent a lot of time in class making fun of other students and cracking jokes. He tries to rely on personality to get by. . . . He passed the first semester by the skin of his teeth and thereafter did almost no work and consistently came to class without supplies.

At the end of ninth grade, Charles passed all his classes except English. He claimed that his teacher told him that there was not anything he could do to bring his grades up because he had missed so much of her class. He remained, however, unwavering in his desire to continue in school, graduate, and go to college. His mom was living back with the family, and Charles was feeling particularly supported by his grandmother and by his uncle, who "tries to keep me in check all the time . . . on my butt. Makes sure I don't fall too far behind . . . just get on my butt. Talk to me and all that."

Charles in Tenth Grade. The summer between ninth and tenth grade was a time of dramatic transition for Charles. His mom regained custody, and he moved in with her. He had mixed feelings about this move because of his attachment to his grandmother and uncle. His father also got out of jail. Charles entered tenth grade resolving to do things differently. It did not work that way. In his first quarter, he flunked English, geometry, and his shop class. It was clear he was not attending classes. Although he was only absent one day, he missed more than 10 days in almost every core subject and more than 18 in geometry. As Charles explained, "I've been fooling around. Fooling around period. In class. Go to lunch and, uh, just walk around the hallways. Stupid stuff." He went to school each day because he knew his grandmother would not stand for it, but he just could not get himself to go to class.

> I do not know. It'll be, like, I don't even feel like going class. I been hanging out with my friends or else not. . . . Just walk around.

Part of the problem was that because first quarter grades did not count, Charles thought he could goof off and then make it up. He would just get lazy when it did not count. His grandmother and uncle knew what he was doing because they had come for report card pickup. They reinforced to him how smart he was and how important it was for him to change his behavior. True to his word, he managed to pass all his classes, getting Ds and Cs in his core subjects but failing shop.

The third quarter was pretty much the same, significant cutting, significant failure. Although he managed to pull his grades up first semester, he did not manage to do it second semester, and at the end of the year, Charles failed history and shop and ended with a D in English and a C in geometry. His teachers were even more negative than the year before. During the middle of the year, Charles got a different geometry teacher. His geometry teacher commented,

> Charles was a behavior and academic problem this year. I had a great deal of trouble from him. He didn't settle down until the last marking period.

Despite this negative assessment, this teacher was seen by Charles as his most important teacher. When asked if there was teacher who made a big influence on him that year, he named her because she was constantly riding him and pushed him to pass her class, arguing, "'Don't you fail my class, and it's very easy to pass my class,' and all that, she'd say, 'It is easy to pass your class if you do work.'"

Charles's home situation changed again in tenth grade. His mom started having drug problems again and "wasn't sharing no money." His grandmother was ill, so he moved in with his uncle. His uncle was strict and made Charles do chores and homework every night. He also made Charles participate in an after-school program to make up his English credits from the year before. He went on Saturdays and after school and totally enjoyed the class. When asked what was something he really enjoyed doing that year, he explained,

> Yep. . . . if you mess up, they don't give you credit. You go after school, and after-school people don't have time to mess on, you gotta push yourself. [Interviewer: So that's a really challenging thing for you, going there, two hours, you're working hard.] Yep.

Charles at the End of High School. Charles's eleventh grade was even worse. He was skipping so much that he was essentially an in-school truant. Charles missed only four days of school the first semester but was absent 23 days in two classes and more than 10 days in his remaining classes. His twelfth grade was better. Despite continued skipping, he managed to pass all his classes and received just enough credits to graduate. Charles graduated 335 out of 372 students. His remaining high school year was marked by more moves between his mother, his grandmother, and his uncle. Charles, however, saw his family as the main support in his life, constantly pressuring him to do well in school. As Charles explains,

> That's all they talk about, school, school, school, school, school. . . . Stay off the streets, go to school, get you a nice girlfriend, and just settle down . . . they always stay on me about school.

Like many students in the study, Charles's performance in school did not deter him from his goals to go to college and be a professional. Even at eleventh grade, Charles was talking about going to Florida State University.

Case 5: William, Becoming a Really Good Student

William in Eighth Grade. In eighth grade, William was one of the top students. His achievement scores placed him on grade level in reading and a year above grade level in mathematics. He had the second-highest eighth-grade GPA and was recognized by his teachers as being "serious about academic pursuits." William wanted to be an engineer, like his father who was out of work at the time. He talked in detail about circuits and wires and connected his schoolwork to getting the skills he needed for the future. William was very positive about his elementary school. He felt his teachers cared and "they'll try to push you ahead . . . they're dedicated to pushing you up to the top, that's their main goal."

William's family was very involved in his education. He lived with both his parents and his older brother. William's mom defined herself as a "stay-at-home" parent. His family left no room for excuses or alternatives for not completing homework. His brother and father frequently helped him with homework, and his parents had firm rules. When asked what happens if he does not do his homework, William explained, "I get in real trouble. . . . They take away my phone privileges, and I can't go outside or watch TV." As an example of his family's involvement and commitment, William's mom organized a family business on the front porch where the kids sold ice cream and candy to the neighborhood. Because this was the summer of the Chicago heat wave, the business was lucrative. The money went to a family fund for school. As William explains,

> It was my mother's idea, originally . . . she sent my sister around the block, and, um, asked her what kind of candy they would like, to, um, to buy from us. This year, soon as it start gettin' hot, my mother, she got her money together, she went up and got the supplies and everything. . . . My big brother, um, the one that's 16, he works at the snow cone, and then my big sister, she's stands there with him to make sure no one cheats him or anything. And then I work in the candy and my little sister we switch up. . . . I enjoy it, but, like, it's hard work.

William felt positive about going to high school and was mentally preparing himself for the changes he would face. As William explained, "High school is, like, a lot more freedom, but a lot more responsibilities, I may have to, um, be prepared to take on that responsibility." His goals were to be on the football and wrestling teams.

William in Ninth Grade. The ninth grade brought immediate difficulty. Although William was making friends and was actively involved in the football team, he was not doing as well as he had expected. Indeed, he was failing two classes. He felt that teachers were not as available to explain information, and lessons moved along much more quickly than in eighth grade. When asked what advice he would give an eighth grader, William explained,

> I'll tell you to get as much as you can out of grammar school 'cause you're gonna need that education in high school. 'Cause the teachers, most of 'em don't have time to slow down the whole class just for you.

He admitted he was having problems in algebra and was often tired. His coach pushed him to pay attention and let him know that his behavior needed to change. William was getting a lot of peer pressure to skip and reported that he was trying to stand his ground.

He thought good advice for an eighth grader was not to rely on friends because "if you're so dependable on your friends, you probably won't be that much into doin' your school work everything. 'Cause you'll probably be wantin' to hang out with your friends."

William's family reacted strongly to his first quarter grades. When William brought his report card home, his mother questioned the Cs, "especially if other grades were higher and certainly anything below a C." She declared that "dropping out of school is not an option." She tried to help him manage his time better by waking him up earlier and preparing him each previous night. She also got William extra tutoring for algebra. His oldest brother, a truck driver who was very involved in William's life, also reacted strongly. All of this made William want to turn himself around.

> 'Cause first time I almost failed, then I got in trouble. I had to improve my grades, to make my parents proud, so then I just did real good, did all my studying and everything. [Interviewer: How come you think you weren't studying?] 'Cause, um, I didn't think it was that important. [Interviewer: What changed your mind?] 'Cause when I got home . . . according to the grades, we get, my brother, he'd give us some money. And then, um, last marking period, when I didn't have that many good grades, he didn't give me any money.

To William, an important factor in ninth grade was his growing focus on being a Christian. This developing role and identity appeared to involve preaching to his peers, avoiding troublesome associates, and performing at his best. His friends took to calling him "preacher."

> They be calling me "Preacher Man," 'cause . . . I be coming and I be preaching. Some people, they'll come and listen. [Interviewer: When did this happen?] I think since the middle of the school year. 'Cause some people, they be like, [you're] not like the beginning of the school year, we used to curse and fight and do all kinds of other stuff. And they'll ask me, "Now you're real religious, why don't you just be like you used to be?" I tell them, "No, the Lord, he called on me, so I got a mission to fulfill." [Interviewer: The Lord called on you one day?] At first, at

the beginning of, I wasn't really into the Word. . . . But then, um, as I progressed and get older, it's like the Lord, he revealed a lot of stuff to me I can understand.

William felt that wrestling was also a positive influence on him, in contrast to his football, which took him away from his academic pursuits. His teachers concurred. His English teacher commented,

William has made much progress during the last 6 months. When he came to South Side, William was more interested in football than anything else. . . he was not encouraged by his coach to focus on his academics first. William wrote some interesting poems. One, "Son to Mother," based on Langston Hughes's poem "Mother to Son," won 1st place at our Craftsmen's Fair. But recently, William has lost his focus. He was absent on a day of a major exam and did not turn in a major required assignment and an extra-credit assignment. I submitted his name for one of the most-improved-student awards but pulled the certificate before the assembly. I feel he must put all that he does into perspective. He must learn to find a place for football, academics, and friends. He also must learn that spurts of excellence do not replace consistent excellent work throughout the year.

His English teacher's comments suggest that even though William found a way to be successful in high school, he was still struggling. In the third quarter, William received Bs and Cs in most of his subjects, but by the end of the year, his grades were slipping and his class attendance decreased. William admitted that after such a successful quarter, he began to coast again and despite a burst of effort, he went from a B to a D in English and B to a C in algebra. He was embarrassed. When asked how his parents responded, William commented,

They was angry. 'Cause, um, they said, they, that they knew I had more potential than that. . . . I was apologizing. [Interviewer: Do you think that's gonna happen again?] Absolutely not. 'Cause next time, um, I'm, I'm gonna be on the ball. I'm gonna try to get straight A's, 'cause I want a be a scholarship for college.

William in Tenth Grade. William's tenth grade experience reflected none of the difficulties he had in ninth grade. William became an A and B student, making the honor roll. He attended classes regularly and got very involved in activities in the school. William seemed happy to go back to school.

> It's a lot of fun, I look forward to coming to school. . . . And when I stay home, my mother, she has some of those chores for me to do. So I just hurry up and try to get to school.

He attributed his success to his relationship with his teachers. During the second year, students at South Shore pick occupation majors. William chose horticulture largely because of the teacher. Although electronics was a choice, his brief experience with that major the year before made him feel that he would get more support in horticulture.

> Because . . . right now, my shop is horticulture and I'm getting more insight in that, and seeing that I like it more than electronics. And, and I'm on this side of the building, it's like, when I'm on the electronics wing compared to over here, my, my grades have changed. 'Cause when I'm over there, it's like the teachers, they're not that close to the students 'cause, many students, you know, um, disrespecting, disrespect 'em and everything. The teachers over there, they let any students slack, but teachers over here, they'll help me, um, get through my grades. 'Cause my horticulture teacher, she said her goals for our junior and senior year are to have everyone on honor roll.

Horticulture provided him with a group of supportive teachers. The horticulture school was organized in a separate area of the building. All classes were located together and organized by block scheduling. William liked this because he was never late for class, a constant problem the year before, and because the block scheduling meant that he really had to keep on task and could not blow off quarters.

He was again on the wrestling and football team, but the highlight of his year was getting involved in Gallery 37, a public arts program. Gallery 37 recognized his talents in art and provided him with pay. His teachers recognized his growing leadership. As one teacher commented,

Very articulate! Will share personal opinions and will allow others to share! Student has exhibited excellent behavior both in his commitment [*sic*]to his work and his decorum! Enjoyed the competition and motivation that he provided for all of us!

Over the course of the year, William's success made him even more committed to schooling. He was particularly proud that his tenth-grade test score showed that he had increased his skills and he was now scoring two years above grade level in math and reading. Now, work came first even if it meant missing matches. As William explained,

'Cause, it's a lot of times, like, people be, um, trying to convince me or peer pressure to ditch my class, but, like today, I was supposed to go with the wrestling team, but I know I have so much work to catch up, up on in class, but I, um, make a dedication to my class work and know that I have to do it to reinforce it. It's, it's sort of hard 'cause for a while I, I've been going to wrestling as much as I haven't missed a, um, a match yet, but when it comes down to it, I want, 'cause the first thing, soon as we came into wrestling, they told us, grades come first, then your wrestling season. So that I'm just doing what they told us.

Throughout his high school career, his family continued to work with him on his school performance, pushing him while continuing to celebrate his accomplishments. Increasingly, William realized how far apart he had grown from his peers with whom he had graduated eighth grade.

It was my family motivated me but my friends . . . the things they were doing, like, they were used to going out and hanging out, everything. But they weren't used to working their butts off in school. . . . 'Cause I was talking to my brother and he said, "Like, look at most of your friends. Down the line, everybody is used to kicking it, going out, hanging out, and no one's not used to being in school and working their butts off like we do." He said, um, "You keep on hanging with 'em and try to be just like 'em, in life, you're not gonna make very much."

William in Eleventh and Twelfth Grade. William continued to maintain his school performance and involvement. In addition to the arts program, William attended football summer camp and continued wrestling. In his senior year, he was captain of the wrestling team. A local newspaper wrote a story about William's leadership, recognizing him as one of the state's top athletes and scholars. He graduated 71st in his class of 372. William kept in regular contact with his interviewer. After graduating from high school, he entered the Army.

NOTES

1. These so-called on-time graduation rates are based on unpublished tabulations from official school transcripts based on analysis conducted at the Consortium on Chicago School Research, Chicago, IL.

2. Early research on school transitions postulated that girls may experience more difficulty in the transition to junior high school because of the coincidence of the transition to puberty with a change in school status (Simmons & Blyth, 1987). Some studies found that, on average, girls experience declines in self-esteem and increases in depressive symptoms during the first year in junior high school, whereas boys, on average, do not (Blyth et al., 1983; Hirsch & Rapkin, 1987; Simmons & Blyth, 1987). This finding, however, has not been consistently replicated in studies (Crockett et al., 1989; Seidman et al., 1994). Although new research docs suggest that urban males experience greater difficulty, Seidman and his colleagues' (1994) study of the transition to junior high school in six urban school systems did not find significant gender differences in declines in school performance, school attitudes, or self-esteem scores between African American, White, and Hispanic students or between males and females.

3. There were three elementary-high schools in the Student Life in High Schools Project (SLP). The second pair was a predominantly Mexican American elementary school and high school on the West Side of Chicago. The third pair was a mixed ethnic elementary school and high school on the North Side of Chicago. For a full description of the SLP study, sample, and study design, see Roderick et al. (1997) and Roderick, Chiong, and DaCosta (1998).

4. The study had substantial success in retaining students. Even among students who were not interviewed in 10th grade, the SLP has maintained consistent enough contact with students or family members so that progress and outcome information were maintained for 31 of the 35 students in the South Side sample.

5. See Roderick et al. (1997) for a detailed description of the content of interviews and study design. Teachers' assessments were collected from two of the students' eighth-grade teachers and three each of their ninth- and tenth-grade teachers if the student was still in attendance. Teacher assessments

asked specific questions regarding a student's behavior, skill level, effort, and parental contacts. Teachers were asked to rate the student's academic skills, social skills, motivation, and home support for learning relative to others in their grade. Teachers were subject-matched to the extent possible across years. Parent and guardian interviews were conducted during the winter and spring of ninth grade. The interview, which included both open- and close-ended questions, was focused on parental involvement and engagement with school, views of the parenting role and parental goals during adolescents, and parents' assessment of their children's progress and experience in school. The parent survey collected additional background information, including parents' occupations and education levels, family composition, and size.

6. The study recruited high schools that represented average high schools in Chicago in terms of their performance (e.g., dropout rates, course failure rates, and achievement levels of their student body). We then recruited elementary schools that sent enough students to each high school to fill an entire cohort ($n = 30$) of SLP students. In recruiting elementary schools, we focused on selecting elementary schools that had average to good reputations and school outcomes. In selecting high schools, our goal was to represent so-called average schools and students rather than either extremely low-achieving and high-risk or exemplary schools.

7. Eighth graders at South Side Elementary School, when compared with the five closest elementary schools in the same neighborhood on test scores on the Iowa Test of Basic Skills (ITBS), performed comparably in reading but significantly better in mathematics. In the year students in this study graduated from eighth grade, 29% of eighth graders at South Side met national norms on the ITBS in mathematics compared to 14% to 16% of eighth graders at the closest elementary schools.

8. In 1995 to 1996, approximately 33% of ninth-grade students in the Chicago Public Schools had average math and reading achievement 2 or more years below grade level compared to 14% of the SLP South Side sample.

9. Parent/guardian interviews were completed with 28 of the 32 students in the South Side sample.

10. The goal of the study was to obtain a representative sample of students from South Side Elementary who would be attending the high school. The SLP initially recruited 35 students at South Side High among the 49 scheduled. Students were selected based on their prior achievement and gender. Students who attended other high schools were followed during the course of the study unless they declined to do so. Three students dropped out after the first interview, 2 students because of withdrawal of parent consent, and a 3rd because of transfer to a Catholic school.

11. Not all students in the South Side sample who initially planned to attend South Side High School did so. Many transferred to other city and suburban high schools over the course of the study.

12. In 1998, for example, the proportion of 18- to 19-year-old African American males who reported having a high school diploma was only 45.5% versus 57.7% for African American females and 52% for White, non-Hispanic males. These lower rates of high school completion are also observed among 20- to 24-year-olds. In that year, only 78% of 20- to 24-year-old African American males reported completing a high school diploma or equivalent compared to 86% of their female counterparts and 85% of White, non-Hispanic males. But completion of high school diplomas or GED does not differ among 25- to 29-year-olds. This and other research on dropouts suggest that many students who drop out return to school later and eventually complete programs or GED (U.S. Bureau of the Census, 1998).

13. The fifth student in this group never attended high school. He became very involved with gangs early in his first quarter and by the winter of high school, had gotten arrested several times. During the year, his grandmother moved the family to another city. At the 4-year follow-up, he was identified by the Chicago Public Schools as being in a correctional facility.

14. Of the five students in this group, Levon's skills and elementary school grades were quite similar to those of the withdrawers. Levon's case was an exception largely because his mother worked extremely hard to keep him in school. Levon dropped out in the twelfth grade.

REFERENCES

Bae, Y., Choy, S., Geddes, C., Sable, J., & Snyder, T. (2000). *Educational equity for girls and women* (NCES 2000–030). Washington, DC: Government Printing Office.

Baker, D. P., & Stevenson, D. L. (1986). Mothers' strategies for children's school achievement: Managing the transition to high school. *Sociology of Education, 59,* 156–166.

Billson, J. M. (1996). *Pathways to manhood: Young Black males struggle for identity.* New Brunswick, NJ: Transaction.

Blyth, D. A., Simmons, R. G., & Carlton-Ford, S. (1983). The adjustment of early adolescents to school transitions. *Journal of Early Adolescence, 3,* 105–120.

Bowman, P. J., & Howard, C. (1985). Race-related socialization, motivation and academic achievement: A study of Black youths in three-generation families. *Journal of the American Academy of Child Psychiatry, 24*(2), 134–141.

Cook, P. J., & Ludwig, J. (1997). Weighing the "burden of acting White": Are there race differences in attitudes toward education. *Journal of Policy Analysis and Management, 16*(2), 256–278.

Crockett, L. J., Petersen, A., Graber, J., Schulenberg, J. E., & Ebata, A. (1989). School transitions and adjustment during early adolescence. *Journal of Early Adolescence, 9*(3), 181–210.

Csikszentmihalyi, M., & Larson, R. (1984). *Being adolescent: Conflict and growth in the teenage years*. New York: Basic Books.

Davidson, A. L. (1996). *Making and molding identity in schools: Student narratives on race, gender, and academic engagement*. Albany: State University of New York Press.

Easton, J. Q., Rosenkranz, T., Bryk, A. S., Jacob, B. A., Luppescu, S., & Roderick, M. (2000). *Annual CPS test trend review, 1999*. Chicago, IL: Consortium on Chicago School Research.

Eccles, J. S., & Harold, R. D. (1993). Parent-school involvement in the early adolescent years. *Teachers College Record, 94*(3), 568–587.

Eccles, J. S., Lord, S., & Midgley, C. (1991). What are we doing to early adolescents? The impact of educational contexts on early adolescents. *American Journal of Education, 99*(4), 521–542.

Felner, R., & Adan, A. M. (1989). The school transitional environment project: An ecological intervention and evaluation. In R. Price (Ed.), *14 ounces of prevention: A casebook for practitioners* (pp. 111–122). Washington, DC: American Psychological Association.

Felner, R., Primavera, J., & Cauce, A. (1981). The impact of school transitions: A focus for preventive efforts. *American Journal of Community Psychology, 9*(4), 449–459.

Ferguson, R. F. (1994). How professionals in community-based programs perceive and respond to the needs of Black male youth. In R. B. Mincy (Ed.), *Nurturing young Black males* (pp. 59–94). Washington, DC: Urban Institute Press.

Ferguson, R. (1998). Comment on the burden of acting White: Do Black adolescents disparage academic achievement? by P. J. Cook and J. Ludwig. In C. Jencks & M. Phillips (Eds.), *The Black-White test score gap* (pp. 394–397). Washington, DC: Brookings Institution Press.

Fordham, S. (1996). *Blacked out: Dilemmas of race, identity and success at Capital High*. Chicago: University of Chicago Press.

Fordham, S., & Ogbu, J. (1986). Black students' school success: Coping with the burden of acting White. *Urban Review, 18*(3), 176–206.

Galatzer-Levy, R. M., & Cohler, B. J. (1993). *The essential other: A developmental psychology of the self*. Boston: Basic Books.

Hare, B. R., & Castenell, L. A. (1985). No place to run, no place to hide: Comparative status and future prospects of Black boys. In M. B. Spencer, G. K. Brookins, & W. R. Allen (Eds.), *Beginning: The social and affective development of Black children* (pp. 201–214). Hillsdale, NJ: Lawrence Erlbaum.

Harter, S. (1990). Self and identity development. In S. Feldman & G. R. Elliott (Eds.), *At the threshold: The developing adolescent* (pp. 352–387). Cambridge, MA: Harvard University Press.

Heckman, J. J., & Lochner, L. (2000). Rethinking education and training policy: Understanding the sources of skill formation in the modern economy. In S. Danzinger & J. Waldfogel (Eds.), *Securing the future:*

Investing in children from birth to college (pp. 205–230). New York: Russell Sage.

Hill, S. A. (1999). *African American children: Socialization and development in families.* Thousand Oaks, CA: Sage.

Hirsch, B., & Rapkin, B. (1987). Transition to junior high school: A longitudinal study of self-esteem, psychological symptomatology, school life, and social support. *Child Development, 58,* 1235–1243.

Hopkins, R. (1997). *Educating Black males: Critical lessons in schooling, community and power.* Albany: State University of New York Press.

Irvine, J. J. (1990). *Black Students and school failure: Policies, practices and prescriptions.* Westport, CT: Praeger.

Jencks, C., & Phillips, M. (1998). The Black-White test score gap: An introduction. In *The Black-White test score gap* (pp. 1–54). Washington, DC: Brookings Institution Press.

Lee, V. E., & Bryk, A. S. (1989). A multilevel model of the social distribution of high school achievement. *Sociology of Education, 62*(3), 172–192.

Lee, V. E., & Smith, J. B. (1995). Effects of high school restructuring and size on gains in achievement and engagement for early secondary school students. *Sociology of Education, 68*(4), 241–270.

Lee, V. E., Smith, J. B., & Croninger, R. G. (1997). How high school organization influences the equitable distribution of learning in mathematics and science. *Sociology of Education, 70*(2), 128–150.

Lewis, D. E. (1975). The Black family: Socialization and sex roles. *Phylon, 3,* 221–237.

MacIver, D. J., Stipek, D. H., & Daniels, D. H. (1991). Explaining within-semester changes in student effort in junior high school and senior high school courses. *Journal of Educational Psychology, 83*(2), 201–211.

Majors, R., & Billson, J. M. (1992). *Cool pose: The dilemmas of Black manhood in America.* New York: Lexington Books.

Markus, H., Cross, S., & Wurf, E. (1990). The role of the self-system in competence. In R. J. Sternberg & J. Kolligian Jr. (Eds.), *Competence considered* (pp. 205–226). New Haven, CT: Yale University Press.

Markus, H., & Nurius, P. (1986). Possible selves. *American Psychologist, 41*(9), 954–969.

Masten, A. S. (1994). Resilience in individual development: Successful adaptation despite risk and adversity. In M. Wang & E. W. Gordon (Eds.), *Educational resilience in inner-city America: Challenges and prospects* (pp. 3–26). Hillsdale, NJ: Lawrence Erlbaum.

Mickleson, R. A. (1990). The attitude achievement paradox among Black adolescents. *Sociology of Education, 63,* 44–61.

Mincy, R. (1994). *Nurturing young black males.* Washington, DC: Urban Institute Press.

Murray, C., & Fairchild, H. (1989). Model of Black adolescent academic underachievement. In R. L. Jones (Ed.), *Black adolescents*. Oakland, CA: Cragmont.

Newman, B., Myers, M. C., Newman, P. R., Lohman, B. J., & Smith, V. L. (1998). *The transition to high school for academically promising urban low-income African American youth*. Unpublished manuscript, Department of Human Development and Family Science, Ohio State University.

Newmann, F. M., Wehlage, G. G., & Lamborn, S. D. (1992). The significance and sources of student engagement. In F. M. Newmann (Ed.), *Student engagement and achievement in American secondary schools* (pp. 11–39). New York: Teachers College Press.

Ogbu, J. U. (1985). AA cultural ecology of competence among inner-city Blacks. In M. B. Spencer, G. K. Brookings, & W. R. Allen (Eds.), *Beginnings: The social and affective development of Black children* (pp. 45–66). Hillsdale, NJ: Lawrence Erlbaum.

Osborne, J. (1997). Race and academic disidentification. *Journal of Educational Psychology, 89*(4), 728–735.

Oyserman, D., Gant, L., & Ager, J. (1997). A socially contextualized model of African American identity: Possible selves and school persistence. *Journal of Personality and Social Psychology, 69*(6), 1216–1232.

Polite, V. (1995). The method in the madness: African-American males, avoidance, schooling and chaos theory. *Journal of Negro Education, 63*(4), 588–601.

Reyes, O., Gillock, K., & Kobus, K. (1994). AA longitudinal study of school adjustment in urban, minority adolescents: Effects of a high school transition program. *American Journal of Community Psychology, 22*(3), 341–369.

Roderick, M. (1993). *The path to dropping out: Evidence for intervention*. Westport, CT: Auburn House.

Roderick, M., Arney, M., Axelman, M., DaCosta, K., Steiger, C., Stone, S., et al. (1997). *Habits hard to break: A new look at truancy in Chicago's public high schools*. Chicago: Consortium on Chicago School Research.

Roderick, M., & Camburn, E. (1999). Risk and recovery from course failure in the early years of high school. *American Educational Research Journal, 36*(2), 303–344.

Roderick, M., Chiong, J., & DaCosta, K. (1998). *The Student Life in High School Project: A longitudinal study of the transition to high school: First follow-up student outcomes*. Chicago: School of Social Services Administration, University of Chicago.

Roderick, M., & Stone, S. (1998, August). *Changing standards, changing relationships: Building family-school relationships to promote achievement in high schools*. Chicago: Consortium on Chicago School Research.

Rumberger, R., Ghatak, R., Poulos, G., Ritter, P. L., & Dornbusch, S. (1990). Family influences on dropout behavior in one California high school. *Sociology of Education, 63,* 283–299.

Sander, M. (1997). Overcoming obstacles: Academic achievement as a response to racism and discrimination. *Journal of Negro Education, 66*(1), 83–93.

Sebring, P. B., Bryk, A. S., Roderick, M., & Camburn, E. (1996). *Charting reform in Chicago: The students speak.* Chicago: Consortium on Chicago School Research.

Seidman, E., Allen, L. Aber, J., Mitchell, C., & Feinman, J. (1994). The impact of school transitions in early adolescence on the self-system and perceived social context of poor urban youth. *Child Development, 65,* 507–522.

Simmons, R. G., Black, A., & Zhou, Y. (1991). African-American versus White children in the transition into junior high school. *American Journal of Education, 9*(4), 481–520.

Simmons, R. G., & Blyth, D. (1987). *Moving into adolescence: The impact of pubertal changes and school context.* Hawthorne, NY: DeGruyter.

Smerdon, B. A. (1999). Engagement and achievement: Differences between African-American and White high school students. *Research in Sociology of Education and Socialization, 12,* 103–134.

Spencer, M. B. (1995). Old issues and new theorizing about African-American youth: A phenomenological variant of ecological systems theory. In R. L. Taylor (Ed.), *African-American youth: Their social and economic status in the United States* (pp. 37–70). Westport, CT: Praeger.

Spencer, M. B., Dupree, D., & Swanson, D. P. (1996). Parental monitoring and adolescents' sense of responsibility for their own learning: An examination of sex differences. *Journal of Negro Education, 65*(1), 30–43.

Spencer, M. B., & Markstrom-Adams, C. (1990). Identity processes among racial and ethnic minority children in America. *Child Development, 61,* 290–310.

Staples, R. (1984). The mother-son relationship in the Black family. *Ebony, 39*(12), 76–78.

Steele, C. M. (1992, April). Race and the schooling of Black Americans. *Atlantic Monthly,* pp. 68–78.

Steele, C. M., & Aronson, J. (1998). Stereotype threat and the test performance of academically successful African-Americans. In C. Jencks & M. Phillips (Eds.), *The Black-White test score gap* (pp. 401–430). Washington, DC: Brookings Institution Press.

Taylor, R. (1989). Black youth, role models and the social construction of identity. In R. L. Jones (Ed.), *Black adolescents* (pp. 155–174). Berkeley, CA: Cobb & Henry.

Taylor, R. (1991). Poverty and adolescent Black males: The subculture of disengagement. In P. Edelman & J. Ladner (Eds.), *Adolescence and poverty: Challenge for the 1990s* (pp. 139–162). Washington, DC: Center for National Policy Press.

U.S. Bureau of the Census. (1998, March). *Current population reports, Series P-20–513. Educational attainment in the United States* (Table 1). Washington, DC: Government Printing Office.

Walker, G., & Freedman, M. (1996). Social change one on one: The new mentoring movement. *American Prospect, 27,* 75–78.

Wang, M. C., Haertel, G. D., & Walbert, H. J. (1994). Educational resilience in inner cities. In M. Wang & E. W. Gordon (Eds.), *Educational resilience in inner-city America: Challenges and prospects* (pp. 45–72). Hillsdale, NJ: Lawrence Erlbaum.

CHAPTER SEVEN

Black Males' Structural Conditions, Achievement Patterns, Normative Needs, and "Opportunities"

Dena Phillips Swanson

Pennsylvania State University

Michael Cunningham

Tulane University

Margaret Beale Spencer

University of Pennsylvania

This chapter seeks to organize what we know about the effect of affective- and cognitive-linked developmental transitions on achievement outcomes and academic-associated processes,

AUTHORS' NOTE: This chapter was prepared with funding provided by the National Institutes of Mental Health, National Science Foundation, Office of Educational Research improvement (Field Initiated Studies), and the Ford and Kellogg Foundations. Funding of the empirical data presented in the chapter was provided to Margaret Beale Spencer from several sources: Spencer, W. T. Grant, and Ford Foundations, and the Commonwealth Fund.

particularly for African American males. As an organizational strategy for accomplishing this task, the synthesis has three goals that also represent this chapter's organization. This chapter is written with the following three goals in mind: Following the introduction, we discuss the conceptual framework used to examine the integration of affective and cognitive processes with a focus on associated developmental milestones of relevance for all children and adolescents. Next, we review selected data that demonstrates the relation between normative developmental transitions, contextual influences, and life stage outcomes, such as academic achievement for preschool and elementary school-aged African American males. Finally, we report empirical data as an illustration of vulnerability and resilient outcomes for adolescent males.

DEVELOPMENT OF AFRICAN AMERICAN MALES

African American males are probably the most highly stigmatized and stereotyped group in America (Cunningham, 2001). With exemplar images of African American males ranging from the super athlete, criminal, gangster, or hypersexed male, society's views, as portrayed in both empirical and conceptual reports of Black youth, are defined by these stereotypes (Cunningham, 1993; Stevenson, 1997). These race-specific stereotypes are in addition to the global-level sex role stereotypes concerning male instrumentality. The societal stereotypes, in conjunction with numerous social, political, and economic forces, interact to place African American males at extreme risk for adverse outcomes and behaviors, and suggest clear implications for the continued structural conditions that characterize life in the United States for ethnic minorities (Spencer & Dornbusch, 1990).

Although racial tolerance in the United States has increased, evidence of structural racism in American society still exists. This stems from systematic and institutionalized practices resulting in the subordination and devaluation of minority groups (Jones, 1991). The consequences of the process of subordination and devaluation for minority youth are twofold. First, minority youth growing and developing in late 20th- and early 21st-century America often live and mature in high-risk environments characterized by systemic, structural barriers to individual effort and success (Spencer, 1986). These obstacles include conditions within the family, neighborhood, and school contexts and interactions between these different contexts, along with their relationships between these settings and the larger social, economic, and political forces in American society (McLoyd, 1998). Second, instances of resilience, success, and competence displayed by minority youth in spite of adverse living conditions often go unnoticed and unrecognized, thus denying individuals a sense of success and accomplishment. For example, social resources such as caring parents and involvement in extracurricular activities help to facilitate positive youth outcomes (McLendon, Nettles, & Wigfield, 2000; Nettles, Mucherah, & Jones, 2000). However, these activities must exist within a culturally sensitive context. A lack of understanding of cultural context leads to a misinterpretation of minority youth behavior and development (Spencer, 1999). Even when successes are acknowledged, the factors that lead to success and resilience in high-risk environments are neither identified nor considered (Cunningham, 1999). Identification of these factors, along with their implementation within intervention efforts, is crucial to promoting an understanding of resilience of minority youth. Work by Spencer (1995, 1999) and her colleagues (Cunningham, 1999; Cunningham & Spencer, 2000; Dupree, Spencer, & Bell, 1997; Swanson, Spencer, & Petersen, 1998) focused attention on the identification and enhancement of resilience-promoting factors from a contextually and developmentally sensitive perspective.

The most important and critical overarching flaw in research on Black youth, and boys particularly, is the absence of a systems-focused theoretical framework that can analyze, represent, and explain the mechanisms of experiences and outcomes. A comprehensive theory is needed that takes into account both normative developmental processes and specific risks faced by African Americans, the affect of experiences on coping and identity processes, and the effect of these on life outcomes. Spencer's (1995, 1999) PVEST model provides such a framework of life course human development in cultural context.

Phenomenological Variant of Ecological Systems Theory

Spencer's (1995, 1999) Phenomenological Variant of Ecological Systems Theory (PVEST) integrates an explicitly phenomenological perspective with Bronfenbrenner's (1989) ecological systems theory, linking context with perception. Determining how minority youth and community members view and comprehend family, peer, and societal expectations and their prospects for competence and success is central to understanding resilience and devising interventions that promote it and thus also revitalize communities. PVEST consists of five components linked by bidirectional processes; conceptualized as systems theory, it is a cyclic, recursive model that describes identity development throughout the life course. In doing so, it allows one to capture and understand the meaning and underlying identity processes as linked to coping outcomes (Spencer, 1995; Spencer, Dupree, & Hartmann, 1997). Thus, it identifies processes for all members of communities: It is relevant when conceptualizing communities and its members from conception to the end of the life course.

The first component, vulnerability level, represents the net balance between risk contributors and protective factors. The net balance of factors may predispose individuals for adverse outcomes. For urban minority youth, these include socioeconomic conditions such as poverty, sociocultural expectations such as race and sex stereotypes, and sociohistorical processes including racial subordination and discrimination. Temperament and mental health may represent protective factors. As self-appraisal is a key factor in identity formation, how minority youth view themselves depends on their perceptions of these conditions, expectations, and processes. Net stress engagement refers to the balance between stress experienced as challenge and support. It is the actual experience of situations that challenge one's psychosocial identity and well-being. Moreover, experiences of discrimination, violence, and negative feedback are salient challenges that increase stressors for minority youth. In response to the net vulnerability given protective versus risk factors, reactive coping methods are employed to resolve the net stress level of dissonance-producing situations. These include strategies to solve problems that can lead to either adaptive or maladaptive solutions. In addition, a solution may be adaptive in one context, such as neighborhood, and maladaptive in another, such as school disengagement. As coping strategies are employed, self-appraisal continues, and those strategies yielding desirable results for the ego are preserved. They become stable coping responses and collectively yield emergent identities. These emergent identities in turn define how individuals view themselves within and between various contextual experiences.

That is, these thematic responsive patterns show stability across settings and not just within families and neighborhoods.

The combination of cultural/ethnic identity, sex role understanding, and self- and peer appraisal all define one's identity. Identity lays the foundation for future perception and behavior, yielding adverse or productive life state outcomes manifested across settings. Productive outcomes include good health, positive and supportive relationships with neighbors and friends, high self-esteem, and motivation (White, 1959). The PVEST (thematic) framework recycles as one transitions across the life course (across multiple settings including community) and individuals encounter new risks and stressors (as balanced against protective factors and supports), try different coping strategies, and redefine how they and others view themselves. For minority youth, the presence and engagement of structural racism poses severe risks for the learning of adaptive coping strategies and positive outcomes with regard to individual and community-level health and well-being.

The PVEST framework contributes an identity-focused cultural ecological perspective (ICE) on identity formation (Swanson & Spencer, 1995). In doing so, various theoretical positions, including psychosocial, ecological, self-organizational, and phenomenological models are integrated, with emphasis placed on self-appraisal processes (Swanson et al., 1998). The approach takes into account structural and contextual barriers to identity formation and their implication for psychological processes such as self-appraisal. In sum, it enhances our ability to interpret the available work and to recommend future improvements on how we structure studies and ask questions about 21st-century experiences of African American males.

PRESCHOOL TO ELEMENTARY TRANSITIONS

The perspective that guides this review focuses on academic achievement patterns of African American males from a normal human development perspective, emphasizing the interaction between all domains of development in the facilitation of life stage outcomes. An important point to highlight is that the literature exclusively examining the development and education of Black males is sparse (Cunningham, 1993). The majority of research focuses on African American youth, both males and females (Brooks-Gunn,

Klebanav, & Duncan, 1996; Moore, 1985). Furthermore, research on affect and cognition is largely based on predominantly White samples. There are many shared or similar experiences among the genders and races. Thus, some research findings based on White or cross-gender samples (e.g., the experiences of females) could sometimes allow for the imposition of generalizations onto African American males. In this chapter, we contend that the social ecology and normal developmental processes affect Black males differently. Given the dearth of literature available, further research is required, but the existing body of knowledge must be used to make inferences and inform future research agendas.

Starting with the typical preschool years (2 to 5 years of age), many significant cognitive changes that occur can be examined. Infants are born with the most primitive brain structure, the brain stem, already intact. This system is responsible for breathing and heart rate. However, higher order cognitive structures of the brain are just beginning to develop. As reviewed by Dupree et al. (1997), with advances in cognitive neuroscience, we have learned that brain development within the first years of life is rapid and is largely influenced by environmental factors. Most important, research suggests that brain development, the development and reinforcement of neural pathways, plays an important role in determining later academic performance (Byrnes, 2001). Central to the new brain development is the role of parents in establishing a new environment conducive to optimal synaptic growth (McLoyd, 1998). To be sure, this is a return to the old premise that parents matter. This premise is of great importance, particularly as it relates to minority children, specifically African American males, because parents might state that they treat their sons and daughters equally, although observed parenting behaviors appear to be gender specific (Spencer, Dupree, Swanson, & Cunningham, 1996).

One of the earliest educational experiences for many Black youth is federally funded Head Start or state-funded day care programs. This is due largely to the fact that many Black youth grow up in single-parent households with working mothers (Lee, Brooks-Gunn, & Schnur, 1988; Lee, Brooks-Gunn, Schnur, & Liaw, 1990; Slaughter, 1988). The literature suggests that the early educational interventions such as Head Start produce definite short-term cognitive benefits as well as immediate gains for caretakers (Bronfenbrenner, 1974; McCall, 1993). However, there are little or no data that exclusively examines the implications of early educational interventions for Black males. Preschool and Head Start programs are believed to provide children with a significant degree of social and cognitive competence, thereby ensuring their success in schools; future studies need to specifically examine the early preschool success of African American males. These will enable researchers and educators to pinpoint the critical time frames of early formal education when Black males begin to underachieve.

An examination of some of the research concerning elementary-aged African American males notes similar patterns regarding the need for further studies. For example, Entwisle and Alexander's (1990) research findings from the systemwide and large Beginning School Study (BSS), which examined children's competence in math (reasoning) concepts and computation at the time of school entry at first grade, reported that although low-resource Whites and Blacks were included in the sample, there were more lower income Blacks than Whites. Importantly, however, they found them equivalent in terms of computational and verbal skills as measured by the California Achievement Test data at the start of first grade. Yet they found a significant difference of about a quarter of a standard deviation favoring Whites over Blacks in math concepts.

Both Black and White children of all socioeconomic levels responded to parents' psychological resources and expectations. Specifically, children scored higher if parents expected them to do well. Availability of educationally stimulating resources in the home also helped both groups. Both Black and White parents sent their children to public kindergartens in the same school where children enrolled in first grade, so differences of race cannot be attributed to White parents' use of private or other types of preschools. On desegregation of the data by race and gender, Black males outperformed Black females in math reasoning, although White males did not outperform White females. Gender differences for Blacks did not attain significance until parents' economic resources were considered. One explanation offered by Entwisle and Alexander (1990) was the possibility that perhaps males' mathematical development was more sensitive to economic deprivation than was females' mathematical development. They offered a rationale from other research that suggested a greater sensitivity of boys to negative life circumstances than girls (Zaslow & Hayes, 1986, cited in Entwisle & Alexander, 1990, p. 464). This disaggregation showed a significant difference favoring Black males over Black females in reasoning. Finally, the data indicated more positive academic outcomes for males over females regardless of parent education. The authors, however, concluded a possible problem of sampling fluctuation (e.g., retention problems), the beginning of the school year, and discuss the general controversy of gender differences in children's math performance and computational skills.

In another one of the few studies that looked at school relevant outcomes and analyzed the data by race, gender, and socioeconomic status, Patterson, Kupersmidt, and Vaden's (1990) findings are informative. They noted that being Black or male or growing up in a low economic status or single-parent household has been identified as risk factors for childhood maladjustment. In their study of second-through fourth-grade students, they compared predictions of three different forms of teacher ratings of children's competence from each of four variables of concern, which were income level, gender, ethnicity, and household composition. The study included an unusually large sample of 868 Black and White elementary school children from either two-parent or mother-headed single-parent homes. The three aspects of children's competence studied included conduct, peer relations, and academic achievement. Their findings indicated that income level and ethnicity were better overall predictors of academic achievement than were gender or household composition, although each of the four variables made significant contributions. However, the main effects were qualified by significant interactions. Specifically, income level was more strongly related to conduct scores for males than for females. Males from lower income families showed more behavior problems than those from other family types. Although a greater proportion of the sample of Blacks was from low SES homes, the authors suggested that it was more likely low-income level rather than ethnicity that was most strongly associated with teacher ratings of behavior problems for males. In sum, the data showed a greater vulnerability of Black males to teacher ratings of conduct disorder. Males and children from low-income homes were less likely than other children to receive teacher ratings that indicated competence across domains. In fact, the authors indicated that gender emerged as the best overall predictor of (teacher-rated) competence.

The gender-associated role of teachers has also been described by other researchers' classroom studies. Both Dweck (1978) and

Irvine (1990) suggested very different teacher-student classroom experiences for young Black males. Whereas Dweck (1978) made the cogent observation that teacher feedback is expressed in distinctive patterns according to gender, Irvine (1990) further defined this distinction as being more specifically a matter of an interaction between gender and ethnicity. She stated, "The White teachers directed more verbal praise, criticism, and nonverbal praise toward males than toward females. In contrast, they directed more nonverbal criticism toward Black males than toward Black females, White females, or White males" (p. 50). Other research by Aaron and Powell (1983) indicated that Black pupils received more negative academic and behavioral feedback than did White pupils. This inconsistent feedback in teacher ratings is also indicated in research regarding play as well. Teachers often rate their play behavior as more aggressive and threatening, and Black males begin to understand teachers' negative expectations just as they have consistently understood societal biases from an early age (McLoyd, 1985).

As dissonance between teacher perceptions and students' actions prevail and begin to interfere with skill acquisition and development, the school performance of Black children can suffer. The prevalence of dissonance on skill acquisition and development can be detrimental to the academic performance of African American students. For example, Spencer (1986) noted that a decline in scholastic achievement for Black males begins in the second grade and, reinforced by academic tracking and negative stereotyping by influential adults, can become fully entrenched by the fourth grade. African American males are particularly vulnerable because they face significant negative stereotyping. It can be assumed that by early childhood, cognitive egocentrism associated with the preschool years can no longer protect them from negative teacher perceptions (Spencer, 1986). Furthermore, awareness of how others perceive them continues and, in fact, heightens during middle and late adolescence (Cunningham, 1999).

LATER TRANSITIONS TO MIDDLE AND HIGH SCHOOL

Even under well-supported conditions, adolescence is perhaps the most confusing and vulnerable period of development experienced by human beings (i.e., except, perhaps, for the so-called terrible twos) (Randolph, Koblinsky, & Roberts, 1996). It is a time of tremendous physical, cognitive, physiological, and social change. The onset of puberty and resultant physical maturation present new challenges for youth. Physical maturation is accompanied by social changes, such as the definition of one's sexuality, peer group, and interests, along with greater independence (Brooks-Gunn & Warren, 1985). Individuals, as a function of their particular experiences, process all of these changes. One consequence is a continually changing or evolving sense of self and identity during this period.

In addition to normative adolescent developmental processes, which are often challenging, multiple other sources of stress and dissonance characterize the experiences of African American adolescents as they begin the process of self-definition (Spencer, Swanson, & Cunningham, 1991). Negative stereotypes, scarcity of positive role models, lack of culturally competent instruction and direction, and problems associated with low socioeconomic status and high-risk neighborhoods all interact to form complex barriers for these youth (Spencer & Dornbusch, 1990).

By the onset of adolescence, African American and other minority youth have developed an awareness of White American values and standards of competence (Spencer et al., 1991). They can begin to integrate their experiences with future expectations given their own and their family's values and those of the majority culture. During this period of evolving awareness of racial stereotypes and their own cultural group membership, both play a key role in identity formation. Identity and appraisal process of self and others become key.

Issues of cultural dissonance also present salient risk factors for minority youth. As a function of cultural socialization, it also represents a potential protective factor (Spencer, 1983). Adolescents must transition between diverse environments and find ways to integrate their various experiences within each context. If the contexts are relatively compatible, these transitions can be placid. Conversely, the transitions can yield dissonance-producing experiences (Phelan, Davidson, & Cao, 1991). As indicated, cultural socialization by parents provides positive options as protective factors (Spencer, 1983, 1990).

With regard to African American adolescent males, a variety of informal data regarding their experiences are available, from media reports of urban cities to anecdotal accounts of young men who develop both successful and vulnerable trajectories. However, more empirical evidence is needed to inform policy recommendations for this group. A better understanding of why some teen males develop positive identities and engage in socially responsible behaviors, whereas their peers from similar backgrounds and neighborhoods become vulnerable to negative pressures, is needed.

Understanding adolescents from a perspective that considers the interactive nature of culture, context, and gender is particularly important when research efforts are focused on African American adolescent males. Too often, the available theoretical and empirical examples concerning African American adolescent males are developmentally inappropriate and are undergirded with notions of pathology (Cunningham, 1993). With few exceptions (Cunningham, 1994; Spencer, 2001; Spencer, Coles, Dupree, Glymph, & Pierre, 1993; Spencer, Cunningham, & Swanson, 1995; Spencer, Dobbs, & Swanson, 1988), the existing literature ignores the fact that many adolescents are quite successful in spite of extreme reactive coping efforts required for life in high-risk environments. Critical questions include explanations of influences on African American male reactive and adaptive adolescent identity responses that inspire diverse outcomes.

An Empirical Illustration of Resilience and Vulnerability for African American Adolescent Males

When focusing on males who are developmentally transitioning from childhood to adulthood, a focus that highlights how adolescents interact within a cultural ecological niche is needed. Notably, two social settings in which adolescents spend a significant amount of their time are their school and community environments. In our study that investigated African American adolescent males' perceptions of teacher expectations for Black male students and the students' perceptions of the experiences of Black males in community settings, we examined the contents of school and community. In addition, an examination of adaptive and reactive coping responses (i.e., bravado attitudes) to high-risk environments was undertaken. Of particular importance was the focus on understanding developmental pathways for both resilient and vulnerable adolescent males. To examine predictors of bravado attitudes, the following research question was addressed: Do adolescent males who perceive negative social and educational experiences regarding Black males adopt reactive coping attitudes?

METHOD

Sample

The participants in the study were drawn from a sample of African American adolescents participating in a cross-sectional longitudinal study in a large southeastern American city: Promotion of Academic Competence, Project PAC (Spencer, 1989). This multi-year longitudinal study addressed the developmental effects of persistent poverty among African American youth. Poverty status was determined from parent-reported family income information. Spencer and her colleagues determined that 58% of the participants' families met federal poverty guidelines.[1] Data for males collected during the third year (8th, 9th, and 10th graders) were used to predict outcomes ($n = 219$).

Measures

As a part of the PAC sample, students were seen in small groups at their respective schools. Many domains were covered, including the areas of interest for this study. The information included in this report is from the males' responses on three instruments. First, the Black Male Experiences Measure, BMEM (Cunningham & Spencer, 1996), addressed the experiences of Black males in public places such as malls, stores, and neighborhood areas. The 5-point Likert-type questionnaire has four scales. However, further psychometric refinement revealed two subscales with strong internal consistency. The subscales are Personal Negative Inferences and Personal Positive Inferences. The Personal Negative Inferences subscale is made up of five questions and has a standardized alpha of .74. The questions' general theme addresses projected negative imagery toward African American males. The Personal Positive Inferences subscale is composed of six questions and has a standardized alpha of .67. The questions' general theme addresses beneficial, positive African American male perceptions. Second, a revised bravado construct derived from

Mosher and Sirkin's (1984) machismo measure was used to examine the males' responses to questions that addressed exaggerations or stereotypic ideas about male attitudes and behaviors. The construct used in the present analysis has been previously used in other published reports (Cunningham, 1999; Spencer, 1999) and has a standardized alpha of .71. Third, a revised scale of Teacher Expectations of Black Males (STEBM) was used to examine how the adolescents perceived their teachers' expectations of their potential academic successes or failures. The STEBM is a 12-item measure that probes the respondent to answer questions pertaining to Black males in the manner that they believe their teacher would respond (e.g., "Your teachers generally believe and feel that . . ."). The measure is composed of two scales: Perceived Negative Teacher Expectations and Perceived Positive Teacher Expectations (McDermott & Spencer, 1997). The standardized alpha for each scale is .84.

RESULTS

To examine the research question that addressed if adolescent males who perceived negative social and educational experiences regarding Black males adopted reactive coping attitudes, correlations and multiple regressions were computed. First, as indicated in the intercorrelations presented in Table 7.1, the adolescents' perceptions of their negative experiences in their community and school were statistically significant. Specifically, the correlation between Personal Negative Inferences and Perceived Negative Teacher Perceptions was $r = .33$, $p < .001$. In contrast, the correlation between Personal Negative Inferences and Perceived Positive Teacher Perceptions was $r = -.14$, $p = .05$. Interestingly, the correlation between Personal Positive Inferences and Perceived Negative Teacher Perceptions was not statistically significant ($r = .06$, ns. The relation between Personal Positive Inferences and Perceived Positive Teacher Perceptions was positive and statistically significant ($r = .26$, $p < .001$). Second, as indicated in Table 7.2, three separate multiple regression models were used to examine the magnitude of how negative perceptions within the participants' communities and schools predicted a reactive coping attitude: bravado level. Model 1 included age and the subscales of the Black Male Experiences Measure as independent variables.

Table 7.1 Intercorrelations, Means, and Standard Deviations of Variables in the Study

Variable	M	SD	1	2	3	4	5	6
1. Age	15.08	1.09	—	.01	-.00	.00	-.07	.02
				(219)	(213)	(213)	(219)	(218)
2. Bravado	49.75	8.75		—	.34***	.04	.29***	-.29***
					(199)	(199)	(194)	(194)
3. Personal Negative Inferences	49.32	9.84			—	.27***	.33***	-.14*
						(213)	(191)	(191)
4. Personal Positive Inferences	49.28	9.63				—	.06	.26***
							(191)	(191)
5. Perceived Negative Teacher Perceptions	50.17	9.06					—	-.44***
								(218)
6. Perceived Positive Teacher Perceptions	48.62	9.75						—

NOTE: Numbers in parentheses are *n* for each correlation.
*p = .05. **p = .01. ***p = .001.

Table 7.2 Community and School Contexts Predicting Bravado Attitudes

Description	F	df	Adjusted R^2	Equation Variables		
				t	β	SE
Model 1 (community context)	8.42***	3	.10			
Age				-.07	-.04	.55
Personal Negative Inferences				5.00***	.32***	.06
Personal Positive Inferences				-.41	-.03	.07
Model 2 (school context)	8.18***	3	.10			
Age				.60	.35	.63
Perceived Negative Teacher Expectations				2.63**	.29**	.08
Perceived Positive Teacher Expectations				-2.54**	-.17**	.07
Model 3 (community and school contexts)	10.29***	4	.17			
Perceived Negative Inferences				3.70***	.24***	.07
Perceived Positive Inferences				.29	.02	.07
Perceived Negative Teacher Expectations				1.12	.08	.08
Perceived Positive Teacher Expectations				2.74***	-.21**	.08

*$p < .05$; **$p < .01$; ***$p < .001$.

The overall model was statistically significant: $F(3, 195) = 8.42$, $p < .001$, $R^2 = .10$. Within the model, the Personal Negative Inferences subscale was the significant contributor (ß = .32, $p < .001$). In the second model, age and the subscales of the Perceived Teacher Perceptions of Black male students were the predictors. Again, the overall model was statistically significant: $F(3, 190) = 8.18$, $p < .001$, $R^2 = .10$. However, unlike the results that had BMEM subscales as predictors, the statistical significance of Model 2's power was attributed to high perceptions of negative teacher expectations (ß = .29, $p < .01$) and low perceptions of positive teacher expectations (ß = .17, $p < .01$). Because Models 1 and 2 both had statistically significant results, we examined a possible mediation or moderation relation of the predictor variables. In accordance to the procedures described by Baron and Kenny (1986) that a relation between variables changes as a function of other variables, we entered the BMEM subscales and the Perceived Teacher Expectation subscales into Model 3 as predictors of a bravado attitude. The predictors of the third overall model influenced the strongest statistically significant results of all the models: $F(4, 173 = 10.29$, $p = .001$, $R^2 = .17)$. A mediational relationship was also noted. The Perceived Negative Teacher Expectations subscale was no longer a statistically significant contributor to the model (ß = .08, ns). The strongest contributors were Personal Negative Inferences (ß = .24, $p < .001$) and low Perceived Positive Teacher Expectations (ß = −.21, $p = .01$).

DISCUSSION

The purpose of the chapter was to organize what is currently known about the affective and cognitive linked transitions on academic outcomes and academic-associated outcomes for African American males. As indicated, educational settings represent environments potentially attentive to both maladaptive gender and ethnicity/race coping responses of Black males. We demonstrated how their responses to chronic and adverse structural conditions and normal developmental themes (e.g., identity formation tensions, general sex role expectations of males, and unavoidable cognitive maturation that makes hyperawareness and sensitivity both a source of risk and support) are influential at different aspects of the life course.

Providing support for parents, teachers, and administrators to understand what the coping responses do and do not mean may aid the abatement of African American boys' maladaptive response patterns. The support is necessary for helping male youth to focus on their self-conceptions as learners first, as opposed to a preoccupation with structuring scenarios that aid the reaffirmation of a fragile view of self as a man. Providing proactive opportunities for affirming self-beliefs of more positive aspects of manhood supports beneficial coping and more transparent transitioning between contexts. In addition, providing productive opportunities for redefining manhood decreases male youths' problematic contribution to contexts of risk for females. Finally, enhancing teacher-training options to ensure that teachers and administrators become part of the solution (i.e., as mentors, social context translators, and models) as opposed to contributors to the structural conditions should be a primary goal of reform efforts. In sum, such programming directly affects adolescent males while affecting the contextual experiences of female adolescents, thus maximizing the use of resources and supports available. It also enhances the competence and professional successes of teachers. That is, serving as part of the solution for Black males' resilience also enhances teachers' sense of efficacy.

The efforts are especially salient given that the results that indicated low Perceived Positive Teacher Expectations were statistically significant predictors of bravado attitudes. Often, youth expect their teachers and other school personnel to be supportive of their development. So when African American males do not perceive the school environment as supportive of their individual goals and development, they may elect to disregard school as a place to receive positive reinforcement for academic success. To promote resilient academic outcomes, efforts must not focus solely on males as perpetrators of bravado attitudes. Instead, the efforts must include programs that also educate the significant adults who interact with male students and represent sources of translation for insensitive social stereotyping. Providing supportive school environments that allow boys to successfully negotiate normative identity issues associated with the transition from childhood to adulthood are needed.

In sum, PVEST provides insights for informed programming and intervention supports that acknowledge the unavoidable normative developmental contributions to psychological discontinuities that accompany the normal childhood through early adolescent transitions of African American males. Accordingly, through the utilization of supportive "theory of change" perspectives (Weis, 1995), more culturally and developmentally sensitive theory-driven interventions not only ensure the maximization of Black males' developmental outcomes as social capital but also demonstrate that the problem may not be in Black males. It suggests, instead, that the major challenge may lie in the limited ways in which we conceptualize African American males' experiences across the life course. Another critical oversight may be both our penchant to overlook the numerous expressions of Black males' resilience in the face of chronic challenge and our inadequate support of contexts in which they live and engage in normal developmental tasks, albeit under highly stigmatizing conditions.

A supportive context is needed at every developmental stage. As indicated by research highlighting the academic experiences of preschool and elementary-aged children, African American males are vulnerable in the realm of educational attainment. At each level of the educational continuum, Black males tend to underachieve on standardized tests and experience greater "stop out" and "drop out" rates (Garibaldi, 1992; Spencer, 1999). For example, during elementary school, Black males perform well in the early grades; however, a rapid decline in academic performance is evident by age 9 or the fourth grade (e.g., Garibaldi, 1992; Irvine, 1990; Spencer, 1986).

Researchers have posed various theories to explain the academic underachievement of African Americans. Fordham and Ogbu (1986) proposed that African Americans are "involuntary minorities" who have developed an oppositional stance to mainstream American values and equate academic achievement with "acting White." This work can be criticized for drawing psychological inferences from sociohistorical data (Trueba, 1988), neglecting within-group variation, failing to understand the developmental and psychological processes that lead to academic achievement, and combinations of the factors noted (Spencer, 1999). Indeed, a developmental perspective that considers both the normative developmental tasks and specific challenges faced by African American youth at various ages (e.g., PVEST) is generally lacking and has scarcely been applied to analyze academic achievement. However, in a recent publication examining racial identity and academic achievement, Spencer, Noll, Stoltzfus, and Harpalani (2001) invalidated previous research suggesting that African American adolescents associate academic achievement with a Eurocentric orientation. They found that individuals with a Eurocentric orientation exhibited lower academic achievement and lower self-esteem than those individuals who have a proactive or internalized Afrocentric orientation. Although adolescents with a reactive or superficial Afrocentric orientation performed poorly, the study demonstrated the shortcomings of deficit-oriented models, which view academic achievement solely in terms of "acting White" (e.g., Fordham & Ogbu, 1986). Thus, interventions that promote proactive Afrocentricity and a positive sense of self should and could promote academic achievement. For example, Ghee, Walker, and Younger (1997) described an intervention for young African American males that included knowledge of Black history and participation in social activities such as sports to have positive increases in social knowledge and self-esteem and decreases in social influences from peers.

Deficit-oriented models are examples of some of the flaws that characterize available knowledge and science on African American youth generally, and, specifically, the life course experiences of African American males. The implications of research support notions that negative attitudes were learned and associated with negative contextual experiences (Cunningham, 1999; Stevenson, 1997). However, like many adolescent experiences, as Black males develop attitudes about selves and interpret their experiences, they may demonstrate behaviors and attitudes that may be exaggerated at first because the interpretation is quite new. When attempting to make meaning of one's personal and social experiences, adolescents make judgments based on what they know, experience, and feel competent about (Keating, 1990). For example, when adolescent males demonstrate attitudes and ideas about maleness that are exaggerated and often stereotypical, they are basing these learned attitudes on their negative experiences or lack of positive experiences (Cunningham, 1999; Spencer, 2001; Spencer et al., 1995). As indicated by the current research findings, the strongest predictors of bravado attitudes were personal negative experiences in one's context (Cunningham, 1999; Spencer, 2001). Thus, as males continue to develop a sense of who they are and what they want to become in life, their attitudes expressed may be responses to a highly stigmatized and high-risk environment. The reactive identity responses (e.g., bravado attitudes) may be coping strategies for survival.

As noted, the chapter examined the academic achievement patterns of African American males from a normal human development perspective, emphasizing the interaction between all domains of development in facilitating outcomes. The available literature that exclusively examines the development and education of Black males is sparse. The majority of research focuses on African American youth, both males and females. To be sure, there are many shared or similar experiences between genders. However, our contention is that the social ecology and normal developmental processes affect the genders differentially. Thus, further research is required. At the same time, the existing body of knowledge must be used to make inferences to the overall male population of African Americans.

African American male adolescents' pursuit of respect from others (e.g., teachers, police officers) can be problematic at best. Teachers uniformly expect studentlike behavior from children regardless of the problematic affective school climate experienced by many African American children and the group's unique historical conditions in America. Gender would appear to be an exacerbating factor for African American students. It results in a heightened salience of respect as a pursuit and often takes on an "in the moment or reaction which appear of more importance than the highly shared and valued acquisition of academic achievement" (Spencer, 1999, p. 51). As suggested, if generalized respect and understanding from the broader society and the school are not forthcoming, adolescent males' "reactive or less constructive" coping response may be the taking on of "habitual right actions," which are polar opposites to those generally valued by society and anticipated by schools.

Specifically, as suggested by Spencer (1999), gender intensified behavior, such as hypermasculinity, may be seen by youth as potentially more effective in generating respect than the instrumentality- and future-linked outcomes associated with academic achievement. The relatively late acquisition of a time perspective or a true sense of the future, as linked to the present and past as a cognitive construction and acquisition, are usually reserved until mid- or late adolescence. Before then, young people require significant aid in understanding and implementing the links between current behavioral investments (e.g., studying and school engagement) and long-term valued outcomes (e.g., secondary school graduation and successful career preparation). Thus, the roles of parents, teachers, mentors, and other adults as social translators are evident. It is not surprising that many young men do not understand that the 12 years of primary and secondary school preparation and academic engagement provide an important opportunity of life course salience. It increases (not guarantees) the probability of acquiring the very long-term respect that hypermasculine behavior connotes and that Black males and adolescents desperately seek and need. However, the variety of historical, structural, and contemporary barriers and challenges make the process inopportune at best.

Promoting issues of academic resilience within multiple perspectives is needed. The present study is an example that future prevention and intervention efforts must be made aware of: The consideration of multifarious foci for effective programming is a necessity. Programs that focus on facilitating males' positive achievement must be accompanied with training adults who interact with males as well. Because the Black males' perceptions of negative experiences were the strongest and most consistent predictor of bravado attitudes, changing the attitude alone will not suffice. Changing the environment that influences the reactive attitude is not merely needed but, in fact, is essential.

NOTE

1. During the period of data collection, for a family of four, the criterion for poverty was an annual family income of $13,950 or less.

REFERENCES

Aaron, R. L., & Powell, G. (1983). An investigation of the relationship between intelligence score and rate for word recall in a naturally occurring classroom setting. *Educational and Psychological Research, 3,* 219–234.

Baron, R. M., & Kenny, D. A. (1986). The moderator-mediator variable distinction in social psychological research: Conceptual, strategic, and statistical considerations. *Journal of Personality and Social Psychology, 51*(6), 1173–1182.

Bronfenbrenner, U. (1974). Is early education effective? In M. Guttentag & E. Struening (Eds.), *Handbook of evaluation research.* Beverly Hills, CA: Sage.

Bronfenbrenner, U. (1989). Ecological systems theory. In R. Vasta (Ed.), *Annals of child development* (pp. 187–248). Greenwich, CT: JAI.

Brooks-Gunn, J., Klebanav, P. K., & Duncan, G. J. (1996). Ethnic differences in children's test scores: Role of economic deprivation, home environment, and maternal characteristics. *Child Development, 67,* 396–408.

Brooks-Gunn, J., & Warren, M. P. (1985). Measuring physical status and timing in early adolescence: A developmental perspective. *Journal of Youth and Adolescence, 14,* 163–189.

Byrnes, J. P. (2001). *Minds, brains, and learning: Understanding the psychological and educational relevance of neuroscientific research.* New York: Guilford.

Cunningham, M. (1993). African American males' sex role development: A literature review. *Journal of African American Male Studies, 1,* 20–37.

Cunningham, M. (1994). Expressions of manhood: Predictors of educational achievement and African American adolescent males. *Dissertation Abstracts International, 34,* 5-A. (University Microfilms No. 1223)

Cunningham, M. (1999). African American males' perceptions of their community resources and constraints: A longitudinal analysis. *Journal of Community Psychology, 27,* 569–588.

Cunningham, M. (2001). African American males. In J. Lerner & R. Lerner (Eds.), *Adolescence in America: An encyclopedia* (pp. 32–34). Santa Barbara, CA: ABC-CLIO.

Cunningham, M., & Spencer, M. B. (1996). The Black Male Experiences Measure. In R. L. Jones (Ed.), *Handbook of tests and measurements for Black populations* (pp. 301–310). Hampton, VA: Cobb & Henry.

Cunningham, M., & Spencer, M. B. (2000). Conceptual and methodological issues in studying minority adolescents. In R. Montemayor, G. R. Adams, & T. P. Gullota (Eds.), *Adolescent diversity in ethnic, economic, and cultural contexts* (pp. 235–257). Thousand Oaks, CA: Sage.

Dupree, D., Spencer, M. B., & Bell, S. (1997). African American children. In G. Johnson-Powell & J. Yamamoto (Eds.), *Transcultural child development: Psychological assessment and treatment* (pp. 237–268). New York: John Wiley.

Dweck, C. S. (1978). Achievement. In M. Lamb (Ed.), *Social and personality development* (pp. 114–130). New York: Holt, Rinehart & Winston.

Entwisle, D. R., & Alexander, K. L. (1990). Beginning school math competence: Minority and majority comparisons. *Child Development, 61,* 454–471.

Fordham, S., & Ogbu, J. U. (1986). Black students' school success: Coping with the "burden of 'acting White.'" *Urban Review, 18,* 176–206.

Garibaldi, A. M. (1992). Educating and motivating African American males to succeed. *Journal of Negro Education, 61*(1), 4–11.

Ghee, K. L., Walker, J., & Younger, A. C. (1997). The RAAMUS Academy: Evaluation of an educultural intervention for young African American males. *Journal of Prevention and Intervention in the Community, 16,* 87–102.

Irvine, J. J. (1990). *Black students and school failure: Policies, practices and prescriptions.* New York: Greenwood.

Jones, J. M. (1991). Racism: A cultural analysis of the problem. In R. L. Jones (Ed.), *Black psychology* (3rd ed., pp. 609–735). Hampton, VA: Cobb & Henry.

Keating, D. P. (1990). Adolescent thinking. In S. S. Feldman & G. R. Elliott (Eds.), *At the threshold: The developing adolescent* (pp. 54–89). Cambridge, MA: Harvard University Press.

Lee, V., Brooks-Gunn, J., & Schnur, E. (1988). Does Head Start work? A 1-year follow-up comparison of disadvantaged children attending Head Start, no preschool, and other preschool programs. *Developmental Psychology, 24,* 210–222.

Lee, V., Brooks-Gunn, J., Schnur, E., & Liaw, F. (1990). Are Head Start effects sustained? A longitudinal follow-up comparison of disadvantaged children attending Head Start, no preschool, and other preschool programs. *Child Development, 61,* 495–507.

McCall, R. (1993). *Head Start: Its potential, its achievements, its future— A briefing paper for policy makers.* Pittsburgh, PA: University of Pittsburgh, Office of Child Development, Center for Social and Urban Research.

McDermott, P. A., & Spencer, M. B. (1997). *Measurement properties of revised scale of teacher expectations of Black males in interim research report no. 26.* Philadelphia: University of Pennsylvania, Center for Health, Achievement, Neighborhood, Growth, and Ethnic Studies.

McLendon, C., Nettles, S. M., & Wigfield, A. (2000). Fostering resilience in high school classrooms: A study of the PASS program (Promoting Achievement in School Through Sport). In M. G. Sanders (Ed.), *Schooling students placed at risk: Research, policy, and practice in the education of poor and minority adolescents* (pp. 289–307). Mahwah, NJ: Lawrence Erlbaum.

McLoyd, V. C. (1985). Are toys (just) toys? Exploring their effects on pretend play of low-income preschoolers. In M. B. Spencer, G. K. Brookins, & W. R. Allen (Eds.), *Beginnings: The social and affective development of Black children* (pp. 81–100). Hillsdale, NJ: Lawrence Erlbaum.

McLoyd, V. C. (1998). Socioeconomic disadvantage and child development. *American Psychologist, 53,* 185–204.

Moore, G. E. (1985). Ethnicity as a variable in child development. In M. B. Spencer, G. K. Brookins, & W. R. Allen (Eds.), *Beginnings: The social and affective development of Black children* (pp. 101–115). Hillsdale, NJ: Lawrence Erlbaum.

Mosher, D. L., & Sirkin, M. (1984). Measuring a macho personality constellation. *Journal of Research in Personality, 18*(2), 150–163.

Nettles, S. M., Mucherah, W., & Jones, D. S. (2000). Understanding resilience: The role of social resources. *Journal of Education for Students Placed at Risk, 5*(1/2), 47–60.

Patterson, C. J., Kupersmidt, J. B., & Vaden, N. A. (1990). Income level, gender, ethnicity, and household composition as predictors of children's school-based competence. *Child Development, 61,* 485–494.

Phelan, P., Davidson, A. L., & Cao, H. T. (1991). Students' multiple worlds: Negotiating the boundaries of family, peer, and school cultures. *Anthropology & Education Quarterly, 22,* 224–250.

Randolph, S. M., Koblinsky, S. A., & Roberts, D. (1996). Studying the role of family and school in the development of African American preschoolers in violent neighborhoods. *Journal of Negro Education, 65,* 282–294.

Slaughter, D. T. (1988). Black children, schooling, and educational interventions. *New Directions for Child Development, 42,* 109–116.

Spencer, M. B. (1983). Children's cultural values and parental child rearing strategies. *Developmental Review, 3,* 351–370.

Spencer, M. B. (1986). Risk and resilience: How Black children cope with stress. *Social Science, 71*(1), 22–26.

Spencer, M. B. (1989). *Patterns of developmental transitions for economically disadvantaged Black male adolescents.* Proposal submitted to and funded by the Spencer Foundation, Chicago.

Spencer, M. B. (1990). Parental values transmission: Implications for Black child development. In J. B. Stewart & H. Cheatam (Eds.), *Interdisciplinary perspective on Black families* (pp. 111–130). New Brunswick, NJ: Transactions.

Spencer, M. B. (1995). Old issues and new theorizing about African American youth: A phenomenological variant of ecological systems theory. In R. L. Taylor (Ed.), *Black youth: Perspectives on their status in the United States* (pp. 37–70). Westport, CT: Praeger.

Spencer, M. B. (1999). Social and cultural influences on school adjustment: The application of an identity-focused cultural ecological perspective. *Educational Psychologist, 34*(1), 43–57.

Spencer, M. B. (2001). Resiliency and fragility factors associated with the contextual experiences of low-resource urban African-American male youth and families. In A. Booth & A. C. Crouter (Eds.), *Does it take a village? Community effects on children, adolescents and families* (pp. 51–78). Mahwah, NJ: Lawrence Erlbaum.

Spencer, M. B., Coles, S. P., Dupree, D., Glymph, A., & Pierre, P. (1993). Self-efficacy among urban African American early adolescents: Exploring issues of risk, vulnerability, and resilience. *Development and Psychopathology, 5,* 719–739.

Spencer, M. B., Cunningham, M., & Swanson, D. P. (1995). Identity as coping: Adolescent African-American males' adaptive responses to high-risk environments. In H. W. Harris, H. C. Blue, & E. H. Griffith

(Eds.), *Racial and ethnic identity: Psychological development and creative expression* (pp. 331–352). Boston: Routledge Kegan Paul.

Spencer, M. B., Dobbs, B., & Swanson, D. P. (1988). Afro-American adolescents: Adaptational process and socioeconomic diversity in behavioral outcomes. *Journal of Adolescence, 11,* 117–137.

Spencer, M. B., & Dornbusch, S. (1990). American minority adolescents. In S. Feldman & G. Elliot (Eds.), *At the threshold: The developing adolescent* (pp. 123–146). Cambridge, MA: Harvard University Press.

Spencer, M. B., Dupree, D., & Hartmann, T. (1997). A phenomenological variant of ecological systems theory (PVEST): A self-organization perspective in context. *Development and Psychopathology, 9,* 817–833.

Spencer, M. B., Dupree, D., Swanson, D. P., & Cunningham, M. (1996). Parental monitoring and adolescents' sense of responsibility for their own learning: An examination of sex differences. *Journal of Negro Education, 65*(1), 30–43.

Spencer, M. B., Noll, E., Stoltzfus, J., & Harpalani, V. (2001). Identity and school adjustment: Revisiting the "acting White" assumption. *Educational Psychologist, 36*(1), 21–30.

Spencer, M. B., Swanson, D. P., & Cunningham, M. (1991). Ethnicity, identity and competence formation: Adolescent transition and identity transformations. *Journal of Negro Education, 60,* 366–387.

Stevenson, H. C. (1997). "Missed, dissed, and pissed": Making meaning of neighborhood risk, fear and anger management in urban Black youth. *Cultural Diversity and Mental Health, 3*(1), 37–52.

Swanson, D. P., & Spencer, M. B. (1995). Developmental and contextual considerations for research on African American adolescents. In H. Fitzgerald, B. M. Lester, & B. Zuckerman (Eds.), *Children of color: Research, health and public policy issues.* New York: Garland.

Swanson, D. P., Spencer, M. B., & Petersen, A. (1998). Identity formation in adolescence. In K. Borman & B. Schneider (Eds.), *The adolescent years: Social influences and educational challenges* (Ninety-seventh Yearbook of the National Society for the Study of Education, Part 1, pp. 18–41). Chicago: University of Chicago Press.

Trueba, H. T. (1988). Culturally based explanations of minority students' academic achievement. *Anthropology & Education Quarterly, 19*(3), 270–287.

Weis, L. (1995). Without dependence on welfare for life: Black women in community college. *Urban Review, 17,* 233–255.

White, R. (1959). Motivation reconsider: The concept of competence. *Psychological Review, 66,* 297–333.

CHAPTER EIGHT

Athletics, Academics, and African American Males

Jomills Henry Braddock II

University of Miami

Preparing and motivating adolescents for high school and beyond involves structuring environments where appropriate intellectual, academic, personal, and social skills that will enable them to think independently and act responsibly will be developed. Because schools often find it difficult to provide appropriate *new* or *extra* incentives that encourage academic investment and prosocial behaviors among students, it is essential that educators find more effective ways of utilizing *existing* programs and activities.

The athletic programs in middle and high schools represent a unique interface between the adolescent subculture and the school, and they claim a significant amount of student time, interest, and effort. School-based athletic activities are pervasive features of most American middle and high schools, yet their potential for creating major changes in student motivation, development, and success remains untapped. School sports activities are not widely or routinely

AUTHOR'S NOTE: An earlier version of this paper was presented at the Symposium on African American Male Achievement sponsored by the Office of Educational Research and Improvement (OERI) and hosted by Howard University, Washington, DC, December, 2000.

examined for such purposes. As a result, the role of athletic activities in schools continues to generate considerable debate.

In this chapter, athletic involvement is examined as a learning, socialization, and social bonding context that can be particularly important in fostering both social and academic development outcomes among African American males. Reviewing extant studies and using data from national surveys, this chapter has the following goals. First, it examines athletic participation patterns among African American males. Second, it reviews evidence on the relationship between athletic involvement and academic resiliency and achievement. Third, it describes a conceptual framework for understanding the relationship between athletic involvement and academic success. Fourth, it discusses possibilities for expanding the role of athletics in *curricular* and *extracurricular* settings. Finally, it suggests that increasing and diversifying opportunities for athletic involvement may be especially useful strategies for facilitating academic achievement and attainment among African American males.

WHY SCHOOL SPORTS MATTER

The argument that participation in athletics provides youth "value-added" opportunities to acquire, develop, and rehearse attitudes and skills that provide a foundation for future educational and economic success has been recognized for some time (Commission on the Reorganization of Secondary Education, 1918; Hanks & Eckland, 1976; Braddock, 1980, 1981; Hartman, 1990; Otto, 1975).

School-based athletics are ubiquitous components of American secondary schools. According to tabulations based on nationally representative data on schools and students, collected in the National Educational Longitudinal Study (NELS: 88), 82% of middle schools and 98% of high schools provide *interscholastic sports* participation opportunities (competition between teams from different schools) to their students; while 72% of middle schools and 56% of high schools also offer *intramural sports* programs (competition among teams within the same school) to their students.

Athletic programs in middle and high schools also involve significant numbers of students. Tabulations that are also based on the NELS: 88 data show that in the middle grades, 66% of the males and

54% of the females report active involvement in interscholastic sports programs. At the high school level, the data also show broad-based participation among 10th-grade males (57%) and females (38%).

According to Ewing, Seefeldt, and Brown (1996), estimates from the National Center for Education Statistics (NCES) indicate that in 1995, of approximately 48 million eligible participants, ranging in age from 5 to 17, approximately 22 million participated in agency-sponsored sports, over two million (2,368,700) participated in club sports, over 14 million (14,512,200) participated in recreational sports programs, 5,776,820 participated in interscholastic sports, and 451,000 participated in intramural sports. These results indicate that many of our nation's youth are involved in organized sport activities at school and in their communities.

Sports are important activities for many students. For example, preliminary tabulations from NELS: 88 reveal that 81% of 10th-grade males and 71% of 12th grade males, report that, among their friends, it is important to play sports. Among females, 66% of the 10th graders and 50% of the 12th graders report that their friends think it is important to play sports. Additionally, 49% of 10th-grade males and 34% of 10th-grade females report having athletes as role models.

Sports are also important to parents. According to a recent Gallup survey, when asked if they would prefer their oldest child to be "a straight A student" or "an average student who is involved in sports and extracurricular activities," only 29% of parents chose the former, while 60% of the parents chose the latter (Phi Delta Kappan, 1996). These results suggest that parents appear to value the role of sports and extracurricular activities in their children's development. Given the widespread availability of athletics and their appeal to adolescents and their families, it is possible that school- and community-based sports could be useful in enhancing academic resilience and prosocial behaviors among young people.

AFRICAN AMERICAN MALE PARTICIPATION IN HIGH SCHOOL VARSITY SPORTS

Media portrayals and popular stereotypes might suggest that African American male youth participate excessively in sports. To examine African American and non-Black male participation patterns in varsity interscholastic sports, we use data from high school senior participants in both the High School and Beyond (HSB) and the National Educational Longitudinal Study of 1988. The comparison strives to examine *parity* trends over time in African American and non-Black males' participation in varsity athletics using *social indicators* (U.S. Civil Rights Commission, 1978). Social indicators generally refer to statistical indices by which demographers, population analysts, and social policy analysts estimate the state-of-being of a given population, at a given time, with respect to a particular set of characteristics (Bauer, 1966).

Statistical comparisons of 12th-grade African American and non-Black male participation in *varsity sports* are presented in Table 8.1.

This table shows that interscholastic sport participation was common among male high school seniors in 1982 (35% for African Americans and 36% for non-Blacks) and 1992 (54% for African Americans and 50% for non-Blacks). Among both African American and non-Black males, overall interscholastic athletic participation increased comparably from 1982 to 1992 (19% and 14%, respectively). When African American and non-Black males' participation patterns are examined by SES level, the parity indicators reveal that the groups were comparable within the upper half of the SES distribution in 1992. In contrast, in 1982, the parity indicator (.79) for African American males in the highest SES quartile shows that they were only 79% as likely (or 21% less likely) as non-Blacks to participate in varsity sports.

These parity indicators also reveal that the groups differed significantly within the lower half of the socioeconomic status (SES) distribution in 1992. The parity indicators for African American males in the lowest SES quartile shows that they were 18% more likely than non-Blacks to participate in varsity sports. Similarly, the parity indicators for African American males in the second lowest SES quartile shows that they were 24% more likely than non-Blacks to participate in varsity sports. This stands in contrast to 1982 where the parity indicators for African American males in the bottom two SES quartiles shows that they were 6% or 7% more likely than non-Blacks to participate in varsity sports.

Examining participation patterns by test scores, the parity indicator reveals that the groups were roughly comparable across categories of the test score distribution in 1982. However, in 1992, the parity indicator (.56) for African American males in the highest test quartile shows that they were 44% less likely than non-Blacks to

Table 8.1   Patterns of Male Seniors Participating in Interscholastic High School Athletics by Race

	1982			1992		
	African American Males N = 710	Non-Black Males N = 4,993	All Males N = 5,703	African American Males N = 516	Non-Black Males N = 4,854	All Males N = 5,370
Total	34.9	36.1	36.0	53.9	50.3	50.7
Parity indicator	*.97*	*1.00*	*1.00*	*1.06*	*.99*	*1.00*
SES						
Highest quartile	28.7	37.0*	36.4	61.5	59.6	59.7
Parity indicator	*.79*	*1.02*	*1.00*	*1.03*	*1.00*	*1.00*
Third quartile	27.7	35.0	34.2	52.3	52.2	52.2
Parity indicator	*.81*	*1.02*	*1.00*	*1.00*	*1.00*	*1.00*
Second quartile	40.8	37.6	38.1	58.0	45.4*	46.8
Parity indicator	*1.07*	*.99*	*1.00*	*1.24*	*.97*	*1.00*
Lowest quartile	36.4	33.9	34.3	48.4	39.5*	41.0
Parity indicator	*1.06*	*.99*	*1.00*	*1.18*	*.96*	*1.00*
Test Scores						
Highest quartile	34.5	35.9	35.8	31.3	56.1*	55.5
Parity indicator	*.96*	*1.00*	*1.00*	*.56*	*1.01*	*1.00*
Third quartile	38.5	34.8	35.3	58.0	50.0	50.6
Parity indicator	*1.11*	*.99*	*1.00*	*1.15*	*.99*	*1.00*
Second quartile	35.3	36.5	36.3	53.1	50.4	50.7
Parity indicator	*.97*	*1.00*	*1.00*	*1.05*	*.99*	*1.00*
Lowest quartile	32.1	36.9	36.0	58.6	42.4*	45.6

(Continued)

Table 8.1 (Continued)

	1982			1992		
	African American Males N = 710	Non-Black Males N = 4,993	All Males N = 5,703	African American Males N = 516	Non-Black Males N = 4,854	All Males N = 5,370
Parity indicator	.89	1.02	1.00	1.29	.93	1.00
Academic Program						
General	34.1	34.9	34.8	47.7	46.5	46.7
Parity indicator	.98	1.00	1.00	1.02	1.00	1.00
Vocational	35.9	37.8	37.6	46.4	32.2*	33.8
Parity indicator	.95	1.01	1.00	1.37[a]	.95	1.00
Academic	34.9	35.7	35.6	62.4	60.1	60.3
Parity indicator	.98	1.00	1.00	1.03	1.00	1.00
School Location						
Urban	39.1	35.8	36.7	51.0	47.6	48.1
Parity indicator	1.07	.98	1.00	1.06	.99	1.00
Rural	22.1	34.0*	33.3	56.6	52.0	52.2
Parity indicator	.66	1.02	1.00	1.08	1.00	1.00
Suburban	33.7	37.4	37.1	57.1	51.6	52.0
Parity Indicator	.91	1.01	1.00	1.10	.99	1.00

SOURCES: 1992 data based on tabulations from second follow-up of National Educational Longitudinal Study of 1988; 1982 data based on tabulations from High School and Beyond sophomore cohort first follow-up.

NOTE: The parity indicator represents the ratio of specific group participation percentages to the total group participation percentage. Values above unity (1.00) reflect overrepresentation; values below unity reflect underrepresentation.

a. This can be interpreted as follows: In 1992, African American males in vocational programs were 37% more likely than their non-Black male peers to participate in varsity athletic programs.

*Indicates that the African American male percentage is significantly different ($p < .05$) from the non-Black male percentage.

participate in varsity sports. In contrast, the parity indicator (1.29) for African American males in the lowest test quartile shows that they were 29% more likely than non-Blacks to participate in varsity sports in 1992.

Examining participation patterns by high school academic program, the parity indicators reveal again that the groups were roughly comparable across academic programs in 1982. However, in 1992, the parity indicator (1.37) for African American males in vocational programs shows that they were 37% more likely than non-Blacks to participate in varsity sports.

When participation patterns are examined by school location, in 1982, the parity indicator (.66) for African American males in rural schools shows that they were 34% less likely than non-Blacks to participate in varsity sports. By 1992, this ethnic difference by school location disappeared.

Thus, while varsity sport participation grew between 1982 and 1992 among all males, the increase appears to have been greater for African American males than among non-Black males. This increase among African American males relative to their non-Black peers was especially noted among males from lower SES backgrounds, among males whose test scores were lower, among males enrolled in vocational programs, and among rural males. Table 8.2 presents 1990 data showing national patterns in varsity sports participation for African American and non-Black male 10th graders.

Compared to non-Black males, African American males were significantly overrepresented in football and basketball, but significantly underrepresented in baseball, soccer, swimming, and other team sports. The parity indicator (1.48) for African American males in varsity football shows that they were 48% more likely than non-Blacks to participate in that sport in 1990. Similarly, the parity indicator (1.82) for African American males in varsity basketball shows that they were 82% more likely than non-Blacks to participate in that sport in 1990. However, the parity indicator (.75) for African American males in varsity baseball shows that they were 25% less likely than non-Blacks to participate in that sport in 1990. The parity indicator (.41) for African American males in varsity soccer shows that they were 59% less likely than non-Blacks to participate in that sport in 1990. For swimming, the parity indicator (.52) for African American males shows that they were 48% less likely than non-Blacks to participate. A similar pattern is observed for other team sports where the

Table 8.2   Sophomore Male Participation in Selected Interscholastic High School Sports by Race (1990)

	African Americans N = 516	Non-Blacks N = 4,854	All Males N = 5,370
Football	38.4	24.6*	25.9
Parity indicator	1.48	.95	1.00
Basketball	31.7	15.9*	17.4
Parity indicator	1.82[a]	.91	1.00
Baseball	11.0	15.1*	14.7
Parity indicator	.75	1.03	1.00
Soccer	3.1	8.1*	7.6
Parity indicator	.41	1.07	1.00
Swimming	1.6	3.3*	3.1
Parity indicator	.52	1.06	1.00
Other team sports	4.3	6.6*	6.3
Parity indicator	.68	1.05	1.00
Other individual sports	24.1	26.3	26.1
Parity indicator	.92	1.01	1.00

SOURCES: 1990 data based on tabulations from first follow-up of National Educational Longitudinal Study of 1988.

NOTE: The parity indicator represents the ratio of specific group participation percentages to the total group participation percentage. Values above unity (1.00) reflect overrepresentation; values below unity reflect undperrepresentation.

a. This can be interpreted as follows: "In 1990, African American males were 82% more likely than their non-Black male peers to participate in varsity basketball programs."

* Indicates that the African American male percentage is significantly different ($p < .05$) from the non-Black male percentage.

parity indicator (.68) for African American males shows that they were 32% less likely than non-Blacks to participate in other team sports in 1990.

African American male varsity sport participation was thus significantly overrepresented in two sports, football and basketball. In other types of varsity sports, baseball, soccer, swimming, and other team sports, African American males were significantly underrepresented.

What Is Known About Sports and Academics?

Over the years, a number of studies have examined the connection between athletic involvement and academic performance, yet this relationship continues to generate considerable debate. Two opposing themes exist in the literature on the relationship between African American involvement in sports and social mobility: the *sports-enhance-social-mobility* hypothesis and the *sports-impede-social-mobility* hypothesis. The sports-enhance-mobility hypothesis assumes that sport have often served minority groups to further their assimilation into American life (Boyle, 1963). Proponents of this perspective point to the highly visible or dramatic social ascent of African American male superstar athletes. The sports-impede-mobility hypothesis contends, on the other hand, that the few African Americans who have become wealthy and successful professional athletes are exceptions. According to Eitzen and Sage (1978: 230), "youngsters who devote their lives to the pursuit of athletic stardom are, except for the fortunate few, doomed to failure in sports and failure in the real world where sports skills are essentially irrelevant to occupational placement and advancement." Despite the paucity of empirical data on this topic, the sport-impedes-mobility hypothesis has become the dominant theme (Coakley, 1978; Eitzen and Sage, 1978; Michener, 1976; Snyder and Spreitzer, 1978). Nevertheless, most of the empirical literature on this topic (Braddock, 1980, 1981; Taylor & Chiogioji, 1988; Trent, 1982; Trent & Braddock, 1992; Braddock, 1982; Dawkins, 1982; Dawkins & Braddock, 1982; Harris & Hunt, 1982; Otto, 1975; Picou, 1978) reports that sport participation is positively associated with a variety of academic achievement outcomes.

In one of the first large-scale empirical studies, Bend (1968) analyzed 6-year interval data from Project TALENT, a 20-year longitudinal study of 400,000 American high school students that began in 1960. He found that high school athletes, compared to non-athletes, were more likely to graduate from college and earn higher salaries even when controlling for social class background and intelligence. Schafer and Armer (1968), in a smaller study, also found that athletes tended to have higher grade point averages than non-athletes, even when intelligence, social class background, and type of curriculum were taken into account. They also found that athletes tended to hold higher educational aspirations than did non-athletes.

Rehberg and Schafer (1968) reported similar results and noted that the association between athletic participation and higher educational expectations was most evident among boys from less advantaged backgrounds. Similar results have also been documented in other studies (Buhrmann, 1972; Picou & Curry, 1974). Otto and Alwin (1977) note not only a positive association of athletic involvement with educational aspirations and attainments but with occupational aspirations and attainments as well.

Spady (1970), on the other hand, found that athletic participation without other extracurricular participation tended to depress aspirations and achievement. High school athletes were less likely to complete college if their educational goals were solely a function of athletic participation or if college was perceived mainly as a vehicle for prolonging one's athletic career. In perhaps the most sophisticated study of its time, Hanks and Eckland (1976) concluded that "Athletics appears neither to depress nor to especially enhance the academic performance of its participants." (p. 292) They argued that athletics and other forms of extracurricular participation "are largely orthogonal to one another, and, further, have both dissimilar antecedents and outcomes" (p. 273). Lueptow and Kayser (1973, 1974) and Hauser and Lueptow (1978) also raised serious questions regarding the causal relationship between athletic participation and academic participation. Analyzing quasi-longitudinal data, they did not find significantly higher school grades among athletes than among non-athletes. They concluded that the often observed differences in high school grade-point averages between the two groups was a function of initial differences between athletes and non-athletes and was not a consequence of athletic participation.

Among the early studies examining the relationship between athletic participation and status attainment, only three considered racial variations. Picou (1978) examined the relationship between athletic participation and educational aspirations separately for African American and White adolescent males. His findings showed positive direct or unmediated effects of athletic participation on educational aspirations for African Americans, while the positive effects of sports participation for Whites were found to be mediated through peer plans and academic achievement. Picou (1978) speculated that, for African Americans, the relationship between athletic participation and educational aspirations might be better understood by considering other intervening mechanisms. For example, self-esteem may be a potentially important intervening mechanism because of the status accorded to sports achievement in the African American community (Braddock, 1978). Additionally, sources other than parents, teachers, and peers may provide interpersonal encouragement to attend college. It has been demonstrated that coaches exert an important influence on the educational and occupational goals of low SES athletes (Snyder, 1972), and coaches may be particularly salient reference individuals for African American athletes. Similarly, the author's early analysis of data from the National Longitudinal Study of 1972 found athletic participation, net of social class and academic achievement tests, to be positively associated with academic self-esteem, curriculum placement, grades, and college plans for African American as well as White males (Braddock, 1981). However, due to methodological and research design limitations, some of the findings of these early studies are not clearly generalizable, nor do they clearly support the implications drawn from them about racial differences in the effects of athletic involvement on mobility.

Most of the recent studies using large national samples (Braddock, Royster, Hawkins, & Winfield, 1991; Hawkins, Royster, & Braddock, 1992; McNeal, 1995) that have examined the relationship between athletic participation and educational attainment within race-ethnic subgroups have often found significant positive associations between athletic participation and educational performance, persistence, attitudes, and future goals among African American males. However, in contrast to most other recent studies, Sabo, Melnick, and Vanfossen (1993) and Melnick, Sabo, and Vanfossen (1992) using High School and Beyond data, analyzed social mobility outcomes (educational and occupational attainment) and educational effects associated with athletic participation and found no significant educational benefits for African American males. Perhaps because of their atypical operationalization of sport (combining "participation" and "leadership roles") and analysis format (separating urban, suburban, and rural youth), their findings are inconsistent with other studies using High School and Beyond data, such as McNeal's (1995) results indicating that athletic involvement exhibited a significant negative effect on school dropout among African American males. Their results are also inconsistent with a number of other recent studies (Picou, 1978; Picou & Hwang, 1982; Picou, McCarter, & Howell, 1985; Braddock, 1981; Braddock et al., 1991;

Hawkins et al., 1992). For example, analyses of base-year data from the National Educational Longitudinal Study (NELS:88) found that sports participation was positively associated with several indicators of academic success among African American male eighth-graders (Braddock et al., 1991) such as stronger aspirations to enroll in academic or college preparatory programs in high school, definite plans to complete high school (interscholastic sports only), and higher expectations for attending college.

A subsequent analysis also found a similar pattern of effects among female African American eighth graders (Hawkins et al., 1992); however, females' plans to graduate from high school and attend college were found to be more strongly influenced by intramural sports participation than by interscholastic participation. These recent NELS:88 studies also showed that African American male and female interscholastic and intramural sports participants derived social status advantages, including popularity and a sense of importance, among their schoolmates that were directly related to their involvement in athletics. This is not surprising, given the special prominence that researchers have found athletes to occupy within the adolescent subculture of schools (Coleman, 1961; Braddock, 1982).

Additionally, some of the NELS:88 studies have shown positive links between athletic participation and several indicators of pro-academic investment behaviors and attitudes. Male athletes have been shown to be less likely to be involved in school-related social misconduct problems (interscholastic only), more likely to look forward to their core curriculum classes (interscholastic only), and less likely to be judged by their teachers as not giving full effort in their class work (intramural only). Their female athlete counterparts were less likely to miss classes and more likely to look forward to their core curriculum classes (interscholastic only). These positive associations appear to be largely direct and unmediated when other important student background variables (age, SES, standardized test scores, and family composition) and school characteristics (urbanicity, enrollment size, poverty concentration, and students' ability group placement) were statistically controlled.

Taken together, these data offer evidence that athletic participation can and often does have a positive impact on student motivation and engagement in traditional pro-academic norms and behaviors for males and females. There is an obvious need for further, higher-quality research in this area. Only a small number of studies employed national samples, while less than half employed what could nominally be termed quasi-longitudinal designs. Variable operationalization and measurement was also problematic in a number of instances.

Although several studies have identified a consistent pattern of positive associations between sport participation and pro-academic behaviors among high school students, there are still questions to be answered regarding the lasting effect relationship/associations between sport participation on students' academic investment and achievement behaviors, how different levels and types of sport participation affect academic investment, and whether athletic participation varies by student ethnicity and gender. In addition, despite the finding that sport participation may be particularly helpful in encouraging academic persistence among at-risk students (Picou, 1978; Braddock, 1981; Braddock et al., 1991), few studies have actually suggested ways in which schools might link sport participation with specific academic goals (see Braddock et al., 1991 for an exception). That is, despite a growing body of correlational studies finding positive associations between sport involvement and diverse academic outcomes, few researchers examining this relationship have sought to specify and operationalize what it is about sports that raises student achievement. The next section offers a conceptual framework that identifies a broad set of potential influences and mediating processes linking athletic involvement and academic success.

TOWARD A CONCEPTUAL FRAMEWORK FOR UNDERSTANDING THE RELATIONSHIP BETWEEN ATHLETIC INVOLVEMENT AND ACADEMIC SUCCESS

Clearly, participation in and mastery of certain physical activities associated with sport can enhance certain skills associated with cognitive functioning (e.g., hand-eye coordination, spatial relations). Physical conditioning and fitness may also be important to young people's academic well-being. However, theory and research suggest that the *learning, socialization,* and *social bonding* experiences associated with involvement in organized sport contexts can have a major impact on youth development outcomes, including academics. Consequently, the consistently observed positive association

Figure 8.1   A Model of Athletic Participation's Influence on Academic
Success

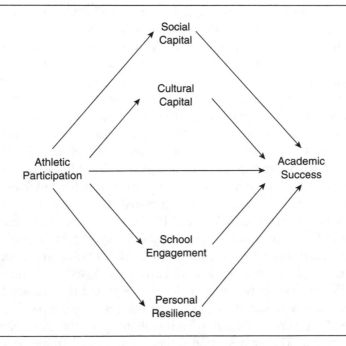

between athletic participation and academic success might best be
understood by examining the varied mediating channels through
which sport involvement can affect academic performance. A review
of the pertinent literature shows that *social capital, cultural capital,
personal resilience,* and *school engagement* are essential correlates
of academic success and are associated with participation in athletic
activities. Figure 8.1 provides a model of the potential relations
between these factors.

As the model depicts, organized school-based sport contexts are
assumed to be sites where adolescent involvement can promote school
engagement and nurture the development of social capital, cultural
capital, and personal resiliency that lead to academic success.

Athletic Participation and School Engagement

School engagement has been defined as "active involvement,
commitment, and concentrated attention, in contrast to superficial

participation, apathy, or lack of interest" (Newmann, 1992). Research has shown that students who are not engaged are less involved, committed, and attached to school and are less likely to internalize the educational material into their lives. Furthermore, students with low levels of engagement become increasingly at risk for school failure and dropout (McNeal, 1995). Finn (1993) and McNeal (1995) note the importance of identifying aspects of schools that can be used to encourage student engagement.

Academic investment refers to the amount of time and effort students spend on school activities. Snyder and Spreitzer (1990) argue that it is a misperception that involvement in school athletics will necessarily detract from time available for academic pursuits. As a consequence, they contend that involvement in athletic activities can lead to academic enhancement due to increased interest in school, motivation to perform in order to remain eligible and heightened self-worth. Furthermore, special attention from parents, teachers and coaches, may lead to membership in elite peer groups and involvement in sport with an orientation toward academic success. All of this "may lead to experiences, attitudes, self-perceptions, and treatment that enhance the academic role" (Snyder & Spreitzer, 1990).

The sport experience could be perceived as an agent for socialization. Eitzen and Sage (1989) contend that participation in sports programs encourages allegiance and loyalty to schools, a unification of students, and social control in that it instills the societal values of working hard work and discipline. They note that organized youth sports, such as programs found in schools, have a formal division of labor, with an emphasis on such traits as hard work, obedience, punctuality, and respect for those in authority. Such socialization skills could help prepare students for classwork and may foster respect for authority figures in school. Similarly, Fejgin (1994) asserts that high school competitive sport involvement can provide positive experiences that enhance student adjustment to school rules, schoolwork, and the basic values of an achievement oriented society. Lamborn et al (1992) suggest that involvement in non-instructional contexts, such as school sport, may result in a sense of bonding to the school that enhances the student's academic commitment indirectly, and may offer the opportunity for students to mix with academically oriented peer groups.

Research has examined school engagement in the context of student academic investment behaviors. Consistent with general patterns in the literature on this topic, research found that sports participation is positively associated with African American eighth-grade males, aspirations to enroll in academic or college preparatory programs in high school, to have definite plans to complete high school (interscholastic sports only), and to attend college (Braddock et al., 1991). The research also found that both interscholastic and intramural sports participants derive social status advantages—popularity and a sense of importance—among their schoolmates that are directly related to their involvement in athletics. Additionally, our data showed some positive links between athletic participation and several indicators of pro-academic investment behaviors and attitudes. Athletes were found to be less likely to be involved in school-related social misconduct problems (interscholastic only), more likely to look forward to their core curriculum classes (interscholastic only), and less likely to be judged by their teachers as not giving full effort in their class work (intramural only). These positive associations appeared to be largely direct and unmediated when other important student background (age, SES, standardized test scores, and family composition) and school characteristics (urbanicity, enrollment size, poverty concentration, and students' ability group placement) are statistically controlled.

Research suggests that large numbers of young people, and especially minority and low income students, lack a strong sense of hope and may therefore become "at risk" for early school failure. Several studies have shown that although most students begin school with high levels of enthusiasm, many lose this early enthusiasm over time and respond less and less to academic demands. This is especially true among African American males (Simmons & Grady, 1990). Rutter (1987) defines resilience as an individual's positive response to situations of stress and adversity. Thus, resilience may be seen as a protective mechanism that is likely to emerge from such specific personality features as self-esteem and self-efficacy, or from family cohesion and the availability of external support systems that are designed to reinforce coping efforts. Braddock et al. (1991) adopt a slightly modified interpretation of academic resilience, conceptualizing resilience not as a personality or individually held trait that emerges in response to academic failure but as a quality more akin to the kind of persistence that develops as a result of participation in athletic activities (Campbell, 1983). In this sense, academic resilience and attachment parallel the persistence and determination generated in the daily athletic activities of coming to practice, stretching and conditioning the body, competing, and finally, starting the process all over again, despite occasional setbacks. Braddock et al. (1991) describe how sport involvement meets each of Rutter's (1987) four mechanisms that help individuals to mediate adverse circumstances or demonstrate resilient behaviors. These mechanisms: (1) reduce the impact of risks, (2) reduce the likelihood of negative chain reactions associated with adversity, (3) establish and maintain self-esteem and self-efficacy, and (4) create new opportunities for success.

In athletic participation, the major *risks* involved are competitive losses. However, the structure of sport competitions generally guarantees several chances to "place" before losses take on a permanent status. Examples include preseason games, scrimmages, and losses early in the season. This sort of structure reduces the impact of the risk of competing so that students are able, between risks, to regroup, restrategize, and practice in order to make a better showing in the next competition (Dane, 1990). Each effort to prepare anew is a resilience mechanism that could be applied within the academic setting. If, for example, students were provided several opportunities to master certain academic tasks and were given time between tasks to analyze weaknesses and to practice, then academic performance and mastery would very likely improve. Indeed, recent remediation reform suggestions often emphasize such strategies.

A related aspect of athletic participation involves how losses are interpreted and negotiated. After games are lost, coaches and players usually review the overall game strategy, make note of problem areas, and devise a plan of action for practice the following week that is designed to improve performance in problem areas. This kind of strategy significantly reduces the likelihood of *negative chain reactions* following game losses and promotes constructive analysis of strengths and weaknesses with an eye toward improvement. We see such a coaching strategy as a particularly effective classroom strategy, allowing teachers and students to analyze academic strengths and weaknesses and to work out plans of action together that may prevent consecutive failures and encourage continuous positive interactions between students and teachers.

Winning in sport competitions is commonly thought to enhance *self-esteem* and *self-efficacy* among students, but even losses may convey a sense of accomplishment. A game, well-played, tends to generate respect between teams and players and the wider student population, which not only reduces the impact of loss, but also contributes to the self-esteem and self-efficacy of players. Rutter (1987) contends that self-esteem and efficacy are in large measure based upon an individual's successful accomplishment of tasks that are important to that individual. Sports, as shown earlier, are clearly important to the many youngsters who devote considerable time, energy, and other resources to its pursuit. Sport involvement can be conceptualized as an investment and is, unlike many other school-based adolescent activities, usually a function of a student's own choosing rather than the decision of parents and teachers (Nettles, 1989).

Finally, sports create important *opportunities for students to excel* and to fit into the school community in a meaningful way (Coleman, 1990; Dane, 1990; Wilson, 1990). Such opportunities are especially important for at-risk students, who may lack legitimate opportunities for investment of their skills and efforts outside of the school setting (Nettles, 1989; Segrave & Hastad, 1984; Trent, 1982). In addition, sport involvement may provide many young males with positive rewards for prosocial behavior both in the wider social environment and among their peers. This intersection of peer/societal endorsement of prosocial conduct is important to the young males and may help to encourage future legitimate pursuits in both educational and economic arenas (Dane, 1990; Wilson, 1990).

Athletic Participation and Cultural Capital

Empirical studies document a strong link between certain family characteristics and student academic success. Yet familial contributions to students educational experiences vary in myriad ways, even within socioeconomic strata. These differences have been associated with variations in "cultural capital" among families. First introduced by Bourdieu (1977) and extended by DiMaggio (1982), the concept of cultural capital has been used to explain how social inequality is reproduced through institutions such as schools. Cultural capital refers to cultural signals such as attitudes, behaviors, preferences, and credentials that are commonly used for social and cultural inclusion and exclusion (Lamont & Lareau, 1988). Thus, cultural capital is those nonmaterial aspects of the middle-class lifestyle that serve to separate its members from working- and lower-class individuals. Cultural capital is often characterized by elite practices such as participating in cultural trips (to museums, art galleries, and the like) or taking extracurricular classes in culture areas (dance, art, and music). According to Bourdieu (1977), children who had such cultural opportunities were more likely to fare well in middle-class institutions (such as schools) because these institutions value and reward such experiences. Lower- and working-class youth were less likely to have these cultural experiences , were also are at a disadvantage in school. However, Lareau and Horvat (1999) suggest that race has an independent effect on social interactions within schools and between parents and schools. They argue that while the presence of cultural capital is important, the activation and acceptance of that capital in educational settings may differ by race. In other words, the return on cultural capital and other educational resources may be different for White students than it is for African American students. Roscigno and Ainsworth-Darnell (1999) also found that African American and low-SES students receive less educational return for their level of cultural capital than do White and higher-SES students.

This topic has not been well studied among African Americans or with regard to interscholastic sports. However, Eitle and Eitle (2000) have recently examined the effect of cultural capital on African American male participation in basketball and football. Using data from the National Educational Longitudinal Study of 1988, they found that "a lack of cultural capital greatly increases the likelihood that African American males will play these sports (relative to whites)." McNeal's (1999) analysis suggests that participating in high school extracurricular activities (including sports) serves to increase levels of human, social, and cultural capital.

Athletic Participation and Social Capital

According to Bourdieu (1977, 1986), social capital refers to "the sum of resources, actual or virtual, that accrue to an individual or a group by virtue of possessing a durable network of more or less institutionalized relationships of mutual acquaintance and recognition." Parental involvement and peer networks are often examined in research focused on social capital and educational outcomes. For example, Finn (1989), Horn and Chen (1998), and McNeal (1995, 1997) have documented the connections between parental involvement, peers, student engagement, and several key indicators of educational success. These studies suggest that the frequency of parent-child school-related discussions and pro-academic peers affects students' likelihood of educational success. O'Bryan and Braddock (1999), using NELS:88 data, found that high school students' (including African American males) participation in sports is positively associated with increased social capital in the form of enhanced parental educational involvement, especially in the frequency of home discussions of educational matters. Additionally, Rodriguez and Braddock (2000) found that the effect of the "parental" and "peer" *social capital* measures operated with different degrees of intensity among males and females. Although both parental involvement and pro-academic peers were significantly related to life-chance perceptions among males and females, the magnitude of the relationship between parental involvement and life-chance perceptions is over twenty times larger among males than females, while the magnitude of the relationship between pro-academic peers and life-chance perceptions among males was twenty times smaller than among females.

New Directions for Sports in Educational Contexts

Building on current knowledge about how young people learn, this section describes emerging ideas for incorporating sport themes in school curriculum and classroom pedagogy. The principle that when students are taught educational concepts in a manner that is meaningful and important to them, they will more completely master and retain them, is both simple and time-tested. While this fundamental principle does not represent everyday practice in the typical American public school classroom, there are some excellent examples of this principle at work with sports. In "Scoring points with physics," Richardson (1995) describes how, as a middle-school teacher, she noticed that her students were most interested in topics that could be connected to their own interests, and observed that athletics was a major part of her students lives. She decided to develop strategies to use sports to teach physics, mathematics, and writing skills. She began with basketball and provided raw data for students to calculate percentages and averages and to graph the results of basketball shots made from three different positions on the court. Following the mathematics components, she provided lessons in the basic physics concepts involved in shooting a basketball, and why the ball is more likely to go in from certain areas on the court than from others. She then added a writing lesson where students researched the physics principles involved in their favorite sports and prepared brief research papers. There are other examples of using sports in teaching core subject matter in areas as diverse as history, physics, and mathematics at both the secondary and postsecondary levels (Bachin, 1999; Berntsen, 1995). Unfortunately, such examples are atypical and isolated, with the result that they rarely extend beyond the classrooms of uniquely innovative teachers. These strategies, while effective, have not become part of school-wide or systemic reform efforts.

Teaching Excellence Achievement and Motivation through Sport (TEAMS)

To explore the potential for comprehensive application of this type of teaching and learning strategy, the University of Miami Center for Research on Sport in Society (CRSS) has recently begun to develop a school-based, after-school intervention TEAMS (Teaching Excellence Achievement and Motivation through Sport). TEAMS is designed to harness children's natural interest in and enthusiasm for sports by embedding instruction in core academic subject matter (reading, writing, mathematics) into a sports context as a means of improving student motivation, engagement, and achievement. As currently implemented, TEAMS involves a partnership between CRSS and the YMCA, YWCA, Big Brothers/Big Sisters, and other United Way agencies to provide after-school programs that focus on improving children's academic performance and that are fully integrated into the life of the school. TEAMS targets four inner-city elementary schools that have a high concentration of students who are at great risk for school failure. Highlights of TEAMS include:

- Focuses on the power of sports to enhance children's psychosocial and cognitive development and to promote self-discipline, drive, goal-setting ability, resiliency, ability to encounter setbacks, and team spirit that can be applied to any area of endeavor and can contribute to future success in life.

- Harnesses children's natural interest in and enthusiasm for sports in the service of academic achievement by using sports to teach and engage children in math, reading, and writing.
- Uses sports to improve student achievement, engage students with school, and motivate children to learn.
- Fully integrates existing after-school programs into the academic and social life of the school
- Provides existing after-school programs with a fully developed, intensive, sport-based academic curriculum to improve children's academic performance.
- Empowers and increases the effectiveness of principals at five target elementary schools by providing sport-themed academic resources, material resources, and professional consultation in the areas of curriculum and staff development.
- Empowers teachers and other school personnel to participate in the program design, implementation, and/or evaluation
- Empowers parents and children as respected advisors to the program developers and to the evaluation team.
- Places the children in classroom settings (rather than the usual cafeteria setting) and environment most conducive to learning.
- Makes full use of the schools' computer labs (currently not a resource for the existing after-school programs).
- Provides educational sport-themed computer software to enhance the resources of the computer labs.
- Provides a fully developed sports-based curriculum that is compatible with and can be used in the regular classroom environment.

TEAMS After-School Program Design

The curriculum developers of TEAMS will create a rigorous academic after-school program curriculum based on the concept of sport that will serve as an accelerated/enrichment experience for participating students. This sport-based curriculum will tie into both the Sunshine State standards as well as the FCAT.

A typical after-school day would include:

1. Intensive, enjoyable group activities that incorporate sport and physical movement to
   a. Enhance student learning in basic academic subjects
   b. Relax, stimulate, and ease kids into further learning

2. Individual tutoring, computer activities, and homework completion time, during which teachers will integrate sport-related content as appropriate. Lead teachers will meet with the regular classroom teachers to identify the areas of needed improvement of the students in the after-school program, in order to individualize the curriculum and meet the needs of the children.

The TEAMS strategy assumes that sports can be used as an educational tool to enhance academic resilience and attachment in ways that allow both athletes and non-athletes opportunities to experience academic benefits associated with sport's broad appeal among young people. Currently underway, the TEAMS project focuses on curriculum development for the elementary grades. There is reason to expect that similar approaches could also be designed for middle grades and high schools.

Informal Strategies

In addition, there are other, less formal ways of incorporating sports into normal teaching and learning routines (Braddock et al., 1991). For example, both athletes and non-athletes could write or contribute to sport columns in school and local newspapers, thereby enhancing student writing and language skills. Students could collect and generate team and player statistics for a variety of school and local sport activities, enhancing their crucial and often underdeveloped mathematical skills. Several types of academic curricular and extracurricular activities that already exist might attract more African American males if participation in sports can be incorporated. Examples include encouraging students to organize the sport sections of school yearbooks, participate on a sports debate team, or perhaps start a sport enthusiast club. Given the interest in sport among African American male students, who may be the least attached to the existing academic programs of public schools, sport incorporated into the English, mathematical, science, and social studies programs of schools offers tremendous potential for making academic investments more salient for their existing interests. This article suggests that educators capitalize on students' athletic investments by creating sport-related opportunities that entail simultaneous academic investments and helping students to apply the skills developed in athletic competition toward the academic arena.

IMPLICATIONS

A stronger emphasis on African American students is long overdue in the current national school reform movement. Although recent reforms emphasizing assessment, higher standards, and more rigorous curricula are important, we must ensure that the diversity of needs and interests of African American and other students of color are adequately met by American schools. Public schools are in dire need of effective programs that create a challenging and supportive learning environment— to motivate all students to care about and dedicate themselves to their schoolwork.

Current evidence suggests that athletic participation can and often does have a positive impact on student motivation and engagement in traditional pro-academic norms and behaviors.

Research and development can best help the reform movement maintain its momentum by demonstrating how the effectiveness of existing school resources can be enhanced. Further research about the role of sports as an educational tool can yield practical new ideas for the use of sports and extracurricular activities in facilitating positive academic and social investments among African American males. Such new knowledge and practical suggestions should be helpful to educational practitioners and policy makers as they proceed with reform efforts. Results of such research will contribute to a clearer definition of the role and importance of sport and extracurricular involvement in the educational system. As many school districts decide what aspects of their traditional school programs should be retained and which should be discarded, extracurricular programs and sports may become especially vulnerable to abandonment if uninformed decisions hold sway. For African American males and other underserved students, the important results of improved academic and athletic connection should be: higher rates of attendance, fewer retentions, more students on grade level in core subjects, more students prepared for and enrolling in academic programs in high school, more students with clear aspirations for high school and postsecondary education and careers, more students with positive attitudes about themselves as students and about school as a place that helps them prepare for their future, and fewer dropouts in the middle grades and in high school.

Most developed societies recognize the important role sports can play in education (MacAloon, 1991). It is puzzling how Americans can devote so many resources to the practice of school sports and so few toward integrating them into the general curriculum.

REFERENCES

Bachin, R. (1999, April). *Sport, pedagogy, and American history.* Paper presented at the American Educational Research Association annual meeting, Montreal, Canada.

Bauer, R. A. (Ed.). (1966). *Social indicators.* Cambridge: MIT Press.

Bend, E. (1968). *The impact of athletic participation on academic and career aspiration and achievement.* New Brunswick, NJ: National Football Foundation and Hall of Fame.

Berntsen, T. (1995). Let it snow, let it snow. *Physics Teacher, 33*(8), 500–501.

Bourdieu, P. (1977). Cultural reproduction and social reproduction. In J. Karabel & A. Halsey (Eds.), *Power and ideology in education* (pp. 487–511). New York: Oxford University Press.

Bourdieu, P. (1986). The forms of capital. In J. G. Richardson (Ed.), *Handbook of theory and research for the sociology of education* (pp. 241–258). New York: Greenwood.

Bourdieu, P., & Wacquant, L. J. D. (1992). *An invitation to reflexive sociology.* Chicago: University of Chicago Press.

Boyle, R. (1963). *Sport: Mirror of American life.* Boston: Little, Brown.

Braddock, J. H. (1978). *Variations in patterns of socialization into sport among Black and White male youth.* Unpublished manuscript. University of Maryland, Department of Sociology.

Braddock, J. (1980, Spring). Race, sports and social mobility: A critical review. *Sociological Symposium, 30,* 18–38.

Braddock, J. (1981). Race, athletics, and educational attainment: Dispelling the myths. *Youth & Society, 12,* 335–350.

Braddock, J. (1982). Academics and athletics in American high schools: Some future considerations of the adolescent subculture hypothesis. *Journal of Social and Behavioral Sciences, 29,* 88–94.

Braddock, J., Royster, D., Winfield, L., & Hawkins, R. (1991). Bouncing back: Sports and academic resilience among African-American males. *Education and Urban Society, 24,* 113–131.

Buhrmann, H. G. (1972). Scholarship and athletics in junior high school. *International Review of Sport Sociology, 7,* 119–128.

Campbell, S. (1983). Persistence behavior of Black children: Some influencing factors. *Journal of Social and Behavioral Sciences, 29,* 53–63.

Coakley, J. J. (1978). *Sport in society.* New York: Mosby.

Coleman, J. (1961). *The adolescent society.* New York: Free Press.

Coleman, J. (1990). Sports as an educational tool. *School Sports & Education, University of Chicago* (National Conference Issue), 3–5.

Commission on the Reorganization of Secondary Education. (1918). *The cardinal principles of secondary education: The report of the Commission on the Reorganization of Secondary Education* (Bulletin, U.S. Bureau of Education: Vol. 35). Washington, DC: Government Printing Office.

Dane, S. (1990). Sport is more than just a game: A study of the use of sport as an academic and life goal enhancement for high school students. *School Sports & Education, University of Chicago* (National Conference Issue), 19–23.

Dawkins, M. (1982). Sports and mobility aspirations among Black male college students. *Journal of Social and Behavioral Sciences, 28,* 77–81.

Dawkins, R., & Braddock, J. (1982). Race, athletics, and delinquency. *Journal of Social and Behavioral Sciences, 28,* 82–87.

DiMaggio, P. (1982). Cultural capital and school success: The impact of status culture participation on grades of U.S. high school students. *American Sociological Review, 47,* 189–201.

Eitle, T., & Eitle, D. (2000, April). *Making sense of the treadmill to oblivion phenomenon: Race, cultural capital, and sports participation.* Paper presented at American Educational Research Association annual meeting, New Orleans, LA.

Eitzen, D. S., & Sage, G. H. (1978). *Sociology of American sport.* Dubuque, IA: W. C. Brown.

Eitzen, D. S., & Sage, G. H. (1989). *Sociology of North American sport* (4th ed.). Dubuque, IA: William C. Brown.

Elam, S. M., Rose, L. C., & Gallup, A. M. (1996). The 28th annual Phi Delta Kappa/Gallup poll of the public's attitudes toward the public schools. *Phi Delta Kappan, 78*(1), 41–59.

Ewing, M., Seefeldt, V., & Brown, T. (1996). *Role of organized sport in the education and health of American children and youth.* New York: Carnegie Corporation.

Fejgin, N. (1994). Participation in high school competitive sports: A subversion of school mission or contribution to academic goals. *Sociology of Sport Journal, 11,* 211–230.

Finn, J. (1993). *School engagement & students at-risk.* Washington, DC: National Center for Education Statistics.

Finn, J. D. (1989). Withdrawing from school. *Review of Educational Research, 59,* 117–142.

Hanks, M., & Eckland, B. (1976). Athletics and social participation in the educational attainment process. *Sociology of Education, 49,* 271–294.

Harris, O., & Hunt, L. (1982). Race and sports involvement: Some implications of athletics for Black and White youth. *Journal of Social and Behavioral Sciences, 28,* 95–103.

Hartman, R. (1990). Trinity Lutheran: Anatomy of a school that successfully combines athletics and education. *School Sports and Education, 6,* 8–10.

Hauser, W. J., & Lueptow, L. B. (1978). Participation in athletics and academic achievement: A replication and extension. *Sociology Quarterly, 19,* 304–309.

Hawkins, R., Royster, D., & Braddock, J. (1992). *Athletic investment and academic resilience among African American females and males in the middle grades* (Research Report No. 3). Cleveland, OH: Cleveland State University, Urban Child Research Center.

Horn, L., & Chen, X. (1998). *Toward resiliency: At-risk students who make it to college.* Washington, DC: U.S. Department of Education, Office of Educational Research and Improvement.

Lamborn, S. D., Brown, B. B., Mounts, N. S., & Steinberg, L. (1992). Putting school in perspective: The influence of family, peers, extracurricular participation, and part-time work on academic engagement. In F. M. Newmann (Ed.), *Student engagement and achievement in American secondary schools* (pp. 153–181). New York: Teachers College Press.

Lamont, M., & Lareau, A. (1988). Cultural capital: Allusions, gaps, and glissandos in recent theoretical development. *Sociological Theory, 6,* 153–168.

Lareau, A., & Horvat, E. M. (1999). Moments of social inclusion and exclusion: Race, class, and cultural capital in family relationships. *Sociology of Education, 72*(1), 37–53.

Lueptow, L. B., & Kayser, B. K. (1973–1974). Athletic involvement, academic achievement, and aspiration. *Sociological Focus, 7*(1), 24–36.

MacAloon, J. (1990). What does school sport teach? *School Sports & Education, University of Chicago* (National Conference Issue), 9–14.

McNeal, R. (1995, January). Extracurricular activities and high school dropouts. *Sociology of Education, 68,* 62–81.

McNeal, R. (1997). Are students being pulled out of high school? The effect of adolescent employment on dropping out. *Sociology of Education, 70,* 206–220.

McNeal, R. (1999). Participation in high school extracurricular activities: Investigating school effects. *Social Science Quarterly, 80,* 291–309.

Melnick, M., Sabo, D., & Vanfossen, B. (1992). Educational effects of interscholastic athletic participation on African American and Hispanic youth. *Adolescence, 27*(106), 295–308.

Michener, J. A. (1976). *Sports in America.* Greenwich, CT: Fawcett Crest.

National Center for Education Statistics. (1988). National education longitudinal study (NELS 1988) methodology report. Washington, DC: U.S. Department of Education.

Nettles, S. M. (1989). The role of community involvement in fostering investment behavior in low-income Black adolescents: A theoretical perspective. *Journal of Adolescent Research, 4,* 190–201.

Newmann, F. (Ed.). (1992). *School engagement and achievement in American secondary schools.* New York: Teachers College Press.

O'Bryan, S., & Braddock, J. (1999, August). *Sport participation and parental educational involvement.* Paper presented at the Association of Black Sociologists annual meeting, Chicago.

Otto, L. B. (1975). Extracurricular activities in the educational attainment process. *Rural Sociology, 40,* 162–176.

Otto, L. B., & Alwin, D. F. (1977, April). Athletics, aspirations, and attainments. *Sociology of Education, 50,* 102–113.

Picou, J. S. (1978). Race, athletic achievement, and educational aspiration. *Sociological Quarterly 19,* 429–438.

Picou, J. S., & Curry, E.W. (1974). Residence and the athletic participation-educational aspirations hypothesis. *Social Science Quarterly 55,* 768–777.

Picou, J. S., & Hwang, S. (1982). Educational aspirations of educationally disadvantaged athletes. *Journal of Sport Behavior 5*(2), 59–76.

Picou, J. S. McCarter, V., & Howell, F. M. (1985). Do high school athletics pay? Some further evidence. *Sociology of Sport Journal, 2*(1), 72–76.

Rehberg, R. A., & Schafer, W. E. (1968). Participation in interscholastic athletics and college expectations. *American Journal of Sociology 73,* 732–774.

Richardson, J. (1999, April). *Scoring points with physics.* Paper presented at the Meeting of the annual American Educational Research Association (AERA) Conference, Montreal.

Rodriguez, A., & Braddock, J. (2000, April). *Athletic involvement and life-chance perceptions.* Paper presented at the American Educational Research Association annual meeting, New Orleans, LA.

Roscigno, V., & Ainsworth-Darnell, J. (1999). Race, cultural capital, and educational resources: Persistent inequalities and achievement returns. *Sociology of Education 72,* 158–178.

Rutter, M. (1987). Psychosocial resilience and protective mechanisms. *American Journal of Orthopsychiatry, 57,* 316–331.

Sabo, D., Melnick, M., & Vanfossen, B. (1993). High school athletic participation and postsecondary educational and occupational mobility: A focus on race and gender. *Sociology of Sport Journal, 10*(1), 44–56.

Schafer, W. E., & Armer, J. M. (1968). Athletes are not inferior students. *Transaction, 6*(1), 21–6, 61–62.

Segrave, J., & Hastad, D. (1984). Interscholastic athletic participation and delinquent behavior: An empirical assessment of relevant variables. *Sociology of Sport Journal, 1*(2), 117–137.

Simmons, W., & Grady, M. (1990). *Black male achievement: From peril to promise.* Upper Marlboro, MD: Prince George's County Public Schools.

Snyder, E. (1972). High school athletes and their coaches: Educational plans & advice. *Sociology of Education, 45,* 313–325.

Snyder, E. E., & Spreitzer, E. (1978). *Social aspects of sport.* Englewood Cliffs, NJ: Prentice Hall.

Snyder, E. E., & Spreitzer, E. (1990). Sports within the Black subculture: A matter of social class or a distinctive subculture? *Journal of Sport and Social Issues, 14*(1), 48–58.

Spady, W. G. (1970). Lament for the letterman: Effects of peer status and extracurricular activities on goals and achievement. *American Journal of Sociology, 75,* 680–702.

Taylor, J., & Chiogioji, E. (1988). The Holland and Andre study on extracurricular activities: Imbalanced and incomplete. *Review of Educational Research, 58,* 99–105.

Trent, W. (1982). Contributions of athletic participation in high school to adult outcomes for college and non-college trained young men. *Journal of Social and Behavioral Sciences, 28,* 104–112.

Trent, W., & Braddock, J. (1992). Extracurricular activities in secondary schools. In *Encyclopedia of educational research* (Vol. 2, pp. 476–480). New York: Macmillan.

U.S. Commission on Civil Rights. (1978). *Social indicators of equality for minorities and women.* Washington, DC: Government Printing Office.

Wilson, W. J. (1990, September 21). *School sport: An educational tool.* Plenary address at the Conference on School Sport as an Educational Tool, University of Chicago.

CHAPTER NINE

Conclusion

Olatokunbo S. Fashola

Johns Hopkins University

The entire process of assembling and expanding this edited volume has been nothing short of enjoyable and thought-provoking. As the process draws to a close, I have a few thoughts to share. As I wrote in the preface, the authors approach the various topics influencing African American male education from several interesting and unique perspectives. They have eloquently and passionately presented theories, perspectives, research, and ideas that the stakeholders as a whole can choose to address or to ignore. The views presented in this volume are not necessarily conclusive, but they do open the door for dialogue, research, and practice among all groups working with and interested in African American male students.

As I conclude the work of editor and author for this volume, I cannot help but ask, Who will read these chapters? Who will act on the authors' recommendations? What will happen next? To best answer these questions, let me draw an analogy to another concern addressing gender and athletic achievement. Thirty years ago, educators, parents, policy makers, and researchers, among other stakeholders, addressed a problem related to gender and achievement. Females did not have the same opportunities as males to succeed and perform athletically. Title IX was created and passed by Congress as a means to address this issue and attempt to provide females with much-needed opportunities.

As we contemplate this edited volume's theme of educating African American males, certain similar steps could be taken. For example, in light of the shortage of African American male teachers in the classroom, we should create extra incentives that would encourage more African American males to teach in urban and suburban schools. This seems like a reasonable approach to addressing the teacher shortage, but to do this, legislators, funders, and additional stakeholders must be willing into invest skill, time, and money to realize this goal. This means we must begin now to reverse the current trend of African American male lack of achievement in the classroom by exploring what successful educators of African American males have done. If we are unwilling or unable to reverse this trend, then we must ask, How can we train future African American male graduates, role models, teachers, and overall successful members of society if they are not even enrolled in school, let alone graduating?

It is time to realize that the lack of academic achievement for African American males presents a major crisis, and it is a great disservice to all if we do not act on the clear pictures presented by researchers. We must begin to create a prototype of a mechanism that will address these issues and continue to eventually serve as a buffer against the factors that continue to work against the academic success of African American males. In the process of educating all students, it is incumbent on us to (a) present positive images of African American males, (b) debunk hypermasculine stereotypes, (c) put more "heart" into high school dropout prevention programs, (d) create a reservoir of educators who will best serve this population, (e) engage these students in quality activities away from school that will continue to create more positive opportunities for them during the nonschool hours, (f) understand the communities they come from and some of the challenges that members of these communities face, and (g) take personal interest in these young men by being available to them during the elementary, middle, and high school years. We must do what it takes to keep positive males present in their immediate communities and provide more opportunities for mental health and emotional outlets for the students as they continue to strive for success.

Researchers show that the cards are stacked against this population both in the community and in the schools. In addition to making them passive recipients, it is also important to give them opportunities to define themselves by the successful images we present to them. This means providing them with opportunities to participate in community service; to be positive role models to younger males through activities such as tutoring and mentoring; and, finally, to engage in established community organizations that foster positive development, especially those organizations that have success working with this population.

In conclusion, it is my dream that within the next 5 years, when the fall season approaches, we will collaborate and talk about African American males celebrating success, excitement, and academic achievement in school. Ideally, when statewide, districtwide, and even local data are disaggregated, the low test scores, high dropout and expulsion rates, and high rate of disciplinary problems that plague African American males will no longer be issues of concern. Rather, the occasion will call for articles celebrating the successes of this population and about lessons learned. Until then, Colleagues, the struggle to achieve high-quality education for African American males continues, and we have only just begun.

Index

**CORWIN
PRESS**

The Corwin Press logo—a raven striding across an open book—represents the union of courage and learning. Corwin Press is committed to improving education for all learners by publishing books and other professional development resources for those serving the field of K–12 education. By providing practical, hands-on materials, Corwin Press continues to carry out the promise of its motto: **"Helping Educators Do Their Work Better."**